3 0132
D0542176

Innocent

Innocent

A murdered son.
A grieving mother.
The fight to clear her name.

SARAH ROSE
WITH ELLIE PIOVESANA

EBURY
PRESS

1 3 5 7 9 10 8 6 4 2

Ebury Press, an imprint of Ebury Publishing
20 Vauxhall Bridge Road
London SW1V 2SA

Ebury Press is part of the Penguin Random House
group of companies whose addresses can be found
at global.penguinrandomhouse.com

Penguin
Random House
UK

Copyright © Sarah Rose 2015

Sarah Rose has asserted her right to be identified as the
author of this Work in accordance with the Copyright,
Designs and Patents Act 1988

First published by Ebury Press in 2015

www.eburypublishing.co.uk

A CIP catalogue record for this book is available from the British Library

ISBN 9780091960407

Printed and bound by CPI Group (UK) Ltd, Croydon, CR0 4YY

Penguin Random House is committed to a
sustainable future for our business, our readers
and our planet. This book is made from Forest
Stewardship Council® certified paper.

Typeset in India by Thomson Digital Pvt Ltd, Noida, Delhi

For Nanny Iris and Kam Kam.
I miss you both every day.

PROLOGUE

I've replayed it over and over. There was nothing extraordinary about that morning. No little warning signs, no gentle heads-up that life as I knew it was about to be completely and utterly destroyed.

The alarm on my phone went off at 7.30am. Nicholas stirred next to me but didn't open his eyes. I reached out for my mobile and hit cancel.

Silence.

I climbed out of bed and went to the toilet. Thierry was at his dad's, and I hadn't heard a peep out of Kamran all night but I knew he would be awake now. Sure enough, I opened his bedroom door and found him sat up in his cot. His face lit up and I smiled. He looked so cute in his big brother's *SpongeBob SquarePants* vest.

'Morning!' I whispered, lifting him up.

I admired him for a moment; the chubby cheeks, the thick black eyelashes any girl would kill for. I squeezed him tight and pressed my lips against his cheek.

Just as I always did, I carried Kam into the living room and plonked him on the sofa.

'Do you want *Milkshake* on Kam Kam?' I asked, pointing the remote at the TV and pressing Channel 5.

I left him watching telly while I made us both a drink – strong tea for me and hot chocolate in a sippy cup for Kam.

I put a good dash of cold water in it, checked the temperature with my little finger then screwed the lid on tightly. He bounced excitedly and reached out for it as I walked in and handed the cup to him. I took mine into the bedroom.

'Morning,' Nicholas said, rolling onto his back and yawning.

He got up and used the bathroom while I put on my black trousers and green Ladbrokes' shirt. I slipped my feet into a pair of black ballet pumps and brushed my hair up into a pony. I grabbed my tea and walked through to the kitchen, where Nicholas was making Kam's Weetabix.

'I need to get going,' I said, kissing him on the lips and picking up my bag. 'See you in a few hours.'

'Bye, Kam Kam!' I shouted as I pulled my coat on. I was out the flat and down the first set of concrete stairs when I realised I hadn't picked up my keys and phone. I had time to dash back up. Nicholas heard me knocking and let me in.

'Sorry,' I said, grabbing my phone and keys off the side. 'Forgot these! See you later!'

Nicholas rolled his eyes, smiled and pecked me on the lips again. As he disappeared back into the kitchen, I decided to stick my head round the living-room door. Kam was still on the sofa, holding his hot chocolate and watching TV, good as gold. My heart swelled and I smiled. He clocked me and smiled back.

'Bye-bye!' I said, waving.

He lifted his hand and waved back.

'Bye-bye, Mommy!'

I made it to the stop in time for my usual bus to Birmingham's Pallasades shopping centre. I spent the journey reading messages on my phone and gazing out of the window. Getting to my job at the betting shop was so much easier now Nicholas was babysitting for me. When Mom looked after the boys, getting them up and over to hers on time was such a stress for us all. Now I only had to worry about myself. Nicholas had even offered to stay a bit later that day so I could meet my close friend Matthew after work. We had decided to go to the local college and put our names down for a course that September. I had to do something. I loved my job but I didn't want to work at Ladbrokes forever.

Already I was on my feet as the bus ground to a halt. The doors swung open and I jostled my way through the commuters. Ladbrokes was already open when I got there, and I walked down the stairs, across the shop floor and out into the staff area. I dumped my things in the cloakroom then sat down at my desk.

It was a fairly steady morning – the usual nondescript kind of day. Around 11.30am, when there were no customers to be served, I told the manager, Charles, I was nipping out the back to use the loo. But, typical me, I couldn't walk past my bag without checking my phone first. And funnily enough, it was ringing.

It was Nicholas.

'Hello?' I answered.

He sounded like he was crying.

'Sarah, the police are coming for you. You need to get to the hospital.'

His voice sounded strange. It scared me.

'What? Why …?'

The phone reception went down. I frantically tried to call him back, my hands trembling. His phone was off. I thought for a moment then tried his mom's landline. It rang twice then she answered. She was crying too.

'Hello? It's Sarah. Nicholas just tried to call me. Is he with you? Is everything OK?'

I could just about make out what she was saying, 'I'm sorry, I'm sorry …'

I was crying now. Something had happened, something bad.

Then she said it.

'Kamran's dead.'

CHAPTER ONE

In the 1950s, an Irish labourer called Tommy Manifold caught a boat to England to seek out a better life for himself. What he found was Iris – a hard-working English girl with a warm heart and a pretty face. Using his gift of the gab, Tommy charmed her into lending him her watch. He pawned it so he could afford to take her out then returned it to her when he'd saved up enough to buy it back. This is the romantic story of how my grandparents fell in love.

Tommy and Iris got married and had six children – three boys and three girls. Thomas was the eldest, closely followed by Margaret. Christina was next, then Martin. Their third son, Anthony, grew up with learning difficulties. Last but not least, the baby of the family was Joanne.

The siblings were raised as Catholics in a cramped house in Birmingham. Tommy was a strict dad, but they were a close-knit family instilled with a good work ethic. They were all expected to go to church and pull their weight, whether it be doing housework or helping care for Anthony.

Christina, or 'Chrissie' as she became known, was the first of the Manifold children to have a baby of her own. I was born in September 1985 and absolutely adored by my grandparents, who we lived with for the first few years of my life. Mom says that when I was tiny and she couldn't get me to stop crying, she would pass me to Nan and I would fall straight to sleep on her boobs. Mom also says that Grandad saved my life. We never found out why but in the first year of my life I had two or three seizures. Well, you can imagine how distraught Mom was, especially the first time. Hearing her screams, Grandad ran in and resuscitated me on his living-room floor. Mom says I wouldn't be here if it wasn't for him and I've never forgotten that.

My parents, Chrissie and Paul Rose, got married on 24 October 1989. It's fair to say it was a shotgun wedding. I was four when Mom fell pregnant again – it was a happy accident, but she didn't want another child out of wedlock. She would have loved the big white wedding but, at the time, a cheap skirt suit and a bus down the registry office was all they could afford.

Stacey, my little sister, arrived on 5 May the following year. As a toddler she was skinny, but super cute. With my jet black hair and hers white blonde, we couldn't have looked more different. I took full advantage of being the bigger sister – if we were given sweets I would scoff all mine then invent games that I would win so I could eat hers too. Despite the fairly substantial age gap, I can't remember a time when she wasn't around.

We lived on Gressel Lane in Kitts Green, Birmingham, in a rented two-bed council maisonette. We were on the middle floor of three and had a balcony coming off our living room. Technically, Stacey and I shared a room. But as I was the eldest, it was basically all mine apart from her bed. I remember having my first stereo in there. It was bright yellow. I think Mom picked the colour to match the candy-coloured stripes on our wallpaper. Every night, right up until I left home, I slept with a soft toy I'd had from birth – a panda called 'Panda'. When I think of my childhood, I think of Gressel Lane and Panda. That's where all my happy memories are.

Ours was a fairly traditional set-up. Dad went out to work, Mom ran the house and wore the trousers. She was a stickler for routine – Stacey and I were always bathed and in bed for 7.30pm, no arguments. Mom was also very house-proud. Every Sunday she would tie back her frizzy chestnut hair, open all the windows and stick Patsy Cline or UB40 on full blast while she blitzed every room. The first thing she would say to Dad when he got home from a hard day at the factory was, 'Get your work clothes off!' Heaven forbid he spread muck everywhere.

Dad is six years younger than Mom. He's tall and skinny – well over six foot – with dark brown hair and hazel eyes, and he's always been young at heart. He would tickle us until we cried and throw us around in play fights as if we were boys. We've never been a particularly lovey-dovey family, but Dad was always ambushing one of us with an over-the-top bear hug and smattering of kisses. Me and Stacey would squeal and squirm until he relented and let us wriggle free. Mom would do pretty much the same, but with a half-embarrassed, half-loving it roll of her blue eyes.

I remember Dad coming home one day brandishing a large tattoo on his right arm – a big skull that said 'Stacey' and 'Sarah' on a scroll either side of it. Mom never understood the relevance of the skull. None of us did, to be honest. I just remember thinking he must really love us to have our names inked on his body forever.

Dad did various factory jobs and always seemed to be driving a different car. Mom juggled home life with part-time hours at a local amusement arcade and the occasional bit of bar work. For a while she did a Sunday night shift, so that was our night with Dad. He would bathe us, wash our hair and get us into our PJs. Then we'd have beans on toast in front of the TV – the wrestling first, then *The Simpsons*. We never had much money, but Mom and Dad put a lot of effort into making sure we had quality time together as a family. If we had a spare weekend, Dad would get out his road atlas and let us pick a new place to visit. Mom would make a big packed lunch and we would just get in the car and go. It always felt like such a big adventure. Once, we ended up in Bath, found a good park to spend the day in then drove home exhausted as it got dark. It was the best day, and apart from having to put fuel in the car it must have cost Mom and Dad next to nothing. I remember thinking, *When I have a family, I'm going to make sure I do stuff like this.*

***

Out of Mom's brothers and sisters, all but Thomas stayed in Birmingham. Joanne lived with her husband a few minutes away and Margaret – my Aunty Maggie – was practically on our doorstep. She's blonde, six foot two and the member of the family most likely to tell you exactly what she thinks. Not everyone knows how to take her, but I've always admired her direct nature.

The year after I was born, Aunty Maggie had twins – two little girls called Sam and Kelly. They aren't identical but people always struggled to tell them apart. Because we were so close in age, the twins were like my ready-made playmates. They're dark-haired like me, so when we were toddling around together, strangers would assume I was their big sister.

When it was time for me to start school, I wished I could take Sam and Kelly with me. I was a bubbly kid around people I knew, but painfully shy around strangers. My parents and grandparents assured me time and time again that if I was brave, I would make lots of new friends. They were right, of course. I went to Our Lady's Primary – the local Catholic school – and soon had a whole new social life. A girl named Alexa became my best friend. She had a sharp blonde bob and we spent a lot of time playing at each other's houses. Then there was Natasha, Collette and Kirsty. The five of us were a little girl gang and stayed close right the way through primary school.

I suffered with asthma when I was young. Our flat was a short walk away from Heartlands Hospital and there are chunks of my childhood where it felt like I was always there. If Mom and Dad weren't rushing me to A&E we would be at the asthma clinic for check-ups. I was a bit of a worrier anyway – if I fell over and cut my knee I thought I was dying. Once I got a splinter in my foot and, while Dad was trying to pull it out with tweezers, I fainted three times. So if I ever started coughing or wheezing, I would panic and start hyperventilating – the last thing you want to be doing when you might be having an asthma attack. I would always leave the hospital with a wedge of the chemist's paper bags to breathe into next time it happened.

Mom and Dad were both smokers, which probably didn't help. I never liked it, even though it was much more common and socially acceptable back then. It sounds crazy now but they would smoke everywhere – in the house, the car. Once, during a check-up for my asthma, the doctor warned me, 'If you smoke you will die.' I've never forgotten that. But even before then, if Mom lit up while we were watching telly I would make a fuss and move away. I always hated the smell.

Despite all this, somehow I was a reasonably fit and healthy kid. As well as new friends, primary school also led me to discover new talents. A couple of years in, the teachers noticed I was good at running. I was one of the fastest at cross-country and was put forward for several local competitions, including one in Birmingham's Cannon Hill Park. When I was whizzing around outside in my trainers I was in my element. I much preferred it to being sat inside learning. Stacey was a typical girly girl who loved to play with dolls, while I was the tomboy – climbing trees and playing football with the boys in our street or riding my bike with Sam and Kelly. Behind their house there were some stepping stones and a brook we used to paddle in, although I discovered years later that the water was actually coming from a sewage pipe!

In school holidays we would take our nets down to the local lakes and spend hours catching fish and throwing them back in. Back then, it was still pretty rare for your average working-class family to afford a holiday abroad, so if we did go away it was a cheap and cheerful caravan holiday somewhere in the UK. It didn't matter to Stacey and me as long as we got to see the sea. Midlands' kids especially are suckers for it, because we live so far away from the coast. I remember the smell of the seaside in the air as we craned our necks out of the car windows, desperate for that first glimpse of sparkling water. The novelty never wore off.

One year, a big group of us went to Great Yarmouth and piled into a 12-berth static home. Uncle Martin came and one afternoon he must have won a dozen soft toys at the amusement arcade. He was so chuffed with himself that it made Mom all competitive. She had a go on a few games but didn't win a thing and went in a huff. It still makes me laugh remembering Martin's stash of toys all over the caravan and her face when he rubbed it in by trying to offer her one.

When I was about seven, Mom let me go on holiday with Aunty Maggie. It was so exciting. We spent a week on Barry Island in a little chalet with me, Sam and Kelly sleeping on two single beds pushed together. We sat up giggling all night then spent hours at the fair and on the beach. I remember us having a pair of those glasses with the funny eyes on the lenses, and laughing our heads off every time one of us put them on.

The twins inherited their mom's height but got their dark colouring from their dad. He walked out on them later, when they were ten. It can't have been easy, but I think it brought Mom and Maggie even closer. And the closer they were, the more I got to see of Sam and Kelly.

***

Despite having more grandchildren, I was still the apple of Nan's eye. She was always slipping me 50 pence or a pound.

'Don't tell your cousins!' she would whisper.

Nan was a grafter and always had a job. For years she was the cleaner at the local working men's club. I used to love it when she took me along with her and let me help. I would follow her around with a duster in my hand and she would give me enough change out of her wages to make me think I was rich. Grandad was a man's man who liked a drink and a cigarette, while Nan was a traditional woman who took looking after her house and her family very seriously. She liked to make sure everyone was fed. She always had biscuits in the cupboard and whenever anyone had a birthday she was the one who made the show-stopping cake. She was a real early bird too. On a Saturday you could guarantee she'd been to the market and done her weekly shop before you'd even had your breakfast. Then she would catch a bus to ours, usually with a huge bag of chips for us to share. I would sit at the front window, watching every bus come and go until she arrived.

My final year at primary school was 1996 – the year the Spice Girls came out. I remember the single 'Wannabe' being huge and, because there were five of us, every chance we got, me, Alexa, Natasha, Collette and Kirsty were singing it and pretending to be them. I always wanted to be Sporty Spice, but because I had curly dark hair they made me be Scary. Take That split up the same year and when we found out, Kirsty and I were so devastated we cried for the whole of break time.

Me and the girls got separated when we all moved up to different high schools. It was a bit of a wrench, but whereas my primary school was mainly for Catholics, Byng Kenrick Central School consisted of faces I already knew from my estate. I clicked with a petite brown-haired girl called Chantelle who was always up for a laugh, and Grace who was already friends with Sam and Kelly. One of my best friends was a boy called Matthew. He was black and a real smiler, with a gold cap on one of his front teeth. He was a lovely, funny, good-natured lad and we became really close. The other kids teased us because they thought we were secretly a couple, but it was never like that. We were like brother and sister.

I hadn't been at Byng Kenrick long when my asthma all but disappeared. My doctor told me that some kids grow out of it and luckily I turned out to be one of them. I still carried my little brown inhaler around with me, though, just in case.

I wish I could say I carried on excelling at sports but sadly, like childhood hobbies and passions so often do, it fell by the wayside as I came into my own as a teenager. Happy, confi-dent and a bit of a joker, I suppose you could say I was one of the popular crowd. The teachers liked me but my school work suffered because I spent so much time talking in class. We lived for mucking about at break times. I remember climbing a tree for a dare. I left my shoes on the grass and while I was boldly negotiating my way up the branches, one of the lads nicked them. I could barely run after him for laughing. Some people have a tough time at school, but hand on heart, I don't remember a single person in my year being bullied. I just remember laughing all the time.

***

It was around this time that lots of girls started pairing off with boyfriends. I developed feelings towards boys, but was always far too shy to do anything about it. I was 13 when I had my first kiss. It was with a boy called Andrew when a few of us were hanging out at Sam and Kelly's house.

'He likes you,' Kelly said, nudging me. 'Kiss him! Go on! Kiss him!'

We shared an awkward snog then never spoke again.

At 16 I had quite a big crush on a guy called Timothy. I found myself befriending him – the only thing I really knew how to do was be one of the lads. Eventually I kissed him and told everyone I liked him in the hope he would find out and confess that he felt the same. Only he didn't. It fizzled out and my pride was a little wounded, but I was too busy being a teenager to dwell on it too much.

I cringe when I think about the things I used to wear back then. There was a market stall in Birmingham that did skinny jeans in all the colours of the rainbow for about seven quid a pop. Nearly every weekend I'd be down there, buying a new colour – green, pink, yellow. If I wasn't in a pair of my signature rainbow jeans I'd be in an Adidas tracksuit or a Berghaus jacket. I couldn't wear a skirt and tights without laddering them so for school I mostly wore trousers. I remember thinking I was so cool when I turned up for lessons in my black trousers and a brand new pair of Rockport boots.

Jennifer Lopez was big back then – all the girls wanted to be her. Every day, without fail, I would scrape my hair back in a ponytail then use a toothbrush and almost a whole tub of hair gel to stick all the baby hairs along my hairline to my forehead. I was obsessed with jewellery, gold in particular. I had sovereign rings on every finger and wore the huge thick hoop earrings with the ball on them. Every birthday and Christmas I asked for more gold. I remember Sam and Kelly getting those clown pendants on gold chains. I was so jealous! There's no getting away from it – I was what you would probably call a chav. But hey, I fitted in. All my friends looked pretty much the same.

We had a half-decent youth club nearby where I would hang out with Matthew or Chantelle, listening to music or playing pool. Sometimes me and Chantelle would go to an under-18s night – it was called Holy Bash, on account of it being held in the local church hall.

***

I had less and less time for Stacey and we started to drift apart a bit. If I had friends round at the house, I would pretty much tell her to get lost. I feel awful about it now, but five years can seem a huge age gap when you're a teenager, and you're so busy doing your own thing you don't see your actions through others' eyes.

Neither of us was particularly naughty, so it was a bit of a shock when I caught her smoking outside the local shop. She must have been about 11.

'Ew!' I exclaimed loudly. 'What do you think you're doing? That's so disgusting. I'm telling Mom.'

And that's exactly what I did – I went straight home and grassed her up. When Mom collared her she pulled out all the classic lines. 'It's bad for you ... It stinks ... It will stunt your growth.'

Stacey's natural response was, 'But you do it, Mom.'

'Well,' Mom snapped, flustered. 'You're not old enough!'

Stacey carried on smoking. She just took greater care to hide it from us. I wound her up constantly with my favourite warning, 'You're gonna die!'

Despite my bossiness, when Stacey started Year 7 at high school and I was in my final year, she came over and pointed me out to one of her mates. There was pride in her voice as she said, 'That's my sister.' That took me by surprise.

We were a bit like chalk and cheese, I suppose. She had Mom's fair skin and Dad's height. By the time she was into her teens she towered over me. She's over six foot now, only an inch or so smaller than Dad. I got Mom's height – five foot seven – and, I'd always thought, Dad's dark hair and olive complexion. I thought him and me were lucky to catch the sun so well. I got called a Paki by a boy once, which didn't make any sense because I always thought I was white. But when I was 15, this relatively minor incident took on a whole new meaning.

* * *

I was at home having a soak in the bath one night when Stacey burst in. She had a look of concern on her face I'd never seen before.

'Dad's not your real dad,' she whispered.

'You what?' I replied, confused.

She repeated the sentence, slower this time.

'Dad's not your real dad.'

Her words hadn't sunk in but I was already crying as I climbed out of the bath, wrapped myself in a towel and went to speak to Mom. She was sat chatting to a friend and Stacey had overheard them.

'Is Dad not my real dad?' I asked, tears streaming down my face.

She froze for a moment then answered.

'No. Oh God, love, I'm so sorry. I never wanted you to find out like this.'

So the man I thought was my dad hadn't always been in my life. He and Mom met at a New Year's Eve party when I was two. He adopted me when they married and I took his name. My biological dad was Asian and a Muslim. He and Mom were together for around 18 months, but when she fell pregnant at 20 she found out he was already married. He wanted to carry on seeing her but she ended it. So the real reason we lived with Nan and Grandad when I was born is because Mom was on her own.

In that moment, I didn't really take her explanations and apologies in. All I wanted to do was slam the breaks on.

'Please don't tell Dad I know,' I begged. My first instinct was that I didn't want him to feel awkward or treat me any differently. I couldn't undo what I knew but maybe if Dad had no knowledge of this conversation we could pretend it never happened.

Of course, the cat was well and truly out of the bag and she had no choice but to tell him. The next morning he sat me down and told me how sorry he was.

'I know this is a big thing for you,' he said, 'but I promise, it doesn't change anything between us. I still love you and Stacey exactly the same.'

It still breaks my heart knowing how upset he was, how concerned he was for my feelings and that I might stop loving *him*. It was never discussed in depth again. I suppose we just all tried to carry on as normal.

I can honestly say my feelings for Dad didn't change but, looking back, my behaviour certainly did. I started spending more and more time with my friends and less and less time at home. Some days the only time I'd see my parents was when I nipped in to ask for a pound so I could get a bag of chips for my tea. I guess I felt lost, like I'd lost my place in the family. I never told her, but I resented Stacey for being Dad's biological daughter. I wanted to be his more than anything in the world and there was absolutely nothing I could do about it. Despite what he'd said to reassure me, I couldn't shake the feeling that he must love her more. I felt like the black sheep.

As far as I know, my real dad has never tried to get in touch and I've never had the desire to go looking for him. I've had moments where I've wondered if I have brothers and sisters out there, but despite being affected by what came out that night, I still felt like I had a dad – and a good one at that.

CHAPTER TWO

For the next year I immersed myself in my social life. I was happiest just hanging out with my mates having a laugh. School just kind of ticked by. I guess I never really took it that seriously, even when it got to GCSE time I didn't get stressed. What was there to get stressed *about*?

Revising consisted of the odd cramming session the night before. Or I would see my friends as usual and do absolutely no revision at all. I remember sitting in the exam room, staring at the papers with no idea what I was supposed to be doing. The day I opened my brown envelope and saw all those Ds and Es I regretted not working harder. That's when the seriousness of it all hit me. I had always seen myself doing something with troubled kids – a probation worker or something along those lines. But I lacked the self-confidence to seek out what steps I needed to take to get into it. When I got home and showed Mom and Dad my results I could tell they were disappointed.

'What are you going to do now then?' Dad asked sternly. 'If you're not going to college then don't think you can sit around here all day. You have to get a job.'

'Alright, Paul,' Mom cut in. 'Don't give her a hard time. She'll get herself sorted.'

Typical Mom – Grandad had been so strict when she was young that she was always mindful of putting too much pressure on us. She was right, though. I had no aspirations to go to college or university, but I knew I definitely wanted a job.

In the two months after I left school I did little more than hand out a few CVs. I spent a lot of time with Gemma, who lived in the same maisonettes as us on Gressel Lane. Our moms became firm friends when we moved in there all those years ago and they really brought the fun out in each other. Like when Gemma and me were about five or six and they couldn't afford proper nights out or babysitters, they would throw a girly night in for the four of us. They would go to town, putting crisps and nuts out in bowls as if it was a proper party. Us kids would get a glass of pop while the moms shared a cheap bottle of wine. They'd put music on and tell us to dance by the window.

'Come on!' they would say. 'If you dance by the window people will think it's busy!'

Me and Gemma thought it was hilarious. On one particularly funny night, the four of us ended up doing handstands up against the walls!

I was a day older than Gemma. We always felt there was something special about being born at almost exactly the same time. She was five foot five and super slim with green eyes. We got into our fair share of trouble together. When we were eight we stumbled across some pots of paint that had been left outside the flats. Naturally, we picked up the used brushes and started painting the walls and the concrete floor. When it dawned on us what we'd done we were so terrified. We grabbed some old newspaper and tried to scrub the paint off, which was obviously a waste of time. We never told anyone it was us. The imprint from the paper was still there years later.

Gemma went to the same high school as me but was a bit of a social butterfly, flitting between her own group of friends and mine. One day, we went off the school grounds at lunchtime and just didn't bother going back. Our master plan was foiled when Gemma's mom drove past and saw us. She was furious. She drove us back to school and marched us inside. It's a funny story now, but at the time we were so scared.

We had a few scrapes but school really was the best days of our lives. When it ended we didn't know what to do with ourselves. With no jobs to go to, me and Gemma sat watching TV at the flat while my parents were at work. She was with me the day I had a run-in with a lad called Tony. He lived in a house across the street from us. Two or three years older, he was a bit of a troublemaker. He flirted with us once, but we were completely oblivious to that kind of thing. He took it badly though and we got an earful of abuse pretty much every time we saw him after that. But today was worse than usual.

Mom and Dad were working and Stacey was at school. It was a sunny day so me and Gemma were stood talking outside on the balcony. Tony appeared in the street and started shouting at us.

'Nigger lover!' he bellowed. 'Paki!'

I'm guessing he must have seen me with Matthew. Growing up in Birmingham, I was so used to being around people from all different backgrounds I didn't even see colour. But not everyone felt the same.

I'll admit, back then I had a mouth on me. When he used the N word I couldn't help but say something back. But what happened next came as a complete shock. He started running at full speed towards the maisonettes. Next thing we knew he was using one of the ground-floor balconies to climb up to ours, like Spider-Man. We watched, frozen with fear, not knowing what he was going to do. Then he was there, on my balcony. I turned and made for the living-room door but he already had me pinned up the wall by my shoulders.

'Not shouting back now, are ya?' he sneered threateningly.

His face was almost touching mine. I had never seen anyone so angry. In that moment, I honestly thought he was about to kill me. Gemma was screaming at him to get off me. A second later he let go. Without saying another word he strutted out through the flat and let himself out the front door. We stood on the balcony in a daze, hearts racing, not even sure what just happened. I think he wanted to frighten us – and it worked. Dad would barely raise his voice to me and Stacey, let alone lay a finger on us. I had never seen a man behave in such a threatening and aggressive way. It really unnerved me.

Gemma and I were so shaken up we sat in silence for over an hour, desperate for my mom and dad to get home. My eyes were fixed on the window and when I saw them I was so relieved I burst into tears.

'What's happened?' Mom asked when she came in and saw the state we were in.

When we told them what had happened they were furious. They knew who Tony was and had always suspected he was trouble.

'We phone the police, right now,' Dad said.

An officer came out and interviewed us later that day. Tony was charged with aggravated assault and Gemma and I were warned we may have to give evidence in court, which to two relatively naive teenage girls was an absolutely terrifying thought. The whole thing was really upsetting for all of us. Tony kept a low profile after that, but the fear of bumping into him hung over us every day.

Dad was so concerned he phoned the council and told them we wanted to move immediately. When he explained the circumstances they agreed and within four weeks we were packing up our family home. The new flat was five minutes away in Clopton Road, Sheldon. It was another maisonette, this time on the ground floor. The blow of being uprooted was softened by the fact it had three bedrooms. For the very first time me and Stacey could have our own room.

'You can decorate them however you like,' Mom said.

I knew exactly what I wanted.

'I want mine pink,' I said. And I meant pink *everything*; pink bedclothes, pink walls, pink carpet, pink rug.

'Like I said,' Mom smiled, rolling her eyes, 'however you like.'

I don't remember the move being at all stressful. I just remember me and Stacey turning up and the whole flat was done. It was freshly painted and spotlessly clean. Every box was unpacked and everything was in its place, just how Mom liked it. She and Dad must have bust a gut getting everything done.

We'd been living on Clapton Road for two or three months when we had to go to court and face Tony. Courts are big, scary places, especially to a 16-year-old. But Birmingham Magistrates' Court in particular is like something straight out of an old horror film. An elaborate nineteenth-century building made from terracotta-coloured brick, it dominates Corporation Street with its huge windows and gothic spires. Inside, the hallways are vast, cavernous places, lit by chandeliers. Serious-looking people wearing suits and carrying briefcases march around at high speed, the combination of high ceilings and tiled floors making every footstep audible. And just in case you're not nervous enough when you walk in, the entrance is a gigantic archway with a stern statue of Queen Victoria in the centre, looking down on you with cold, hard eyes. Honestly, it's like a gateway to hell. I had walked past the court many times, but never entertained the idea that I would be one of the people who had to go inside.

The day Gemma and I went we were like frightened rabbits. The thought of having to stand up and speak in front of all those important-looking people shredded nerves I didn't even know I had. Thankfully, we were offered a lifeline. Before the hearing our solicitor sat us down and explained that Tony had agreed to plead guilty to the assault. He would face the Magistrates and be dealt his punishment and we could go home without having to set foot in the witness box. We were so relieved. Tony got community service and a fine and we drove home, thanking our lucky stars it was over. I hoped I would never have to see the inside of a court again.

CHAPTER THREE

It wasn't too long before a job opportunity came my way. Hayley, a neighbour and good friend of mine and Gemma's from school, had got a position at Merrell Casting, a small factory in Birmingham's Jewellery Quarter. One night she phoned to tell me there were some vacancies.

'You should give them a call,' she said. 'You'd be great. And the money's good too!'

So that's what I did. I made the call, was invited in for an informal interview and found myself being offered a full-time job on the spot. The work was injecting wax into the moulds they used for rings, making sure there were no air bubbles. It was quite fiddly. If the air gauge on the wax machine wasn't exactly right, everything you did that day would be sent back. But once I got the hang of it I was pleasantly surprised by how much I enjoyed it.

Hayley and I would meet in the mornings and do the two-bus journey together. By 9am we would be upstairs, overalls on, ready to start work. At lunch we would get a cheap sandwich and sit in the cemetery in the grounds of Birmingham Cathedral like all the other city workers. Then at 5pm we would get our two buses home. We loved it. We loved it so much we worked nearly every Saturday, even though we didn't have to. Saturdays were the best day because it was a half day and everyone would order a hot bacon, sausage and egg sandwich from the cafe over the road.

***

For a 16-year-old the wage was pretty decent – well over £200 a week. Every Friday I would be given my earnings in a little brown envelope. That night I would give Mom and Dad the £50 we'd agreed for board money then I would blow the rest over the course of the weekend, either on new clothes or going out.

'Don't go wasting all your wages on your friends!' Mom would shout as I disappeared out the front door.

'I won't, Mom!' I'd lie.

Hardly any of my mates worked. Some were still at school or college, so I would happily foot the bill so we could all have fish and chips or a load of sweets from the shop. I suppose you could say I was a bit too generous; if I was lucky, come Monday morning I would have just enough left to buy my bus pass and lunch for the week.

My other new expenditure was the pub. Legally, I wasn't old enough to drink, but with my hair done and a bit of make-up on I had no trouble getting served. Every other Friday night I would get Dad to drop me off at the Waggon and Horses on the Warwick Road, and my cousins Sam and Kelly would meet me in there.

We've been going there pretty much since the day we were born. Grandad used to drink in there – everyone knew Tommy Manifold – and we used to go for Sunday dinner.

In the summer they'd put on a barbecue and have a bouncy castle for the kids. It closed down and changed hands a few times but it's always been a good local. Even though I was underage Mom and Dad didn't mind me going there because everyone knew me – I was Chrissie's daughter, Tommy's granddaughter. They knew I would be safe.

On a Friday and Saturday the pub attracted a younger crowd with half-decent DJs who played garage and R&B. There was a guy called Mark Rowe who was in the Waggon most weekends. His mate was one of the regular DJs so he could usually be found standing next to him, helping with the records or filling in. One night, he came over and started talking to us. He was tall, black and wearing some kind of branded tracksuit with expensive trainers – the typical uniform for Birmingham boys. He was good-looking, although I can't say I was struck by an immediate attraction. I slowly realised he had taken a shine to me, however. What started out as friendly group chat quickly became just him and me.

At 21 he was a few years older than me. He had a job, a car and rented a bedsit on Sampson Road in Sparkbrook. He also knew my friend Matthew. Leaning in close to hear me over the music he asked about my job. He said he could pick me up after work one night and take me out for something to eat. It caught me off guard a little. I laughed it off but didn't say no.

Barely anyone had a mobile phone back then so it took a few more weeks of our paths crossing at the Waggon before I actually agreed to anything. I'd never been on a date before so was avoiding saying yes out of shyness and nerves. But in the end, I couldn't help but be flattered by his persistence.

He arranged to pick me up from work one night in the week, just like he said. I spent the whole day injecting wax trying to ignore the butterflies in my stomach. We were so used to talking to each other when we were in a busy pub with other people. What was it going to be like when it was just us?

When I finished work at 5pm he was sat outside waiting for me in his old Astra. Trying to stay cool, I walked over, climbed into the passenger seat and put my seatbelt on.

'Good day at work?' he asked, starting up the car.

'Yeah, fine.'

It was all I could think of to say. Our eyes met, he smiled and I did a stupid giggle.

We went for a Pizza Hut then walked round to the Odeon and saw a film. He paid for everything. *So this is what boyfriends and girlfriends do*, I thought. It all felt very grown up.

There was a bit of a bombshell, however. Over the pizza he dropped into conversation that he had a daughter – Mya. He said he hadn't been with his ex-girlfriend, Marie, for long and they had split up while she was pregnant.

'I've been looking after Mya most weekends,' he explained. 'I pay Marie's rent to help her out. We didn't get on when we were together, but things are OK now.

'I've got Mya this weekend,' he went on. 'You could come round and meet her if you want?'

***

I don't know what I was expecting when I rocked up at his place with Gemma that weekend, but it certainly wasn't a baby. Mya must have only been about eight weeks old. And that wasn't all – he was babysitting Mya's half-brother, Marie's son from another relationship, too.

I should have been freaked out. I probably was at first. But any rumblings that this was a slightly weird set-up for a second date were forgotten as Mark handed me the baby. Me and Gemma took turns holding her and giving her a bottle. She was so cute. To naive teenagers it was like playing mom with a live doll.

There was no doubt in my mind that I wanted kids one day. Despite being a tomboy I used to sit and write lists of the names I would call my children. The boys' names I liked best were Kaden and Jaden. I laugh now, but for girls I liked Shania and Shakira. I was obviously quite swayed by whoever was famous at the time!

I always imagined myself having lots of boys. I wanted what I had growing up – stability. I wanted the husband, the kids, the house. But as far as I was concerned, having babies was something way off in the distant future. Or so I thought.

We'd both turned 17 when Gemma fell pregnant. When she broke the news to the teenage father, he dumped her. I remember thinking how strong she was – she wanted the baby and just got on with it. She didn't cry about it, not to me at least. If anything she seemed excited. I tried to imagine what she was going to look like with a bump and wondered what it would feel like to have a baby moving inside you.

***

There was no big discussion, but after our first couple of dates there was an unspoken understanding that Mark and I were now together. We saw each other a couple of times a week. We would go to the pub in a group, to the cinema or just hang out on our own at his flat. Even though I had my own money, he always paid for everything. It was nice. He was nice. I liked having a boyfriend.

I was a virgin when we met and felt comfortable enough with him to take the next step. I was so nervous the first time, though. I don't remember much about it but I know I definitely didn't enjoy it. It's not that he did anything bad or wrong, it was just nerves on my part. And I think it was a while before I felt ready to do it again.

One night, after a bit of a fall out with a friend, I stormed round to Mark's place. He sat calmly, listening to me rant, then put his arm round me.

'Don't worry,' he smiled. 'You know I love you, right?'

'I love you too,' I said.

My parents had no idea I was seeing someone. I was still avoiding being at home unless I really had to be, so it was easy to say I was staying at a friend's when really I was sleeping at Mark's. I think they might have even seen me with him but because I had so many male friends they assumed he was a mate.

For a couple of months things were going great. Then suddenly I felt different. We did use condoms, but not every single time. It sounds so naive but it had never really crossed my mind that I might get pregnant. We certainly hadn't talked about it. I think deep down I already knew. But without telling a soul, I went to the chemist on my lunch break and picked up a test. When I got home that night, everyone was in. Without saying hello, I went straight to the loo, locked the door and peed on the stick. The box said to wait for a minute so I flushed the chain, put the test up my coat sleeve and made a beeline for my room. My heart was thumping as I stood with my back against the door. I pulled out the test. It was positive.

I stood there for ages, just staring at the test. I felt scared, overwhelmed. I was still only 17 and had a job I really enjoyed. I would never judge anyone for having an abortion, but I've always felt strongly that for me personally, it's not something I would be able to do. If this was happening my only choice was to go through with it.

I ran a hot bath, undressed and submerged myself in the bubbly water. Closing my eyes and taking a few deep breaths, the questions began ticking over in my mind ... I had always wanted children, but was I ready? What was Mark going to say? What were my *parents* going to say?

Well, I didn't have to wait too long to find out. I opened my eyes to find Mom standing over me, the positive pregnancy test in her hand. I'd stuffed it in my coat pocket and she'd found it as she tidied round. *Why does she have to be so bloody tidy?*

'What's all this?' she asked. She wasn't angry, but her face said it all – she was upset, disappointed. The life she had imagined for her eldest daughter was taking a completely different turn.

'Sarah,' she sighed, 'you're 17! You've got your whole life ahead of you! I didn't even know you had a boyfriend!'

'Please don't tell Dad!' I said, bursting into tears.

I told her about Mark, that he was a good boyfriend and treated me well. I think she was worried he had taken advantage of me because he was older, but I never felt that way. I told her I didn't want to get rid of the baby. A life was growing inside me and I had no intention of stopping it.

Mom understood. I think she felt guilty – she'd never really sat me down and given me the birds and the bees talk. She thought I told her everything and assumed I was still a long way off even thinking about having a boyfriend.

'Me and your dad will help you,' she said. 'We'll face it together, as a family. Everything will be OK.'

I told Mark face to face the next day. I remember him smiling and putting his arms around me. He didn't freak out. If anything, he seemed happy. I, on the other hand, had never been more terrified.

CHAPTER FOUR

Getting pregnant changed everything. Dad gave me the silent treatment for a few weeks. Mom liked having an excuse to mother me, while Stacey took great pleasure in winding me up. 'Look at you, all *pregnant*!' she mocked. 'I'm never going to end up like *you*!'

I remember Nan coming to see me and dreading her reaction, but she was really sympathetic.

'You'll be fine, bab,' she winked. Part of me felt like I'd let my parents down. I wouldn't have been able to cope if Nan had been disappointed in me too.

I was the first one in my main social circle to get pregnant, and certain friends disappeared off the face of the earth. Gemma, on the other hand, couldn't believe her luck.

'We're only two months apart!' she said, almost jumping for joy. 'They're going to grow up together like we did! Man, we have got so much shopping to do!'

Unfortunately, I soon realised there was more to pregnancy than getting fat and shopping for baby clothes. I felt absolutely awful. The morning sickness was so rough that it wasn't long before I stopped going into work. When I told Mom and Dad I'd quit they weren't happy. Not only was I leaving a decent job, it meant I would have to rely on them financially. But they could hardly force me to keep going when I was throwing up several times a day. I regret not sticking it out and maybe taking proper maternity leave but – typical teen-ager – I just didn't fully consider the long term.

I carried on treating Mom and Dad's like a hotel, eating and sleeping there, but spending my days hanging out at either Grace or Chantelle's house. Sometimes I would see Sam and Kelly. We would go into town and window shop. There were no more nights out or under-18s parties, I just relied on whoever was around to fill my time.

***

Mark was at work in the daytime so I would see him in the evenings. He saw nothing wrong with still going out on the weekends he didn't have Mya, though, which I resented. I was scared and fed up. Mark thought he should be allowed to carry on living his life and it annoyed the hell out of me that he could and I couldn't.

Just before we were due to have our very first scan the midwife came to my house for a routine check-up. She was filling in a form and when she asked Mark for his home address, he refused.

'Why can't you give her your address?' I asked, puzzled.

'I don't want to,' he said.

I was furious. It just set off this huge alarm bell that he wasn't serious about me.

'Just forget it,' I screamed at him. 'I don't need you! I can do this on my own!'

Mark left with his tail between his legs, no doubt a little embarrassed at my causing a scene in front of the midwife and my mom. I called him to tell him I wanted my CDs back and that I didn't want anything else to do with him. Yes, I was angry, but I was also serious. And Mark must have known I was because he didn't put up a fight. He didn't even try to phone or come round and I never got to the bottom of why he withheld his address. Maybe he was concerned about getting into trouble because I was so young. Maybe he was worrying about having to support another child financially. Whatever it was, it signalled the end of our relationship.

I thought I was in love with him – I'd meant it when I said it – but in hindsight, I didn't know what love was. I was just going through the motions, going along with the idea of being in a relationship. I thought having a boyfriend was a good thing. I thought it was what I wanted. I thought it was what I was supposed to be doing. But actually, even with a baby on the way, I felt better being on my own. I'm shocked by how strong I was about the break up. There were no tears – I barely gave him a second thought. I just remember putting a hand on my tummy and telling myself, 'You can do this.'

***

On the day of my routine 12-week scan it was Mom by my side. She must have sensed I was anxious because as we sat on the uncomfortable chairs in the Heartlands Hospital reception area she clasped her hand tightly around mine. She never said so, but when I think back to that time the worry was written all over her face. Having had two kids of her own, she knew how hard it was. She must have wondered how

I was going to cope with a baby when I was still just a baby myself. *Her* baby.

And she was right to worry. I was so clueless. I had no idea what was even involved in a scan. *IS it going to hurt? What will happen if there is something wrong with the baby?*

'Sarah Rose?'

We were called into a room and I was asked to lie down on a bed. The lady doing the scan lifted up my top and rubbed cold gel on my belly. I wasn't even showing yet. *Is there really a baby in there?*

I glanced nervously at Mom. Her smile reassured me as she placed her hand back on mine. I was so glad it was her in that room with me instead of Mark.

A grainy black-and-white picture appeared on the monitor next to us. I could make out a peanut-shaped blob. It was wriggling.

'And there's your baby,' the lady said, matter-of-factly.

All the tension I was feeling slipped away. A smile spread across my face. I felt a warm rush fizzle in my chest then quickly spread across my whole body. I felt elated. I loved that little peanut. And in that moment, the enormity of the love I felt took me completely by surprise.

'If you see here you can make out the heartbeat,' the lady continued, pointing at the screen.

Sure enough, we could clearly see a little flicker, pumping away. I could have stared at it all day long. It was amazing.

'Your baby is healthy and growing well,' she concluded. 'Keep looking after yourself and we'll see you again at 20 weeks.'

I walked out of Heartlands relieved and excited beyond belief. I couldn't wait for the next scan now, when they could tell me if it was a boy or a girl. I definitely wanted to know.

***

They say you're supposed to feel wonderful once you're past the 12-week mark, but I just couldn't seem to shake the morning sickness. In fact, I vomited my way through pretty much the whole pregnancy. There was none of the eating for two – every time I ate, I wanted to throw up.

The thought of my 20-week scan, of seeing my baby again and finding out the sex, was the only thing that kept me going.

When I finally got back to the hospital, I couldn't get up on that bed and lift my top up fast enough.

My belly was getting round now. It wasn't so obvious that people would fall over themselves to give me a seat on the bus, but it was definitely getting there. The lady applied the gel and started pressing the scanner against my tummy. The grainy blob appeared on the screen again. It was definitely bigger this time. Whatever she was doing seemed to take an absolute age.

'Do you want to find out the sex today?'

I thought she was never going to ask.

'Yes, please,' I said.

My heart was racing.

'So if you just take a little look down here,' she said, zooming in, 'I can tell you you're having a boy.'

I looked at Mom. We both had huge smiles on our faces. I laughed and my eyes filled up, like all the happiness was about to tumble out of them as tears. A boy – just like I'd always imagined.

The prospect of becoming a mom felt more real than ever. I started writing lists of names again. But now I was picking a real name for a real baby, none of the ones I'd liked when I was at school and daydreaming seemed right. I wanted something unusual.

One night, I was round at Matthew's and an Arsenal game was on the telly. When I heard the commentator say the name Thierry Henry it was like a light turning on in my mind.

'That's it!' I said. 'I'm going to call him Thierry!'

You can imagine my mom's reaction when I bounded through the door and broke the news.

'You're not calling my grandson bloody Thierry!'

But I'd made up my mind. That was the one.

**

As my due date drew closer the movements and the kicks got stronger. Despite still being so sick I got anaemic, I couldn't wait to meet my baby. Even Stacey warmed to the idea of being an aunty and was always first in line when it was time to shop for baby things. I think she thought the baby would be like another doll for her to play with.

I spent more and more time with Gemma, too. We would go shopping or put our feet up at her house. We were always comparing bumps in the mirror and whinging about our aches and pains.

Her son Aston was born on Christmas Eve 2003 and I waddled up to Heartlands Hospital to visit them. She'd had a straightforward birth that was over in four hours. *Labour doesn't sound so bad!* I thought. Seeing Gemma with her baby just made me even more excited to meet mine.

By the New Year I was just a huge round bump with skinny arms and legs sticking out. Despite feeling so tired and rotten, I loved the way my belly looked. Everything seemed to be going to plan. The baby was head down and engaged and Mom helped me pack my hospital bag. I was ready.

Unfortunately, the baby wasn't.

***

My due date came and went. I was ten whole days overdue when I finally went to Heartlands to be induced. It was a fresh, sunny morning. Me and Mom caught the bus. I felt so heavy at this point I was struggling to walk.

When we arrived we were taken to a spacious private room with a big bed, a chair and a TV. When the midwife examined me I felt so embarrassed, lying there with my legs apart. I closed my eyes, took a deep breath and reminded myself she'd probably seen more lady bits than I'd had hot dinners.

'Right,' she said. 'We are happy to go ahead and induce you today. I'm just going to break your waters.'

I felt a sharp stabbing pain, a pop, then a gush of water.

'You OK, love?' Mom asked.

'Yeah,' I lied. I didn't like it but I wanted to be brave.

The midwife gave me a pessary and a hormone injection.

'That's it for now,' she said. 'The best thing you can do is keep moving around. Good old gravity should help that baby move down to where he needs to be.'

The contractions started almost straight away. They were mild at first, just like a bit of period cramping. But eventually they got so intense that I would have to stop whatever I was doing and breathe through them.

Grace and Chantelle knew I was being induced that day. Every hour or so one of them would call my phone, excited for news.

'Have you had him yet?' they would ask.

But things were moving very slowly. The contractions were getting stronger but I wasn't dilating.

Grace and Chantelle decided to come to the hospital. They helped me walk around my room, out into the reception area and up and down the stairs. Then when I had to stop and breathe through a contraction they would rub my back and say something funny to take my mind off it.

When visiting hours ended, the girls said their goodbyes and it was just me and Mom again.

'I'm so tired,' I told her. 'Why is it taking so long?'

The pain ramped up overnight. Even with gas and air it was total agony. I was hooked up to a monitor that kept track of how strong the contractions were. Eventually the graph started going off the paper.

'The contractions are really strong,' a midwife said. 'You're handling them really well. But you're still not dilating.'

The more tired I got, the more pain I was in. And the more pain I was in, the less brave I got. It must have been awful for Mom to sit there watching and not be able to help.

Grace and Chantelle came back the next morning, but I was in such a state they didn't stay long.

Shortly after they left the atmosphere changed. The baby's heart rate started dropping and the midwives were concerned he was in distress. I was still only 4cm.

'We think an emergency caesarean section is the best way forward,' one of them said.

'It's fine,' I assured her through gritted teeth. 'I don't care. I just want you to get my baby out. Can you put me to sleep while you do it? I can't bear it any more, I can't bear it. Please, please, just put me to sleep. I don't want to be awake for it, please.'

They must have taken pity on me because they got me straight into theatre and knocked me out with general anaesthetic.

***

The next thing I remember was waking up in the recovery room. Mom was stood over me, smiling, and there was a baby boy swaddled in a blanket lying peacefully in the crook of my arm. He was so chunky! Eight pounds two ounces, they said. I couldn't believe he was here and he was mine. I stared in wonder at his face and his tiny fingers. It felt like a miracle had happened. He was amazing. And he definitely looked like a Thierry.

My moment taking it all in was cut short. A midwife pulled back my white bed clothes and realised I was soaked in blood. Thierry was taken off me so they could deal with what turned out to be a pretty serious haemorrhage. The whole experience of giving birth was traumatic from start to finish, never mind that I was still only 18 years old.

The memory that stands out the most, however, is seeing my dad hold Thierry for the very first time. He was one of the first to come and visit us, bringing Stacey with him as soon as he'd finished work. I watched him cradle my tiny little bundle, tears filling his eyes. I still have the photograph that one of us took.

That moment was a turning point for me. Suddenly, it didn't matter that he wasn't my real dad. This was his first grandchild and he loved us unconditionally as his own. Thierry had repaired our bond.

CHAPTER FIVE

In hindsight, I think the baby blues started before I'd even left the hospital. I loved Thierry completely and never regretted having him, not for a second. But the teenager in me was sulking.

I spent three days in hospital recovering from the surgery. The midwives badgered me to get out of bed, to have a shower, to get dressed. I think they were making sure I wasn't just lying in bed feeling sorry for myself, which to be fair, I probably was.

I was too shy and embarrassed to breastfeed, so Thierry had formula from a bottle. He was a greedy little thing, guzzling down every drop of every bottle we gave him. But on day two, despite feeding well, he wouldn't stop crying. The midwives were so concerned they took him into their room to try and settle him for me, away from the other moms on the ward. It seemed a bit strange, but I tried not to worry too much. Then one of them came back with a serious question to ask me.

'Do you have a drug problem?' she asked. 'Have you taken any recreational drugs during your pregnancy?'

I couldn't believe what she was asking me. I'd never touched drugs in my life. I certainly hadn't decided to take them up while I was expecting a baby. Maybe it was common for them to see druggie teenage moms bearing children who then suffer withdrawal, but I assured her I wasn't one of them. Thankfully, she seemed happy to take my word for it and after a couple of hours Thierry settled. They put it down to the trauma of the labour.

The news that I'd had the baby spread quickly. Matthew was one of my first close friends to visit and was all smiles as he held Thierry for the first time.

'I've got something to ask you,' I said. 'I'd really like you to be his godfather.'

Matthew seemed genuinely touched.

'That would be ace,' he smiled.

'Great,' I said. 'You can start by changing your first nappy.'

I watched as Matthew lay Thierry on a changing mat, carefully removed the nappy he was wearing then lifted his legs to wipe his bottom. Right on cue Thierry weed all over him. When we had managed to stop laughing, Matthew told me that Thierry's dad Mark had come with him and was sat waiting in reception.

'I know you said you didn't want to see him,' Matthew said, 'but we hoped you might change your mind. He really wants to meet his son.'

It was nice of Matthew to try, but I was having none of it.

'No,' I snapped. 'I've done all this without him. I don't want him just waltzing in here and taking all the glory. Who does he think he is?!'

Matthew didn't push it. He kissed me and Thierry goodbye and left.

The visitors kept on coming – Aunty Maggie and the twins came, then my nan and grandad with all the booties, hats and cardigans she'd knitted. There was always someone with me during visiting hours. I felt strangely detached from it all, though, like I wasn't really there. The days were busy and the nights were long and lonely.

Once I was allowed home, Mom went into full fussing mode. She had washed all Thierry's baby clothes and laid out a selection on my bed ready for him to wear. She announced that now there was a baby in the house it was strictly a no-smoking zone. As well as welcoming a new addition to the family, we were preparing to move again. Our maisonettes on Clopton Road were being knocked down so the council moved us to a three-bedroom house on Wash Lane in Yardley. It was just what we needed – more space and a huge garden that Mom couldn't wait to throw a party in. Plus, we were even closer to Nan and Grandad.

I was still tired and in a lot of pain from the C-section so for a while Mom insisted on having Thierry in her room at night time so I could sleep. Even when I felt better and we moved the Moses basket into my room, she would hear me get up to do the night feeds and come straight in: 'Let me, let me.' We clashed a bit. She wanted to do everything. Sometimes I took advantage, sometimes I just wanted to shout, 'He's *my* son!' But despite locking horns from time to time, I don't know what I would have done without her.

***

It was a strange time for me. I healed well and got straight back into my jeans. But I was shell-shocked from the birth and overwhelmed about having a living, breathing baby who needed me 24/7. Somewhere during the pregnancy all the confidence I'd had as a carefree teenager had disappeared. I now know that all these feelings are very normal for a new mom, especially a young one. But at the time, all I knew was how to bottle everything up. And with no way of expressing how I was feeling, my inner turmoil snowballed until I felt on edge pretty much all the time.

***

I can't remember exactly when the obsessive compulsive disorder started but Thierry was still only small. If he was asleep, I would check on him constantly, terrified he might have stopped breathing. Then it escalated to other things in the house. If there was a gap in the curtains I would have to get up and adjust it. If I looked in the mirror I would have to walk past it four times. If I turned on a light I would have to pull the cord ten times. My family couldn't help but notice. Mom must have encouraged me to speak to someone because when Thierry was about two months old and had just been christened, I started seeing a counsellor called Julie. She was skinny with short, cropped hair. All she really did was ask a few questions and let me talk, but it helped a lot. I opened up about Dad and how I missed being a normal teenager – things I was feeling but hadn't properly acknowledged or said out loud to anyone. Offloading to Julie once a week made me feel lighter and more in control. She helped me understand that my OCD was a natural result of a stressful time in my life. Gradually, if I felt the urge to engage in any of the habits I'd developed, I could just tell myself to get a grip and not do it.

Mom must have been so worried, though. She continued to bend over backwards for me and Thierry, always encouraging me to go out and keep living my life. After some gentle persuasion, I started having Thursday nights off, where she would babysit and I would go out, just to a mate's house or something. I appreciated feeling like the old – or should I say young? – me for a few hours.

Meanwhile Thierry was becoming this awesome little person. He was a good baby. He always seemed very alert and interested in the world. Stacey couldn't wait to get home from school and play with him. He would be sat minding his own business in his baby bouncer and she would put his arms and legs into different positions, like he was a little doll. When Dad got home he would give him a cuddle and a bottle. It was a team effort. There hadn't been a baby in the house since my sister. It seemed to lift everyone – it was like he was all of ours.

***

For the first six months of Thierry's life, Mark pestered me like mad to see him. He really tried. He would phone or get Matthew to speak to me. Mom and Dad never confronted him, but they were firmly on my side. The feeling was that as long as I wanted him to stay away, he should never darken our door.

Looking back, I was selfish playing God like that and I regret it with all my heart. I've never agreed with stopping dads from seeing their kids, not without good reason. But I was angry and stubborn. And it felt like too little, too late.

The situation really bugged Matthew – he didn't agree with me cutting Mark out of Thierry's life.

'You're wrong,' he would say. 'You have to let Mark see Thierry, he's his dad.'

It annoyed the hell out of me that Matthew – one of my best friends – was fighting Mark's corner. But, eventually, I had to accept that what he was saying was right. I picked up the phone and called Mark.

'You can come and meet Thierry,' I said. 'Let's work something out.'

When he came round he couldn't stop smiling at his son. Suddenly, all the anger and bitterness I'd been feeling seemed like a waste of energy.

'Look,' I said, 'if you want to see Thierry, you can. Come round whenever you want.'

And he did. Sometimes it was twice a month, sometimes he would pop in as much as once a week. Our relationship was over, but he was making an effort to have a relationship with his baby boy. I decided that as long as he kept making the effort, Thierry deserved to have his dad in his life.

***

I was keen to get another job and start supporting myself. I absolutely detested the single mom stereotype. Back then everyone thought teenage girls only got pregnant so they could get a council house. I felt people's eyes tarring me with that brush whenever I was out with the pushchair. I wanted to stand on my own two feet, prove I wasn't that cliché and set a good example for my son.

Thierry was nine months and crawling when I went up town and traipsed round the shops handing out CVs. It paid off. Pretty much straight away I got a call from Poundland. After a brief interview I was offered a part-time position. It was hardly my dream job but I enjoyed it. While Mom looked after Thierry I stocked shelves and worked the tills three times a week. I thought it was great. It didn't even matter that my maths was so bad – everything was £1!

The best thing about the job was the people. Most of the staff were a similar age to me so I made friends with some of the girls. We would have lunch together in the canteen and occasionally, if Mom didn't mind another few hours' babysitting, I would go to the cinema with them after work.

Nabeel was a tall skinny Asian guy who worked in the warehouse. I would see him around, all six foot one of him, either when I was collecting boxes in the warehouse or in the canteen at lunchtime. We started talking more and more and I was surprised by how well we got on. There was nothing that stood out and made me fancy him. And we had absolutely nothing in common – I was a single mom, he was a Muslim who never touched a drop of alcohol. But he seemed like a really nice guy.

He told me about his family. He lived at home with his parents and younger sister. They had a brother too, who had moved away. I talked a lot about Thierry to everyone and Nabeel was no different. I never wanted to hide the fact that I had a son, but there was always the worry that people would think less of me for being a teenage mom. Nabeel probably knew about Thierry way before I dropped him into conversation. If he was ever shocked that I was a mom he certainly didn't show it.

One night over dinner, I told Mom I'd met someone at work. Her eyebrows lifted as she considered what I was saying.

'What's his name?'

'Nabeel. He's a Muslim.'

Given her painful experience with my real dad, Mom's heart must have sunk. She knew first-hand how difficult it was for Muslim men and western women to be together.

'Does he know about Thierry?' she asked.

'Yeah,' I shrugged. 'We're just friends anyway.'

Maybe Nabeel was playing the long game, but at the time that's what I believed we were – just friends. Good friends who laughed and talked.

One lunchtime, I told him it was Thierry's first birthday coming up.

'Are you having a party?' he asked.

'I don't think so,' I replied. 'Maybe just presents and a cake or something.'

'Why don't *we* do something?' he suggested. 'The three of us.'

'Like what?'

'I dunno … What about the zoo? Dudley Zoo is good.'

'He really loves animals actually,' I said.

'Let's do it then! I won't take no for an answer.'

* * *

That day at the zoo, Thierry was in his element. Nabeel got him up on his shoulders and he was pointing at all the animals. Afterwards, Nabeel took us to McDonald's for a Happy Meal. It was a perfect day. I thought it was really sweet of him to make such an effort with my son. Not many young men would have done that.

It wasn't long before our chats got a bit deeper. I never imagined that he would be my type but I liked that he was sensible, calm and thoughtful. He was easy to talk to and made me laugh. He was never cocky. He never turned on the charm like most guys would have done. We had a genuine connection and everything just seemed to develop really naturally. The only sticking point was his parents. He was always completely upfront about the fact he could never tell them he was with a non-Muslim girl. But what 19-year-old really cares about meeting the parents anyway?

'It'll never work,' Mom would say, her tone teasing me but her words desperately trying to make me see sense.

But I didn't listen. I threw caution to the wind and allowed our friendship to become a relationship. We liked each other. I was happy. What could possibly go wrong?

CHAPTER SIX

I stared at the Poundland pregnancy test. Before I'd even disappeared into the staff toilet to pee on it I knew what it was going to say. *Oh my God*, I thought. *What have I done? I'm 19. Two kids by two different men? Two different colours?!*

The walls of the cubicle seemed to be closing in. I sat on the loo with my head in my hands. I couldn't believe this was happening to me again. *How could I have been so careless?*

All I can say is that I must have written off the first time as a fluke. But the reality is I was young and fertile, and those one or two occasions when a condom isn't to hand are all it takes. I've learned that the hard way.

Once again I was flooded with a swirl of conflicting emotions. There was a baby growing inside me. My heart swelled. I thought of Thierry and knew that I loved this baby as much as him already. An abortion was never an option. But the situation was nowhere near ideal. I still lived at home, and Nabeel and I had only been a couple for two months. His parents had no idea I even existed. Apparently he pretended to be working when really he was with me. And now we had an even bigger bombshell – their first grandchild. *Would they disown him? Would they make him dump me? And if he doesn't stick around, can I really do this on my own again? Another pregnancy? Another birth? Raising another baby without its father?*

I wrapped the test in toilet paper, chucked it into a bin and went back to work. I was so deep in thought the rest of my shift seemed to fly. I was glad. I knew one thing for sure, I needed to get home and tell Mom. My stomach was doing somersaults the whole bus ride home. I knew I could count on her to be there for me, but I was still a nervous wreck. I hated feeling like I was letting my parents down.

When I got to the house, Mom was in the kitchen doing dinner. I walked straight in and just blurted it out.

'Mom, I'm pregnant again.'

I covered my face with my hands. I couldn't bear to see the disappointment in her face.

'Oh, Sarah, not again! Did you not learn your lesson the first time? You have to be so careful!'

'What am I gonna do?' I asked, dropping my hands to my sides. 'Two kids by two different men. How did I get into this mess? Nabeel's parents still don't even know about me!'

'Have you told him?'

'No, not yet.'

'Well, sit down with him and talk it out. If he's got a decent bone in his body he *has* to tell his mom and dad. Trust me, the longer the lies go on the worse it gets.'

I started to think that maybe the baby was a blessing in disguise. *Surely his family will have to accept me if I am carrying his child?*

Nabeel was due to come over that night. I watched the clock nervously until he knocked on the door then we went upstairs and sat on the bed. Just like I had with Mom, I decided to blurt the news out immediately.

'So, erm, I'm pregnant.'

I stared at him, waiting to read his reaction.

'Pregnant?'

'Yeah. I did a test today. At work. Mom knows. I had to tell her. What do you think? I mean, I can't get rid of it. I just don't think I could go through with an abortion ...'

'Hey, hey, hey,' he said, shushing me. 'No one said anything about an abortion! It's fine! *I'm* fine! It's pretty exciting actually!'

'Really?'

'Look, we're in this together. I'm here for you. Whatever you need.'

'What about your parents?'

'That's the tricky part. But listen, I'll tell them when the baby comes. It will be fine.'

He put his arms around me and I took a deep breath.

It's all OK, I thought. *He's going to support me. And he'll tell them when the baby comes.*

* * *

The sickness was just as bad as the first time, if not worse. I couldn't even put a toothbrush in my mouth to brush my teeth without throwing up. I was on iron tablets which made me constipated. And I was so tired all the time. I don't know who these women are who feel radiant and wonderful, but I certainly wasn't one of them. The only joy I felt during the whole pregnancy was when the baby moved. Watching my belly jump and wriggle, knowing there was a baby in there, was absolutely magical. Whenever I was at home and felt any movement, I would shout to Thierry, 'The baby's moving! Come and see!'

I would press his hand against my belly so he could feel the kicks. He was completely deadpan at first. But when he started to understand, his little face would light up.

'There's a baba in there, Thierry,' I'd say, and he would kiss my bump. Well, I say kiss – it was mostly dribble.

Thierry was walking now. He was a late starter with some of the physical milestones. Gemma's daughter was walking at 11 months, Thierry was more like 14. He took his first steps for my mom while I was out at work. I was gutted at the time, but soon got over it as I watched him practising. Within a week he was walking perfectly. And he was so inquisitive. He got a real kick out of counting and pointing to all his body parts, so I made sure I did little things like that with him every day. He was obsessed with dinosaurs. He had one that roared when you pressed its tummy. I can't say I was upset when he dropped it in the bath and it stopped working.

The pride I felt for Thierry kind of took me by surprise. Watching him develop into such a bright, clever little boy just made me love him even more. I used to look at him and think, *Wow, he's mine.* When he learnt something new, or even just came over and put his arms around me for a hug, he made me realise I wasn't missing out on anything. It was all worth it: children are a gift.

It was very different being pregnant and having a boyfriend around. Despite keeping his parents in the dark, Nabeel made sure he was at every appointment. At the 20-week scan we took Thierry with us. The sonographer pointed everything out to him as he sat staring at the screen, not really sure what to make of it all.

'Do you want me to tell you if it's a boy or a girl?' she asked.

We said yes. There was no way I could wait.

'We've got another little boy in there,' she smiled, first at me and then Thierry. 'You're going to have a little brother.'

Another boy – I was delighted and so was Nabeel. He couldn't stop grinning.

'I'd really like him to have a Muslim name,' Nabeel said afterwards. I had no intention of raising my son as a Muslim, but maybe a name wouldn't be a bad compromise. I was open to suggestions.

'Omar?' Nabeel said, tentatively.

I scrunched up my nose.

'Fazal? It means grace,' he explained. But he could tell by my face I wasn't feeling that one either.

'What about Kamran?'

Something about Kamran seemed right. As well as being a Muslim name, the spelling 'Cameron' has Celtic roots and is popular in Ireland. I liked it. It just seemed to fit.

We agreed Kamran was the one, and that his surname would be Rose. I felt it was important that the new baby had the same last name as me and Thierry, and Nabeel understood.

Shortly after the scan I stopped working at Poundland and started nesting. I still had all Thierry's baby clothes but that didn't stop us buying more. It was easy to pretend we were a happy family-to-be when we were at the Merry Hill Shopping Centre spending Nabeel's money on cute Babygros and sleep suits, but it was really starting to bother me how much he was lying to his family.

That September, for my twentieth birthday, Nabeel took me to Blackpool for the weekend. I remember us going down for breakfast at our hotel and trying really hard not to laugh when we realised we were the youngest people there by about 40 years. We had a lovely weekend. I couldn't go on any of the rides, but we walked around the fair, the amusements and the waxwork museum. I went home laden with tacky gifts for everybody and toys for Thierry. I held on to all the good times as a sign Nabeel was going to tell his parents one day. But with every week that ticked by, I was getting more and more impatient.

'Have you told your mom and dad yet?'

It went from being a genuine question to a loaded one and he gave me every excuse in the book. 'It's not a good time,' he would say. 'I'll do it next week. Dad's not happy with me at the moment, it'll have to wait.' Nabeel's reasons may have been perfectly valid, but they were sounding more and more ludicrous to me. I was nearing the end of my rope and Mom wasn't far behind. For her it was like watching history repeat itself. I just couldn't get my head around what the big deal was – why couldn't he just tell them? What I understand now, several years on, is that it wasn't about me or what his parents thought of us: it was all down to the fear of what the Muslim community would think of Nabeel's family. He didn't want to bring shame on them. I was so blindsided by how it was affecting me, I never fully appreciated the extent of that pressure.

Towards the end of 2005 we started going to antenatal classes at Heartlands Hospital every Thursday night. My cousin Sam was pregnant too, so sometimes she would come with us.

As my due date drew closer, Nabeel came up with a proposal.

'Would you consider becoming a Muslim?'

He thought that if he could tell his parents I was converting it would make breaking the news a little easier. But I've been brought up Catholic and believe in God 100 per cent. I couldn't even consider it. My answer was no and he didn't push it. I don't think he ever seriously expected me to say yes. All I could do was hold on to his promise, 'I'll tell them when the baby comes.' But I think I already knew he was never going to keep it.

The situation really started to get to me. I just wanted a normal family and a daddy for my baby, but I couldn't see it happening. For the last few weeks of my pregnancy I was an emotional wreck. I think that's how I knew I was in love with Nabeel. Ditching Mark had been relatively easy, even with his baby in my belly. But this time, emotions ran deep. I didn't want to lose Nabeel, but I couldn't see a future for us either, not if the only choice was for him to carry on hiding us.

I cried on Mom's shoulder.

'How am I going to do this?' I sobbed. 'Another baby, another dad that's not around. Why does this keep happening to me?'

She never once said 'I told you so'.

'He said he would tell them when the baby comes,' she soothed. 'There's still time.'

'He's not going to, Mom. I just know. How am I going to cope with two kids?'

She sighed and put her arm round me.

'As long as you have a routine,' she said wisely, 'everything will be fine. And you've got your family, Sarah. We'll get through it. We'll always be here for you.'

CHAPTER SEVEN

After the traumatic arrival of Thierry, I desperately wanted to have my second baby naturally. It's drummed into you that the natural way is the best way and I was in no hurry to go through the grim agony of another C-section, especially with a toddler to look after. I tried to keep my feet on the ground. Surely it couldn't be any worse than the first time? But with the memories of Thierry's birth still fresh in my mind and all the stress of Nabeel, my nerves were getting the better of me.

With four weeks to go, my midwife suggested I try weekly reflexology at the hospital. As well as helping with relaxation, it has been known to give natural labour a little helping hand.

Everyone thought I was mad, letting someone fiddle with my feet. But my God, it was bliss! I think I drifted off to sleep at almost every session.

Excited for the new arrival, Nan knitted booties, hats, cardigans and blankets. Mom prepared for the new baby the best way she knew how – by washing all the tiny clothes and cleaning the house.

'You don't need to do so much this time, Mom,' I told her. 'I relied on you too much with Thierry. I need to do more myself.'

She reluctantly agreed, before insisting that me and the boys take the master bedroom.

'It's the biggest room,' she said. 'It makes sense. Me and Dad will have your room.'

So on Mom's orders, Dad got the Moses basket out and switched all the furniture around. Thierry and I shared a double bed. I know the experts frown on co-sleeping, but he was my first and I liked having him close to me, especially if it meant us both getting a better night's sleep.

Unfortunately, as lovely as it was, the reflexology didn't help bring my labour on naturally. My due date came and went. As I approached the ten-day overdue mark, I started to get déjà vu. On 22 January 2006, I was admitted to Heartlands Hospital and induced. Nabeel was with me, and my mom of course. I wanted her there, although she probably would have been by my side whether I requested it or not. For the best part of two days I lay in that hospital in crippling pain. This time I had some pain relief – regular injections of pethidine in my leg. It didn't stop the pain, but it was strong enough to take the edge off. Between contractions, I was like a drunken lunatic. I kept shouting, 'Mom! I love you! Nabeel! I love you!'

To be fair to him, Nabeel was great. Through the worst bits he held my hand and told me everything was going to be OK. His parents still had no idea their first grandchild was on the way. I've no idea how he explained his absence to them while he was at the hospital with me. By this time I didn't care.

***

After 40 hours of labour I heard the dreaded prognosis.

'Your labour is not progressing sufficiently. We recommend getting you up to theatre for an emergency C-section.'

Just like the first time, I wasn't dilating. I wasn't going to have a natural birth. Only one person was allowed into theatre with me. It must have killed Mom to let Nabeel go, but she quickly agreed that he was the father, he should be there. Maybe part of her was hoping that seeing his son born would be the kick up the backside he needed.

I was wheeled into theatre and given a spinal to numb me from the chest down. Things weren't going the way I had hoped, but I can't describe how relieved I was to not feel the contractions any more. All I could feel was some gentle tugging as they cut me open and pulled my baby out.

I heard crying. They quickly weighed him then wrapped him in a blanket and passed him to Nabeel. He looked so long. And so wrinkly! Like a little old man.

Kamran – born 24 January 2006, weighing eight pounds exactly.

I looked at my baby, then Nabeel. His eyes were full of tears. I hoped that this would be the turning point for us.

***

Despite being my second C-section in two years, I recovered surprisingly well. During the mandatory three-day hospital stay, Nabeel took time off from work and was at my bedside for 8am every morning. The first day he brought flowers. Then he fulfilled my requests for chocolate, crisps and magazines.

I'm shocked, thinking back now. There were a lot of Muslim women having babies at Heartlands Hospital but he never seemed worried about being spotted by someone he knew.

After going home to get some rest, Mom returned with Dad, Stacey and Thierry. I was desperate to see my boy. Even though being in hospital with a new baby was a perfectly good reason, I couldn't help but feel guilty and tearful being away from him. He followed our orders to give his new baby brother a kiss and a cuddle. But, to our amusement, he was far more interested in watching CBeebies on the hospital telly. Everyone else took turns holding Kamran and took lots of photos on their mobile phones, even though the quality was terrible back then.

No one gave Nabeel a hard time. My parents weren't happy that their daughter and new grandson were still a big secret. All any parent wants for their daughter is a decent partner who can be there and support them, especially at a time like this. But, for my sake, they bit their tongues and kept things pleasant.

Nabeel must have been at work the day I brought Kamran home because it was just me, my parents, Stacey and Thierry, who was now a month away from his second birthday. With Dad at work full time, and Stacey nearly 16 and in her last year at school, my days consisted of being at home with Mom, feeding, burping and changing two lots of nappies. It was hard work. Kamran was quite a whingey baby. I was naturally more confident than I had been with Thierry, but even with the strong painkillers I was on, my tummy was still really sore from being cut open again. Sitting down, standing up and getting up stairs was really painful. I wasn't allowed to lift anything heavier than Kamran for six weeks. It broke my heart not being able to pick Thierry up when he reached up to me, wanting cuddles.

On a good day we would get out of the house, even if it was just to the supermarket or to Nan and Grandad's for tea and biscuits. To my relief, Thierry didn't show any signs of jealousy. In fact, he couldn't have been more loving towards his little brother. He was always kissing him and stroking him. I've got a picture of Kam in his baby bouncer with Thierry next to him. They're staring at each other and you can just see the love between them.

Just like Thierry, we had Kamran christened when he was two months old. I still had Thierry's christening outfit so I dressed Kam in that – white booties, a shirt, trousers and a little waistcoat. Nan made a cake. We had the service at the Corpus Christi Roman Catholic Church, where she and Grandad married, then a party in Mom's back garden. I didn't consult Nabeel. I wanted my son christened like everyone else in our family and didn't want to give Nabeel the opportunity to say no.

Mark continued to visit Thierry most weeks. Nabeel would pop round and play with Kamran either on his days off or after work. I started to get annoyed with him, though. He knew the boys were in bed at 7.30pm, yet he would turn up at 8pm, wanting to see Kamran. He told me he wanted me to bring him up eating halal meat and avoiding pork. I told him he had no right to tell me how to raise my son when he couldn't even tell his parents he had one.

By this point I sounded like a broken record. Every time we saw him I would say: 'Have you told your mom and dad yet?' The answer was always no. I remember looking at Kamran, thinking, *How can Nabeel do this? How can he not want to tell the world about his perfect little boy?* I couldn't understand why he couldn't choose, why he couldn't just stand up and face the music now Kamran was here – living, breathing, needing him.

For a brief moment, immediately after Kamran was born, I saw a flicker of hope for us. But as soon as I was home and the reality kicked in again, my dream of Nabeel telling his parents and us being a proper family unit seemed further away than ever. He did try – for a while he said and did all the right things. He gave me money when Kamran needed clothes. But ultimately, the shine was taken off everything because he wouldn't stand up and 'do the right thing'. Mom was right – it was never going to work. I got so sick of it all I would say, 'Don't bother coming round again.' I wasn't going to beg. I knew where his mom and dad lived. I could have gone round there and told them myself – God knows enough people told me to. But I would never do that. It was his family, his mess, his responsibility.

In the end there was no big break up. The situation had eaten away at our relationship until there was absolutely nothing left. For weeks I was heartbroken. I cried in Mom's arms. But he'd had more than enough chances to do the right thing. I had to look forward now.

***

Desperate to stand on my own two feet again, I got my old job back at Poundland. It was a double-edged sword – I was grateful to get out the house but then spent every single one of my part-time shifts wondering what the boys were doing and feeling guilty for not being at home.

Sometimes my hours would clash with Nabeel. But with him in the warehouse and me on the shop floor it was easy to keep my distance.

I started to think about what I wanted long term.

'I think I want to go to college,' I told my manager. 'Maybe I could do an NVQ in retail then apply for some better jobs.'

'They need a supervisor at our store in Erdington,' he said. 'Why don't you apply for that?'

It seemed like a good idea. It was full time but it was a better position and more money. Mom said she would help with the kids so I went for it. I was delighted when I got a call to say I'd got the job.

***

At first, I was in my element. It was June and sunny. The change of scenery and the new challenge put a spring in my step. I enjoyed earning my own money again and was so busy I didn't have time to think about Nabeel.

But two or three weeks in I couldn't shake the feeling that I'd bitten off more than I could chew.

For three months I plugged away, feeling more and more shattered, more and more upset that I was missing out on so much time with the boys. I barely saw them in the week. I felt like my mom was more of a mother to them than I was and it really started to hurt.

Sensing I was down, Mom kept asking when I was going to go out and enjoy myself.

'You know I don't mind babysitting,' she said. 'You're young! Have a night out! Have some fun for once!'

Eventually, I agreed. I hadn't seen my cousin Kelly in a while. I knew she would be up for it.

We arranged to go out on a Thursday night. I had work the next day but didn't start until the afternoon. I made a bit of an effort with my outfit – jeans, but with a nice top and heels. We met at Kelly's then got a bus into town and walked to the Rat and Parrot on Broad Street. As soon as we got there I spotted Duane, a guy Grace went out with when we used to hang out at youth club.

'Alright, Sarah,' he said, seeing me and beckoning us over. 'I'm just getting the drinks in. You want one?'

I've never been a big drinker, but if I do it's only ever one thing.

'Vodka and coke, please,' I said.

'I'll have the same,' said Kelly.

The bar was scattered with lively Thursday night drinkers shouting over the R&B that blared from the speakers. Me and Kelly knew the words to nearly every song.

Duane came back with our drinks.

'Have you met my mates?' he asked. 'This is Andre and this is Nicholas.'

Nicholas was tall with dark skin and a good physique. I felt my heart do a little flip. I could barely look at him. What was going on?

He came over.

'So what do you do, Sarah?' he asked.

'I'm a supervisor at Poundland,' I said. 'And I'm a single mom. I've got two boys.'

I always felt better putting it out there straight away. Like ripping a plaster off. If he didn't like it he would have to lump it.

I needn't have worried.

'I've got a daughter,' he said sympathetically. 'It didn't work out with her mom, but I get to see her most weekends.'

Nicholas was 21, a year older than me. He told me he still lived at home in Castle Vale and was in the process of looking for a new job. I don't know what it was, but just talking to him gave me butterflies.

Kelly and I stayed with Duane, Andre and Nicholas for the rest of the night. The music was great and we were on our feet dancing until it was time to go home. As we got ready to leave, Nicholas asked for my number. I gave it to him and he leaned in to kiss me goodbye. That kiss was the icing on the cake of a really fun night. I went home a very happy girl – I hadn't danced like that in ages and as for Nicholas, well, I'd never felt an instant attraction like I did that night.

'Bet he calls you,' Kelly said with a knowing nod.

I really hoped he would.

CHAPTER EIGHT

In September 2006, my stresses about full-time work came to a head. I was at an all-time low – cramming in over 40 hours per week, exhausted and missing my boys. I wanted a job but felt totally out of my depth. Maybe I aimed too high, too soon.

It sounds daft now, but when my boss at Poundland refused to let me book time off for my twenty-first birthday, it was the final straw. I had a massive strop and quit. If I'm honest, I was happy the situation gave me a way out.

The downside of quitting work was that I was now at home full time. Even before Kamran arrived, Mom's house was feeling cramped. I knew her heart was in the right place but she was driving me batty. If I didn't clean up, I was messy. If I *did* clean up, I didn't do it right. She vacuumed so often the boys became experts at napping through it. I could tell I was getting under her feet. I was far too laid-back for her. If something needs to be done, she'll do it straight away. I, on the other hand, don't mind a bit of washing in the basket or a cup being out of place. I wanted to be able to leave the dishes in the sink overnight if I chose to. I wanted my own space. I wanted to move out.

Mom didn't want me to go. I begged her to tell the council she was kicking me and the boys out. I'd been on the council list since Thierry was born and nothing was happening. This was the only way we could get a place of our own. The council took Mom's word and moved me, Thierry and Kamran to a hostel while they waited for a property to become available.

The hostel was in Small Heath, right near the Birmingham City Football Ground. Just the word 'hostel' conjured up visions of drug addicts and ex-cons. I braced myself for the worst but it really wasn't that bad. It was just a big old house sectioned into flats being used by families like us. I didn't take much with me – just our clothes and the TV from my room. We had our own room with a cot for Kamran and a single bed for me and Thierry. It was cramped to say the least. Up until he was three, Thierry could only go to sleep if he was holding my hand. By the end of the night he would be upside down with his feet in my face. I just kept reminding myself that it wouldn't be for long – four to six weeks according to the housing officer who checked us in.

We shared a small kitchen and bathroom with a polite Somalian family. But as they never used to come in until 10pm at night it felt like we had everything to ourselves. I filled our days by getting up and taking the boys to Mom's. We would spend most of the day there, she would give us our tea, then I'd catch the bus back to the hostel, bathe the boys around 5pm, do their milk and get them to bed.

Twice a week there was a parent and toddler group downstairs so I would make the effort to go. The boys liked playing with other kids and it helped to break up our routine. Thankfully, they didn't seem at all phased by the move.

***

Right on time, around four weeks into our stay, I was called into the housing office downstairs.

'Would you be interested in viewing this flat?' the guy asked. 'It's in Bromford, and it's available ASAP if you want it.'

I phoned Mom and told her the good news.

'Me and Dad will come with you,' she insisted. So the next day, we all piled into Dad's car and drove to Kempson Road, Bromford. The flat was on the top floor of a maisonette. It was a decent street, not far from some shops. There was a school nearby and a doctor's surgery directly opposite. It was perfect for us. I could have kissed the bloke from the council when I realised it was a three-bed – I thought we'd be lucky to get two.

'We'll take it,' I said, without a moment's hesitation.

Thierry's dad Mark had a van so we asked him to help us move. He and Dad loaded all our stuff up and when we arrived at the new flat, Mom entertained the kids while I stood dishing out orders, telling the men where I wanted everything putting. Aunty Maggie gave us a washing machine and Mom rallied round to make sure we had everything else. She gave us her cream sofa – another example of her going above and beyond the call of duty. She and Dad had to watch telly in their bedroom before they could afford a new one, but they never complained once.

As well as all the practical stuff, Mom's advice was never far from my mind. *As long as you have routine, everything will be fine.* So, just as they were at Nanny's house, I made sure Thierry and Kam were always bathed and in bed by 7.30pm.

***

Although I couldn't wait to cut the apron strings, standing on my own two feet and finally being a proper mommy was as daunting as it was exciting. I loved it, though, just me and my boys. Every morning we would sit on the sofa watching *Milkshake* on Channel 5. Then we would get dressed and either catch the bus to Mom's or sit and wait for Dad to drop her off to us on his way to work. Funny, isn't it? I couldn't wait to get away from her then ended up seeing her most days anyway! I suppose the reality was, I wanted my own space but I didn't want to lose the special bond we had between us and the kids. Plus, she lived for us. She was the first person I phoned if the boys got ill. The first one to offer to help when I needed it. She was my rock.

Stacey was a huge help too. I don't know if it was because I wasn't at home any more or just that she was growing up a bit, but I started to feel like we were getting close again. Our flat quickly became her second home. Pretty much every day she would come round after college. She would keep me company, help around the flat and play with her nephews. She was always doing Kamran's hair, styling it with gel when my back was turned, then getting him to pose for photos.

Kamran was a happy little soul who would start dancing the second he heard music. His favourite toy was one of those giraffes that you can clip onto things. I bought it for his cot but he was soon carrying it around everywhere. He was besotted with Thierry. He never bothered crawling, he just started walking at ten months. I'm convinced it's because he was so determined to copy his big brother. They were so cute together. Thierry was always dressed in jeans and tank tops. Kam had a lot of his hand-me-downs, but if we were leaving the flat, my favourite thing was to dress them in matching outfits. I hardly ever bought clothes for myself. Any spare cash went on buying two of something smart from the kids' department in Next.

Nothing made me happier than watching them run around the flat, making each other cackle with laughter. I enjoyed even the simple things like getting to cook their tea at night. They were both good eaters and loved anything with chicken. They had the odd squabble – kids naturally get possessive over toys – but I could just sit and watch them potter about for hours. In all honesty, they were both golden. They knew that as soon as the theme tune for *Emmerdale* came on that it was time for bed. They would just toddle off by themselves – no fuss – and I would follow them up, give Kamran his bottle, tuck them in and kiss them goodnight. Mom's tips about routine really did pay off.

It hadn't been easy getting to this point, but I loved them both so much. My whole life revolved around them. The most special thing in the world to me was seeing their little smiley faces every day. I wanted us to have designated family time, just like I'd had growing up. So every Sunday I took them to the local Wacky Warehouse. I would let them loose in the soft play area then treat them to lunch. It was nothing fancy but to them it was like having a party once a week.

***

Things were going really well when I bumped into Duane one day in the street, the guy Grace used to go out with.

'What are you doing here?' he asked.

'Me and the boys have got our own place on Kempson Road,' I explained. 'It's great. You should come round some time.'

'Are you still in touch with Nicholas?' he asked.

Oh yeah! I thought. *Nicholas!*

'Nah, we haven't spoken in a while,' I said. 'It just fizzled out. I don't think I've even got his number anymore.'

'You should give him a call now you're living here,' he suggested. 'He lives on Dixon Close, it's not far from here.'

Duane dug his phone out of his pocket, found Nicholas's number and read it out to me as I punched it into my phone.

'Thanks, Duane,' I said. 'I'll probably see you around!'

As I walked home I decided I had nothing to lose. I was going to text Nicholas. I fancied him, he seemed to like me. Maybe ending up in Bromford was fate?

* * *

My heart skipped a beat as my phone beeped. Just as I'd hoped – it was Nicholas.

'Mom's out Saturday. Want to come over?'

After texting again for a few weeks, the conversation naturally turned to meeting up.

'Yeah, OK,' I replied. 'I'll ask my sister to babysit. We'll put the boys to bed then I'll be over.'

There were no buses to Castle Vale so I had no choice but to walk the 15-minute journey. I felt a bit sick. A heady mixture of excitement and nerves. *Would we have anything to talk about? Would he still like me?* It had been so long since

I'd been on a date. *Would I even know what to do when I got there?*

I needn't have worried. As soon as I arrived, everything felt easy.

'How's it going?' he asked, showing me through to the front room.

'Good, thanks,' I replied.

'Can I get you a drink?'

'Er, yeah. Just pop is fine, thanks.'

He disappeared into the kitchen then came back with a glass of squash.

'Kids OK?'

'Yeah, fine. My sister is looking after them for me so I can't be too late.'

'My two sisters are asleep upstairs,' he explained.

'Where's your mom?'

'Out with her boyfriend.' He leaned forward and picked up a DVD box. 'I've got this film if you want to watch it?'

It was a pirate DVD. A good copy, though, he claimed.

'Do you want anything to eat?' he asked.

I said no. Even if I was hungry, I was far too shy to eat in front of someone I'd just met.

He put the film on and sat down next to me on the sofa. We talked over some bits, kissed and cuddled over others. I asked about his daughter. She was only around a year older than Thierry and Nicholas seemed genuinely sad that it hadn't worked out with the mom.

'It's a shame, isn't it,' he said, 'when parents can't stay together? But I get to see a lot of my little girl.'

'You know when you were younger,' he continued, 'what did you want to be when you grew up?'

'Don't laugh,' I said.

'I won't!' he promised.

'A probation worker. I always saw myself working with kids who were having a hard time. I thought I'd be good at it.'

'I think you would,' he nodded. 'Have you ever been arrested?'

'No!' I said. 'Why? Have you?'

'Yeah. Only once, like. When I was younger.'

'What for?'

'It sounds bad now … Robbery. We were just kids. We took some other kid's phone.'

I wasn't shocked – it didn't sound that serious. And most lads I knew had been in some scrape or other.

'We all do silly things when we're young,' I said.

The film had finished. I glanced at the clock on my phone. Where had the time gone?

'I should probably be getting back.'

'I'll call you a taxi.'

When the car pulled up outside he saw me to the door.

'I'll call you,' he said, leaning in for another kiss.

I went home with a big smile on my face. Granted, as first dates go it was nothing fancy – but I didn't care about fancy. I was just on cloud nine to have met someone I liked and have them like me back. It was an amazing feeling. I was smitten.

CHAPTER NINE

When Stacey and I were little, Christmas was a huge deal in the Rose household. Mom would spend hours decorating the tree. We were never allowed to help because she liked it done *her* way. On Christmas morning I was always the first one up. I would open all my presents at ridiculous speed then muscle in on Stacey's too. Mom would be in the kitchen cooking a big breakfast while Dad followed us around with a bin bag, collecting all the used wrapping paper, probably on Mom's orders.

It was nearly always just us four on Christmas Day, which somehow made it all the more special.

Boxing Day we would all gather at my nan's. I remember the men would come back from the pub, all merry and rosy-cheeked. The music would go on and everyone would be singing and dancing. We would sleep over and Nan would let us eat as much chocolate as we wanted.

Christmas 2006 was all set to be a special one. I had my two beautiful boys, my own flat and now a boyfriend. Mom treated herself to a new tree and brought the old one round to the flat for us. As usual, she insisted on putting it up and decorating it herself, placing the baubles just so.

'It feels strange that you're not at home for Christmas,' she said. 'It's the first year we haven't been living together.'

'I know,' I said. 'But we're still invited for Christmas dinner, right?'

She laughed. We agreed that me and the boys would stay over at Wash Lane from Christmas Eve until Boxing Day.

I was still out of work, relying on Housing Benefit to pay the rent and Jobseeker's Allowance to buy food. There was very little left for Christmas presents. I hated being so short. Like any mom, I didn't want my kids to go without.

There was a branch of Shopacheck by my parents' house and one afternoon I swallowed my pride, walked in there and took out a loan for £300. It wasn't an ideal situation, but I couldn't bring myself to borrow it off anyone I knew. Most people were as skint as I was anyway.

With the boys at Mom's and the money in my pocket, I went into town and got everything I wanted. I bought toy cars and trains, a tricycle, a rocking horse for each of them, a talking teddy for Kam and aeroplanes for Thierry. For everyone else I picked up gift sets from Boots. I couldn't help but feel excited as I got the bus home with all my bags. I went back to Mom's, wrapped up all my gifts and placed them under her tree, ready for Christmas morning.

The day before Christmas Eve, Mom, Dad, Stacey, me and the boys piled into Dad's seven-seater Zafira to drop presents off at my nan's and Aunty Maggie's. We were all in really high spirits when we arrived back at the house, but we were about to get a nasty shock.

With the front door key in his hand, Dad was first to reach the house. He opened the door, stepped into the hallway and froze. He saw the Christmas tree, then the empty floor beneath it. Every single present we'd put underneath the tree was gone. A second or two later, me and Mom were taking in the same heartbreaking scene.

We stood aghast for a few moments while Dad sprung into action. He headed straight for the back door. Sure enough, it had been forced open. We had been burgled – the night before Christmas Eve. Dad was fuming. Mom and I were in tears. 'Who would do this?' was pretty much all we could say.

The police were called. I remember them coming out to us and dusting for fingerprints but we never heard anything else from them. Dad must have knocked on every door in the street. But no one else had been burgled, and no one had seen anything.

That night I phoned Nabeel in tears.

'Someone's broken in and stolen all the presents. Can you believe it? Kam's first Christmas … I had to take a loan out to afford all the presents. I'm skint now. I don't know what I'm going to do.'

Nabeel doesn't even celebrate Christmas so I don't know why I called him. I think I just felt like he should know that his son's first Christmas had been ruined by some scumbag.

'Don't worry,' he said reassuringly. 'We'll sort something out. Meet me in town tomorrow.'

I met him at the Bull Ring and he gave me £250 in cash.

'Are you sure?' I asked.

'Of course,' he said. 'I want to help.'

Thanks to Nabeel, I raced around Toys R Us and bought all the presents again. He might have let me down in the past, but he was my knight in shining armour that day. He saved Christmas. I couldn't thank him enough.

Despite what happened, the burglary didn't ruin Kam's first Christmas. The boys were none the wiser and it was still a really special day. They tore the paper off their gifts, ate chocolate and played with all their new things. Mom and Dad had been unable to replace the presents they'd bought, but Stacey and I assured them it didn't matter as long as we were all together.

'Look on the bright side,' I said. 'At least they didn't nick any of the food!'

Mom slugged it out in the kitchen to provide us all with a slap-up turkey dinner. We clinked glasses and ate until we were stuffed. If anything, the upset of the burglary made us even more grateful to have each other.

***

I was so busy with my family that I didn't see much of Nicholas over Christmas. We were constantly in touch, though, sending each other several text messages a day and speaking most evenings. I liked that he didn't play games. If I sent him a message he never kept me waiting too long for a reply.

Because of my track record I was wary of rushing things, especially where the kids were concerned. From the beginning I knew there was no way on earth I was introducing Nicholas to the boys, not unless I knew for sure we had something serious that was going to last. I told Nicholas how I felt and he couldn't have been more understanding. He said he felt exactly the same about introducing anyone new to his little girl. We agreed we should just see how things went.

I saw Nicholas every couple of weeks at first. I would put the boys to bed, then leave Stacey babysitting in front of the TV so I could spend a few hours at his. After a month or so he started coming to mine after the boys were in bed. One night, Thierry got up while me and Nicholas were watching telly.

'Who's that, Mommy?' he asked, rubbing his eyes.

'It's Mommy's friend, Nicholas,' I explained. He didn't seem at all phased as I ushered him back to bed.

Once Thierry had seen him I felt a bit more comfortable about the boys seeing me and Nicholas together. He started coming to the Wacky Warehouse with us on a Sunday. Thierry would run around the big kids' soft play on his own while we would sit in the baby area and play with Kam.

He started popping round to the flat during the day, too. On the days we didn't see Mom, he would watch telly with us and play with the kids. He always paid them loads of attention. He would bring his Xbox and give Thierry a control to play with. If Thierry wanted to play dinosaurs, he would be on the floor, getting involved. If they wanted a drink or something to eat, he would just get up and sort it out. He was a natural. I put it down to the fact that he was already a dad. He even helped out around the flat. If there was washing up in the bowl, he would do it. If there were crumbs on the floor, he would hoover them up. *I've got a real diamond here*, I thought.

One afternoon me and the boys walked all the way to the local Sainsbury's to do a bit of shopping. I ended up buying more than I'd planned and was struggling with the pushchair and all the carrier bags when Nicholas phoned.

'Where are you?' he asked.

'Not far from yours actually,' I said. 'Me and the boys have walked to Sainsbury's, although I've bought so much food, I'm not quite sure how I'm going to walk back!'

'Why don't you come here?' he suggested. 'Then I can walk back to yours with you, help you with the bags.'

'Yeah, OK,' I said. 'Thanks.'

I made my way to Dixon Close, saying hello to a neighbour as I struggled past her to Nicholas's house. I'd been there several times, but it was the first time I'd been when his mom was in.

We said hello – she knew who I was and seemed friendly, although we only stayed for about five or ten minutes. Still, it was the first time I'd met any parent of any boyfriend. I finally felt like I was in a proper relationship. There was none of the secrecy and lies I'd had with Nabeel. I was 21, with two kids by two different dads – I felt so lucky to have found someone. I thought any decent bloke would write me off as damaged goods. Yet here he was, not just wanting me, but embracing my kids and introducing me to his family. He seemed too good to be true.

Nicholas fitted into our lives so effortlessly that, before I knew it, we were seeing each other almost every day. He liked to go home to his mom's for dinner and would be at home the weekends he had his little girl, but he popped in on us most days and stayed over three or four nights a week. I was happy with the set-up. I liked having him around but I also liked the fact that he had his friends and I had mine.

I still saw a great deal of Matthew. He would come over in his spare time and play with the boys – they were crazy about him. Every now and then Stacey and her friend Sara would babysit so me and Chantelle could go out for a drink. Knowing I was out, Nicholas would call Stacey to check she was OK. A couple of times he even turned up with a pizza and kept them company until I got home.

Nicholas was never officially living with us and I liked it that way. I liked that the flat was my own, for me and my boys. I was in no rush to give up the little piece of independence I'd worked for. Plus, he was a bit of a mommy's boy. I wasn't sure he would have wanted to leave her anyway.

One day Kamran pointed at Nicholas and said, 'Dada.'

We looked at each other, not sure what to say.

'I don't mind!' Nicholas laughed. 'I *am* your dada, aren't I, Kam Kam?'

We laughed and I thought of me and my dad and how much we loved each other despite not being blood.

'I love you,' I said, pecking him on the lips.

'I love you too,' he replied. 'I love all of you.'

CHAPTER TEN

Kamran's first birthday fell on a Wednesday. With Stacey at college and Dad at work, we arranged to spend the day at Mom's, just her, me and the boys. We got the bus over and stayed all afternoon. We gave Kam his presents – a Winnie the Pooh activity table, a little battery-powered piano that made far too much noise and a rocking horse. We presented him with a cake and sang happy birthday. He was fascinated by the candle.

When I was little and it was my birthday, Mom always used to buy Stacey a present. And on her birthday I would get a gift. So in keeping with tradition, we gave Thierry a little something too, to make sure he didn't feel left out. We needn't have bothered: he was into all the birthday presents more than the birthday boy was!

The day was low-key, but special. The year had gone by so fast. Kam wasn't a baby any more. He was such a plucky little thing – funny, sweet and so affectionate. He was in awe of Thierry and I loved that they were growing up together. They were best buddies.

As I sat watching the two of them playing that day, I felt happier than I had in a long time. It was partly down to having Nicholas around, but mostly because me and the boys felt so sorted. It felt great to be standing on my own two feet. The only thing niggling away at me was having to rely on benefits. The money didn't stretch far and I was all too aware of what people thought of young moms who didn't work. I didn't want to be the girl people looked down on; I wanted to support myself.

***

Chantelle had been working at a city centre branch of Ladbrokes for a while. It was a tiny betting shop in the heart of China Town. She told me they were always getting rich Chinese men coming in and placing huge bets. Occasionally, the friendly ones would slip her a £25 tip. She came round to the flat a lot, popping in to see me and the boys. When money was tight, she would bring bags of food from the supermarket to tide us over. I was so grateful for her kindness. She was a good friend.

One day she mentioned that Ladbrokes had some vacancies. They needed three people at the branch in the Pallasades shopping centre, near New Street station.

'If you're interested, I'll put a good word in for you,' she said.

It was a different branch to Chantelle but it sounded like just what I'd been waiting for.

'Thanks,' I said. 'That would be amazing!'

Chantelle got me an interview with Tracey, the area manager. She was really friendly and once again I was offered a part-time job on the spot. All I had to do was pass the three-day training course.

So the following week I left Thierry and Kam with Mom while I did my training. I'd never put a bet on in my life so it was all new to me and fairly complex. But I soon realised it didn't really matter that my maths was so terrible because the computer system did most of the work. I sailed through the brief exam at the end and got given my uniform – black trousers and a green short-sleeved shirt with a Ladbrokes logo on the breast. Mom was really pleased for me: she knew how important it was for me to have a job. Plus, it meant she got to babysit three times a week and spend even more time with Thierry and Kamran.

Chantelle was excited too.

'You know what we need?' she said. 'A holiday. I'm not going away with my parents this year. Why don't we go somewhere? Somewhere hot! Now you're working, you can afford it!'

'What about the kids?' I asked.

'Bring them too! It'll be ace!'

I'd never been abroad. It did sound tempting.

'Where will we go?'

'I dunno. Turkey? Let's get something booked so we can pay it off!'

I agreed. A holiday would give me something to work towards. And it would be an amazing experience for the boys. I imagined how excited they would be, getting on an aeroplane, playing in the sand and seeing the sea. It would be something for us all to look forward to.

So, Chantelle found a package holiday to Turkey. She booked and paid for it on the agreement I would pay her back a bit each month. She even agreed to pay half towards the cost of the boys' passports. I couldn't wait.

* * *

Setting foot inside Ladbrokes on my very first day was pretty terrifying. It was the biggest branch – in Birmingham, at least. I wasn't used to that kind of environment. And, to put it politely, they attract some colourful customers.

The entrance was on the street but you had to go down a set of stairs to get to the carpeted, brightly-lit shop floor. The walls were covered with TVs and roulette machines. There was a circular desk in the middle of the room, where four of us would be sat with our computers. All the staff were a similar age. We would have a little laugh and a joke when there was a lull in bets. At the back of the shop floor we had a decent-sized staff room, where we would sit and eat lunch. It had a table, chairs and a TV. Because we were underground the phone signal in there was appalling.

Charles was our manager and was only a few years older than me. He was always friendly and pleasant, but at the same time kept us all in check. We all knew instinctively that he wasn't the type to stand for any mucking about.

I soon got used to the daily hustle and bustle. Getting to know the regulars was all part of the fun. One of my favourites was Betty, the archetypal old lady – tiny, slightly hunched over, always wearing a headscarf and dragging a pull-along shopping trolley. She only ever placed ten or twenty-five pence bets on horses that were 100-1. She came in every week without fail and counted a purse full of shrapnel out onto the desk. A little flutter was her weekly treat.

Then there were the blokes who hung around all day in between trips to the pub. I remember one coming in and starting his day with a £1,000 win. You'd think he'd be over the moon to leave with a full wallet. But no! I soon learned that cold hard cash does strange things to people. He thought he was onto a winning streak. He kept placing bet after bet after bet until every last penny of his winnings was gone. Angry and skint, he started ranting and raving at us. Charles told us not to serve him again and asked him to leave. Charles was always asking people to leave. There was a group of Somalian lads who liked to use the shop as a place to doss during the day. They would play on the roulette machines and just sit about, being a nuisance, until Charles told them to get lost. Those kinds of situations weren't nice, but thankfully not quite frequent enough to ruin the job.

If there was something big on, like a big football match or boxing, the place would be humming and we wouldn't be able to put the bets on fast enough. The biggest bet I ever witnessed was placed by an important-looking Asian guy. He came in with three flunkeys and announced matter-of-factly that he would like to put £10,000 on a horse. In cash.

There's quite a buzz when something like that happens. Charles had to take over the transaction, starting with a call to head office to get it authorised. Then, several eye-wateringly large wads of cash were handed over and put through the note counter. In those situations, you know someone on the inside has given them a strong tip. So while Charles took care of the customer, the rest of us took it in turns to sneak out to the William Hill a few doors down and put £10 each on the same horse. It was the favourite anyway, which meant the odds weren't amazing. But still, you could have heard a pin drop when the race came on the telly. The horse won! We were up a couple of quid each. Mr Big Bet, however, left several grand richer. How the other half live, eh?

***

As much as I was enjoying my job, on the days I was working, mornings at home were quite stressful. The alarm on my phone would go off at 7am. I would get the boys up then spend the next hour running around like a headless chicken, trying to coerce two sleepy toddlers with no concept of time into eating their Weetabix, getting dressed and out the door. Poor Kam took ages to wake up properly in the mornings. He would still be half asleep as I stuffed his arms in his coat and strapped him into his pushchair. I would look at his tired little face and feel wracked with guilt. And that was before we'd even got outside. With Thierry walking alongside Kam's pushchair, I would struggle down the two flights of concrete steps and onto the street. We would catch the bus to Mom's, then once I'd dropped the boys off I'd get a bus into town, to be at work for 10am. Home time was the same routine – a bus to Mom's, pick up the boys, then another bus home. It was exhausting. If Dad was around he would give us a lift, but after a few weeks it started to feel like a real slog, especially in February when the weather was chilly and the nights were still dark.

One night I was having a moan about it all to Nicholas when he made a suggestion.

'Why don't *I* have the boys?' he asked. 'I'm here most of the time anyway.'

The idea had never entered my head, but as soon as he put it out there it seemed like the perfect solution. He was still looking for work so he had plenty of time on his hands. And, like he said, he was there most of the time anyway. I could get up and go to work and the boys wouldn't even have to leave the flat. The more I thought about it, the more it made sense. Thierry was at nursery now and spent three nights a week at his dad's. So more often than not, Nicholas would only have to look after Kamran anyway. And the thought of being able to get on a bus and go straight home at the end of my shift felt like a luxury.

It was around the beginning of March when we decided to give it a go. I'd been working part time at Ladbrokes for almost six weeks.

* * *

'Don't worry,' Nicholas said, kissing me goodbye on their first day alone. 'We'll be fine!'

Sod's law, my shift had fallen on a day when Thierry was at home. I looked down at the dinosaurs all over the living-room floor, then up at the two boys tearing around in their pyjamas. I took a deep breath.

'I know,' I said, shaking my head and telling myself to get a grip. 'See you later.'

The first day was one of the hardest. It's not easy looking after two toddlers and I worried they might play up when I wasn't there to keep them in line. I texted and called Nicholas every chance I got. Each time we spoke he assured me everything was fine and when I got home that night, the boys were already bathed and ready for bed.

'Mommy!' Thierry cried, running over to greet me.

'Have you been a good boy for Nicholas? Have you had a good day?'

'Yes, Mommy,' he said.

'They've both been great, haven't you, boys?' Nicholas said, ruffling Kamran's hair.

The flat was clean and tidy. They'd had their tea and mine was on the side, ready to be warmed up.

'Wow!' I laughed. 'I could get used to this!'

* * *

Each time Nicholas babysat, I worried a little bit less. When I got home in the evenings he was always on top of everything. Without fail the flat would be tidy. Thierry would usually be at his dad's, Kam would be bathed and in his pyjamas, ready for me to put him in bed.

When I worked at Poundland and my mom had Thierry I would give her £20 or £30 a week for looking after him. It wasn't much but it covered their food and any activities they might do during the day. I told Nicholas I was happy to pay him the same and he agreed. But in the end I think I only gave him cash for the first two weeks. After that it slipped my mind, and he never asked for it. There was just an unspoken agreement that he was around us all the time anyway. The money didn't matter.

We were two or three weeks into our new routine when something a bit odd happened. I came home to find a vase that had been sitting on the front window ledge had been smashed to smithereens. It was only cheap – from Poundland, probably. But as Mom's old sofa was positioned directly underneath it, I didn't understand how it could have broken.

'How did that happen?' I asked Nicholas.

'It fell,' he shrugged.

I thought about it again. If the vase *had* fallen off the ledge, it would have landed on the sofa. There's no way it would have smashed. Even if it had toppled over on the solid window ledge there's no way it would have broken into so many pieces. *That's strange*, I thought. But within a few minutes of getting on with my usual things, it had completely gone from my mind.

***

By April 2007, everything was in full swing. I was enjoying part-time work, the boys were great and things between me and Nicholas felt really settled.

We never went out much as a couple. Apart from Sundays at the Wacky Warehouse we spent most of our free time just chilling out in front of the TV. I liked cuddling up to him; I felt happy and safe when he was around. I remember getting the hump a couple of times because he wanted to go out with his mates. If I ever gave him a hard time he would just hold his hands aloft and walk out. At the time it would wind me up even more, but we always made up on the phone before we went to sleep.

The sun was still shining when I got home from a shift around halfway through the month. This particular day, Thierry was at home. He was sat watching TV and Kam was playing outside on the balcony.

'Your tea's in the microwave,' Nicholas said, kissing me on the cheek. 'I'm off home. Speak to you later.'

It was quite normal for him to go straight home to his mom's for his dinner. I took off my jacket and flopped down onto the sofa. I gestured to Kam to come and give me a cuddle. He came toddling in. He was wearing a baseball cap and I wondered whether he might be hot.

'Come here, you,' I said, grabbing hold of the peak. 'Let's get this off.'

I lifted the cap off his head and placed it on the sofa. When I looked at Kam's face I saw the hat had left an imprint on his head, as if it had been on too tight.

That's weird, I thought, gently stroking the indent with the tips of my fingers.

'Did that naughty cap hurt you, Kam Kam?' I asked him, kissing his chubby cheek. 'We'll have to get you a bigger one.'

I thought nothing more of it as I pottered about and started heating up my tea but half an hour later I looked at Kam again and he looked even stranger. Bending down to look more closely, I realised his head looked swollen.

'Are you OK, Kam?' I frowned, unable to mask the concern in my voice. 'What's happened to your little head?'

I stood up and grabbed my phone off the kitchen worktop. My first thought was to call Nicholas. He'd been with him all day – maybe Kam had banged his head. He was obsessed with going up and down the small step on the concrete balcony over and over again. Maybe he'd fallen.

It rang a few times then Nicholas answered.

'Has Kamran fallen over today?' I asked.

'No, why?'

'His head is swelling. What do you think it could be?'

'I've got no idea.'

'I think I might take him up the hospital. I'm worried.'

'OK,' he said. 'Call me later, let me know he's OK.'

'Will do, bye.'

My next call was to Mom. She agreed a visit to the hospital was the best plan.

'Bring the boys here,' she said. 'Dad will watch Thierry and I'll walk to Heartlands with you.'

It was about 4.30pm when I first took Kam's cap off. By the time I'd got him in the pushchair and rushed the three of us to the bus stop the swelling looked like it was getting worse. When Mom opened the door to us and saw it for herself she was shocked. Kamran didn't seem unhappy or unwell, he was babbling away like his normal chirpy self. But it was like he had a balloon under his scalp that was steadily inflating. I was struggling to contain the panic rising in my chest. There was something seriously wrong.

We set off immediately only to be greeted by a huge queue at A&E. We had an anxious wait with Kamran sat on my lap. I tried to talk to him and play with him like there was nothing wrong but really I was studying him – his face, his reactions. *Is he hurt? Is he unwell? Is he engaging with me?*

'I think it's getting worse, Mom,' I said, fighting back tears. 'Look.'

Sure enough, the other side of his head was ballooning, and his face. He squirmed so I put him down and let him run around. He went straight over to a little girl, who was drinking a purple Fruit Shoot. He grabbed it off her and started to drink some. I realised I'd been so worried I hadn't even thought to give him a drink or something to eat. Mom got us all a drink from the machine and I tried to relax.

'What's taking so long?' I wondered aloud, looking at the clock on the wall.

It was two hours before we were finally called into one of the bays for a consultation with a female doctor.

'So, how can we help you today?'

'It's my little boy,' I told her. 'His head is swelling. I noticed it at around 4.30pm and it seems to be getting worse.'

The nurse examined Kam's head and took his temperature.

'I'm going to need to do a quick blood test too,' she said. 'He's probably going to cry. Are you OK to hold him still for me?'

I nodded, but knew I wasn't going to like it – I cried when Thierry and Kam had their injections as babies. When they do blood tests on small children, they take the blood from the back of their heel. They have to drain enough to fill a little test tube and it can take several goes to get the right amount. I cuddled Kam close to me, held my breath and waited. I knew the needle had pricked him because he kicked and screamed and clung to me as tightly as he could.

'Mamma! Mamma!' he screamed.

I tried to be brave for both of us but I couldn't stop the tears.

Once the nurse was happy she had enough blood to get it tested, we were shown onto a children's ward.

'You'll be here for the night so we can monitor Kamran. We're going to get him booked in for an X-ray to see if we can find anything, but that will probably be in the morning now.'

***

Kam had a small cot and I had a little bed settee next to him. Once we were settled I decided to call Nabeel. At this point in time we barely spoke, but I felt he should know.

'I don't want to worry you but I'm in the hospital with Kam.'

'Is he OK? What's happened?'

'His head is swelling and we don't know why. We're staying the night so I'll let you know what the doctors say once we get any news.'

'OK,' Nabeel said. 'Do you want me to come to the hospital?'

'There's no point,' I told him. 'We'll just be going to sleep soon. I'll call you tomorrow.'

I put the phone down and called Nicholas.

'Hey. How's Kam?'

'The swelling's worse,' I said. 'We're on a ward. They want us to stay overnight while they monitor him.'

'What do they think it is?' he asked.

'No one's saying anything,' I said. 'They're sending him for an X-ray in the morning.'

Then Nicholas said something weird.

'They're gonna think it was me,' he said.

'Why the hell would they think it was you?' I asked.

'Dunno,' he said.

'Listen, don't worry. We're fine. We're gonna get some sleep. I'll call you tomorrow.'

I thought nothing more of it – my focus was Kamran. It was late now and he was getting tired. After lots of cuddles he settled in the cot. It was well after midnight when Mom left. I pulled out the bed settee, lay down and pulled a blanket over me. I wondered if I was going to be able to sleep. Then I was gone.

* * *

When I opened my eyes there was a nurse stood in the bay, looking at Kamran. I sat up and looked at my phone: it was just after 4am. First light was creeping through the large hospital windows.

'Is he OK?' I asked, pulling back my blanket and standing up.

'He's fine,' she smiled, 'although he seems to have developed some bruising on his face.'

Kamran was still sound asleep. I looked down at his face and had to choke back tears. He looked like he had two black eyes.

'My God!,' I gasped. 'What is it? What's wrong with him?'

'We'll be doing some more tests today,' the nurse said. 'Try not to worry, he's in the best place.'

That morning the doctors came one after the other, each one poking and prodding Kam. He got so fed up with it that he started to cry whenever one of them came within a few feet of us. I hoped the X-ray would shed some light on things, but it came back normal.

'How can it be normal?' I asked. 'Look at him. He can barely open his eyes now.'

'Have you put anything on his head?' a doctor asked. 'A product? Food? Egg, maybe?'

I assured him I hadn't. Everyone seemed as clueless as I was. There was talk of allergic reactions, a possible blood disorder and booking Kam in for a CT scan. Then a doctor came over and said they were sending me to Birmingham Children's Hospital for a second opinion.

I was handed Kam's file, given a car seat and sent to reception. They said a cab would be waiting outside. The car seat was for a newborn so he was way too big for it. I couldn't help but feel tearful as I struggled out to the car. I was tired and lonely, and desperately wanted to know what was wrong with my baby. Kam babbled away to me for the whole 15-minute drive. I wondered how he could be so chirpy when he looked so terrible.

When we got to Birmingham Children's Hospital, we were shown onto a ward with a small play area. I got Kam out of the car seat and he headed straight for the toys. As I sat down, a little boy came over and handed me a plastic car.

'Thank you!' I said.

He looked around Thierry's age. There wasn't a single hair on his head.

We had a short wait before being seen by a female doctor. I don't know if she was having a bad day but she was really abrupt. I was shocked and disappointed – I had assumed all children's doctors were nice. She checked Kam over then told me we could get a taxi back to Heartlands. I was still none the wiser. I felt myself well up with tears of worry and frustration. *Why can't anyone tell me what's going on?*

I was so glad to see Stacey when we got back to Heartlands.

'I thought you could do with some company,' she said.

We dropped our things off on the ward and took Kam into the little sensory room, where there was music playing and lots of pretty lights. It was a really calm, lovely space and Kamran was fascinated.

I was filling Stacey in on our trip to the children's hospital when a song came on that got Kam's attention. It was 'Glamorous' by Fergie from the Black Eyed Peas – one of his favourites. My heart swelled as he started dancing, bopping from side to side like he always did. He looked at us and grinned – he knew he was entertaining us. Stacey laughed and joined in. I choked back more tears – his face was swollen and bruised, he looked so poorly, but he was still dancing.

***

To my relief, that afternoon the swelling started to go down. Even his eyes looked better. When Stacey left, I phoned Nabeel.

'I still don't know anything,' I said. 'They think he might have had an allergic reaction. Or it could be a blood disorder.'

'How long do they want to keep him in?'

'Well, he looks loads better but I've got no idea.'

'Why don't I come to the hospital?' he suggested. 'I bet you could do with a break.'

He was right. A change of clothes would be nice. And a shower.

'OK,' I said. 'See you in a bit.'

So that evening, Nabeel came and sat with Kam for a couple of hours while I nipped home. I had a wash, got changed and threw some clothes in a bag for Kam. When I got back, we got him settled down for the night.

'Listen,' Nabeel said, 'if we don't get any answers from the hospital, I'll pay for him to go private. Get a second opinion.'

'Thanks,' I said, genuinely grateful for the reassurance. 'That would be great.'

He left and I lay down next to my boy. The bed seemed more uncomfortable now. Despite being exhausted I tossed and turned all night. A feeling of unease was knotting my stomach: I just wanted Kamran to be home and well.

The next morning we were discharged from hospital.

'We've ruled out any major problems,' the doctor said. 'We'd like Kamran to have a CT scan, but there's no immediate rush. Give him paracetamol if he needs it and we'll get an appointment for the scan sent out to you in the post.'

'That's it?'

'For now. Like I said, the CT scan should tell us more. But as Kamran is looking better and all our tests have come back fine there's no reason for us to keep you here. Go home and get some rest.'

I told myself I should trust the doctors. Surely they would know if it was something serious? Besides, Kam *was* looking better. The swelling had gone down. He seemed to have lost some hair where the lumps had been, but whatever it was appeared to be going away.

***

Once we were home it was business as usual. I couldn't afford to take any time off so I went back to work, leaving Kamran with Nicholas. I naturally kept a closer eye on Kam, though. When we were at the hospital he seemed well but looked terrible. A week on, it was the opposite. He looked like himself but was behaving differently. He seemed much quieter than usual, more introverted. And he was clingy. Every few minutes he would be whingeing and reaching out to be picked up.

I gave him all the cuddles and attention I could but he always wanted more. I didn't get a moment's peace. There were times I ran out of patience.

'Please, Kam,' I would plead. 'Just give me five minutes! Please!'

He would cry more and the guilt of snapping at him would bring me to tears.

The holiday with Chantelle was only six weeks away and I was worried. We didn't know what had made Kamran's head swell up. *What if he got ill in Turkey? Or on the plane?* I'd been looking forward to it so much. Now I was having stomach-churning visions of his little head exploding from the cabin pressure. I know that sounds far-fetched but without a proper diagnosis my mind was running wild. We'd had the boys' passports done and if we cancelled the trip Chantelle would lose all the money she'd paid. In the end, I decided I would rather leave Kamran at home with Mom. I consoled myself with the fact that he would be too young to remember missing out.

I broke the news to Chantelle when she came round to the flat one evening. She was still a regular fixture at our place on Kempson Road. Quite often we would get the bus home from work together in our Ladbrokes shirts and she would come in to see the boys or talk about the holiday. Thankfully, she agreed it was the best thing.

'Do you mind?' I asked her, guiltily.

'You're right,' she said. 'It's a shame to leave Kam at home but it's probably for the best.'

Before Chantelle left that night, something happened. I was washing up and Nicholas was in the living room, vacuuming. I heard raised voices, then Chantelle burst into the kitchen.

'You want to see what he's just done to Kamran,' she snapped, jabbing her index finger in Nicholas's direction. 'I'm not having that, he's got no right.'

I couldn't help but be taken aback by how angry she was. I went through to the living room to find out what was going on. Kamran was sat on the sofa, looking tearful.

'What's happened?' I asked, turning to face Nicholas. 'What's Kam done?'

'I'm doing the vacuuming!' he replied, hands outstretched. 'Kam was standing in my way. I asked him to move and he wouldn't. So I picked him up, put him on the sofa and told him to stay there.'

Chantelle was behind me now, fuming.

'He's got no right,' she said again. 'He's not his dad!'

I'd never seen her like that before. Whatever she'd seen had really riled her. But then Nicholas's explanation seemed perfectly plausible. You'd be hard pressed to find a parent who hasn't snapped at their kid in that exact situation. And at the end of the day, he was trying to help me by keeping the flat clean and tidy.

'OK,' I said, keen to diffuse the situation. 'Let's all just calm down. Kam's OK, it's fine. But please,' I added, looking directly at Nicholas, 'they're my kids. If anyone tells them off, it's me.'

I was firm with him – not because I believed he'd done anything wrong, but so he was clear where he stood. As Chantelle stormed out, I couldn't help but feel that she'd overreacted.

***

On one of my days off, I decided to take the boys to Poundland to see Nabeel. I thought it would be good for him to see Kam after everything that had happened at the hospital. I was walking down the high street when we were stopped in the street by a man selling AXA health insurance. I was probably the first person to have stopped and listened to his sales pitch all day.

'So, are you interested?' he asked, once he'd finished.

'Yes,' I nodded. 'I'd like to sign me and the kids up.'

When I'd filled in the paperwork we carried on to Poundland. Nabeel came up from the warehouse and spent ten minutes with us.

'Hello, son,' he said, crouching down in front of Kam's pushchair. 'Are you all better now?'

I told Nabeel that Kam wasn't coming to Turkey and he agreed it was best for him to stay at home. When we left, he bent down and gave Kam a kiss.

'I love you,' he said, ruffling his hair.

I wondered if Kam even knew Nabeel was his daddy.

* * *

Saturday, 5 May was Stacey's birthday. The weather forecast was good so Mom arranged a big garden party at hers with food and a bouncy castle for the kids. Although he'd seen Mom in passing, it was the first time Nicholas had met the whole family. He seemed a little nervous, which was perfectly understandable. I thought it was quite sweet.

The four of us got the bus to Mom's. Thierry was excited to see Nanny and go on the bouncy castle.

When we got there we let ourselves in and walked through the house and out into the garden. There was already a good crowd and kids running around everywhere. Mom and Dad were milling about. Stacey was chatting with her friends Sara and Laura. Aunty Maggie and the twins were there and Sam's daughter Shereen, who was two months younger than Kamran, was already on the bouncy castle.

As we said our hellos, Thierry ran straight over to his nan for a hug. When she saw him she crouched down and squeezed him tight. I made a beeline for two empty chairs and as we sat down next to each other, Nicholas lifted Kamran up onto his lap. My backside had barely touched the seat when Aunty Maggie seized her moment.

'So, tell me, Nicholas,' she asked loudly, 'what right have you got to pull Kamran about?'

Chantelle had been so upset about the hoover incident she'd told my mom and aunty.

I was so embarrassed. *Did she really have to do this now – in front of everyone?*

Everything seemed to go quiet as Nicholas squirmed in his seat, racking his brain for the right response. But Maggie wasn't finished.

'Kamran is not. Your. Son,' she said.

Nicholas looked like he was going to cry. He put Kamran down, then he was on his feet and heading back through the house. I went straight after him. Mom followed.

'Nicholas,' I pleaded, 'don't go. Don't get upset.'

He burst out the front door, stopped on the front lawn and turned to face me.

'I love Kam, Sarah. You know I do. I was hoovering and he was in the way. All I did was move him! I love him Sarah! I love him as my own!'

He was wiping the tears off his cheeks with his fingers. Mom was beside us now, her face full of concern.

'Calm down, love,' she said, resting her hand on his shoulder. 'No one wants to see you upset like this. Calm down. Come back inside. Let's start again.'

Before that moment I'd never seen Nicholas cry. It really pulled on my heartstrings to see him like that. Me and Mom felt so sorry for him. I couldn't help but feel Chantelle had exaggerated the whole thing to make him look bad. *Why did she have to go telling tales to my family?* Kamran was fine. Nicholas was good to me and my boys. As far as I was concerned there was no need for any of this.

Once Nicholas had calmed down he agreed to come back inside. He was quiet for the rest of the party but no one mentioned it again. Kam spent most of the afternoon getting on and off my lap while Thierry enjoyed the bouncy castle. The four of us got the bus home around six o'clock so we could get the boys bathed and ready for bed.

'I'm sorry about earlier,' I said to Nicholas once we were alone.

'It's OK,' he replied, giving me a kiss. 'I'm sorry for getting upset.'

'I can't believe Chantelle,' I said, 'and I can't believe how much all this has escalated. Kam wasn't hurt – I don't see what the big deal is. Do they really think I would be with someone who hurt my kids?'

***

The next day, Mom popped round with ice lollies for the boys.

'Everything OK?' she asked, sitting down on the sofa.

'Yeah, fine,' I said. 'It was just all a bit embarrassing, wasn't it? There wasn't any need to bring it all up in front of everyone.'

'I know, love,' she said. 'But you know what Maggie's like. She can't help herself.'

'I hope it didn't ruin the party.'

'Don't be daft,' she said. 'It's fine. Anyway, I'd better be getting back.'

Then, out of the blue, as Mom got up to leave, Kamran burst into tears. He was reaching up to her, sobbing his heart out.

Either he didn't want Mom to leave or he wanted to leave with her.

CHAPTER ELEVEN

The Tuesday after Stacey's birthday, when I arrived home from work, Nicholas was in the living room. As I walked in I heard his phone ring and him answer it. My ears couldn't help but pick up the sound of the voice on the other end. It was female. He ended the call so hastily I couldn't help but feel suspicious.

'Who was that?' I asked.

'No one.'

'It sounded like a girl.'

'It was a friend.'

'What friend?' I snapped. 'Since when did you have any female friends?'

'Don't start, Sarah,' he said.

We argued. He did the usual walking out routine. With Thierry at his dad's, I fixed me and Kamran some dinner while I cooled off. I soon felt silly for making such a fuss about the phone call. I didn't really believe Nicholas was seeing anyone else.

I tried his phone. He answered.

'Sorry about earlier,' I said sheepishly.

'It's fine,' he said. 'No harm done.'

'What are you up to?'

'I'm just out with Duane.'

'Well, Kam will be going to bed soon. Why don't you both come round?'

It wasn't long before they were at the door. Kamran was still up so Nicholas scooped him up into his arms and took him to bed while I put the kettle on. We sat chatting and watching TV, and Duane left around 9.30pm. I had work the next day so I had a quick shower before bed. Nicholas brushed his teeth then got into bed and waited for me. We made love and I fell asleep in his arms.

* * *

The next morning the alarm on my phone went off at 7.30am, and it was the usual routine until I left for work. I gave Kam Kam a hot chocolate, which he drank while watching *Milkshake*, dressed in his brother's *SpongeBob SquarePants* T-shirt. The only thing unusual was that I forgot my keys and phone, and went back to the flat, where I sneaked that last look at Kam. 'Bye-bye, Mommy!' he said.

Then I was at work and found my phone ringing when I went for a toilet break. After a frantic conversation with Nicholas, I spoke to his mom, who blurted out that Kamran was dead.

* * *

I must have been screaming because Charles came running in. He found me slumped on the floor, the phone still in my hand.

'Sarah?'

He crouched down in front of me. His eyes were wide with fear and concern. His face had turned white.

'What's happened?'

'My baby!' I sobbed. 'My baby!'

Not knowing what else to do, he took the phone out of my hand and called Chantelle. Everyone at work knew how close we were. I was so distraught I didn't even notice him make the call. The next thing I knew I was on my feet and putting on my coat.

'I need to be ready,' I said, pulling myself together. 'The police. The police are coming here.'

Charles handed my phone back and I marched out into the shop. The lights felt uncomfortably bright. I felt like everything was spinning.

Chantelle appeared in front of me. She put both her hands on my shoulders.

'Sarah? What's happened?'

'It's Kamran,' I said. 'The police are coming. I need to go to the hospital.'

I was shouting now.

'Where are the police? I need to see my baby!'

Chantelle vanished. Poundland was practically next door so she had gone to get Nabeel.

'Here,' Charles said, shoving a £20 note into my hand. 'When Chantelle gets back, go and flag down a black cab.'

I don't even think I said thank you as I flew up the stairs and out of the shop. To my relief there were plenty of taxis about. As I waved one down, I realised Chantelle and Nabeel were with me. We clambered into the back of a car.

'Heartlands Hospital,' I said loudly.

The cab pulled out. I was sat on the back seat between Chantelle and Nabeel. I crumpled again.

Chantelle put her hand on my knee.

'Kamran's fine,' she said. 'I know it.'

'*How* do you know?' I said, unable to stifle my sobs.

Nabeel stayed silent.

Before we'd even come to a stop outside the hospital I was scrambling out of the door. I could hear alarms going off. Then I saw a man shouting and struggling by the entrance. It was Nicholas. His hands were behind his back in cuffs and there were several police officers trying to restrain him.

His eyes met mine.

'Sarah!' he screamed, struggling again.

I ran towards him.

'What's happened?' I shouted.

'They think I killed Kam! They think I killed him!'

My baby boy. I need to see him. He must be here, in the hospital. Please God. Please let him be OK.

My bag and coat fell to the floor as I forgot about Nicholas and ran towards the hospital building. I'd been there so many times over the years, my gut told me to avoid the main reception. Instead I went through a side door that paramedics use to admit the patients brought in by ambulance. I found myself in a busy corridor. Within seconds I was looking at my sister, standing with her friends, Sara and Louise. They were all crying. Then Mom appeared – she was crying too. My heart was pounding in my ears. *What is going on? Why is everyone here? Where is Kam?*

***

Everything went into slow motion. I realised every single person had stopped what they were doing and was staring at me. Even the people I didn't know seemed to know who I was. I looked at Mom again. She shook her head and I knew. I knew Kam had gone. I fell to my knees, screaming, shouting, crying, willing it not to be true. Some nurses rushed over and tried to help me up.

'It's all your fault!' I screamed. 'I brought him here four weeks ago and nothing was done! He's dead because of you!'

I could hear Mom beside me now.

'Sarah, love, I'm so sorry. Calm down. Please. Come in here. This lady needs to speak to you.'

I was ushered into a small private room with Nabeel. I don't know if it was the shock, but when I saw him, I completely lost control.

'This is all your fault!' I screamed. I pounded my fist into his leg over and over and over. 'If you'd told your mom and dad about Kamran we would still be together! Everything would be OK!'

Nabeel didn't deserve that, but I was out of my mind. Mom grabbed my hand to stop me hitting him.

'Sarah! Please!'

The woman was talking now. She was plain clothes police, around 35, with naturally curly hair. She was wearing a grey suit with a white shirt.

'My name is Kate,' she said. 'I know you've just had a terrible shock, but can we ask you a few questions?'

Through my sobs I managed a nod. I could feel Mom's arm around me now.

'What time did you leave your flat today?'

'Just after 9am,' I said.

'And who was looking after your son, Kamran?'

'My boyfriend, Nicholas.'

Nabeel didn't even know I had a boyfriend. He had his head in his hands. I suddenly remembered his promise of private healthcare.

'You said you were going to pay for us to go private!' I screamed. 'We were going to get a second opinion! You didn't do it in time!'

I broke down again. Nabeel didn't respond, he just sat staring at the floor, pale and in shock, listening to me rant. I was convinced that the NHS had let my son down. That whatever had caused his head to swell had turned out to be fatal.

The policewoman, Kate, was asking me something else now.

'Do you feel well enough to accompany us to the station?'

'Excuse me?' Mom cut in. 'You do realise her son's just died?'

'It's OK, Mom,' I said, suddenly pulling myself together. 'It's alright.'

A child had died – *my* child. The police needed to get to the bottom of what was going on so I had to help them.

***

A man in a black suit appeared – Kate's colleague. He was a bit older, with greying hair, and said he was a detective inspector, and that his name was Chris. They escorted me back through the corridor and out into the car park. I don't know how I managed to put one foot in front of the other. I felt like I was dreaming.

Chris gestured towards an unmarked police car parked nearby. Before we got to it, another car pulled up outside the hospital. It was a taxi, and my dad was getting out.

'Dad!'

'Sarah! What's happened?'

I started to go to him but Chris grabbed me by the elbow. He must have thought I was trying to make a run for it. Instead, I just blurted it out: 'Kam's dead.'

'What? Where's your mom? What's happened?'

'She's inside. I need to go to the police station.'

He was in front of me now. Sam was with him – they were both working at the same factory and had rushed over together. We hugged. Chris opened the rear car door and, as Dad and Sam hurried inside Heartlands, I climbed into the back seat and put on my seatbelt.

Chris drove while Kate sat in the back with me. I was completely in shock – OK one minute, sobbing uncontrollably the next.

'Calm down,' Kate kept saying. 'You'll be alright.'

She kept putting her hand on my knee. She was kind to me. The drive seemed to take a lifetime, though. For some reason we had to go all the way to Sutton Coldfield Police Station, a good 45 minutes from the hospital. All I could think was, *Kamran's dead. Kamran's dead. I'm never going to see my baby again.*

***

We pulled up at the station and Chris opened my door for me. They escorted me through a side door and into a small room, where a man in uniform was waiting for us.

'Empty your pockets, please,' he said.

I didn't have a thing with me. No money, no bag, no phone. Not even my coat. The officer patted me down.

'Shoes off, please.'

I took off my black slip-ons so he could check inside them. Security search over, Chris and Kate showed me into another room. There were tables and chairs scattered about and a white board in the corner. It looked like the kind of room important police meetings were held in. Kate handed me a plastic cup with cold water in it. I sat on one of the chairs and took a sip. Two women walked in – they were plain clothes too, but even more casual. I'm sure they both had jeans on. They were very friendly. They said they were sorry about my son but I struggled to take in what they were saying.

Kate and Chris left the room.

'Can we get you anything to eat?' one of the women asked.

My stomach lurched and I shook my head. I don't think I could have managed a thing even if I'd wanted to.

'I'm really sorry about your son, Sarah. His name was Kamran, wasn't it? What was he like?'

'A little star,' I croaked quietly, wiping my nose. 'He was happy. He was always dancing. He loved his big brother ...' The tears came again. *Thierry ... What am I going to tell Thierry?*

'How old was Kamran?'

'Fifteen and a half months.'

'And you have an older son?'

'Yes, Thierry. He's three.'

'What's Thierry like?'

'Amazing. He's so smart. He loves counting. He knows all his colours. He loves to learn.'

'He sounds lovely. You must be really proud of him. What about the boys' dad?'

'They've got different dads. I was 17 when I got pregnant with Thierry. His dad, Mark ... we split up while I was pregnant.'

'And Kamran's dad?'

'He's Muslim. He wouldn't tell his family about me and Kamran so I ended it.'

'That must have been hard.'

I nodded.

'Did Kamran see his dad?'

'At first. But not now.'

'Who else was involved in Kamran's life? Did you have any help from family? Friends?'

'I had a lot of help from my mom,' I explained. 'She's like a second mom to my boys. They love her.'

'That's great. You need your mum when you have kids, don't you? Is there anyone else?'

'My little sister, Stacey. She helps me. And Nicholas, my boyfriend. A few weeks ago he started having Kamran for me when I was at work.'

'Where do you work, Sarah?'

'Ladbrokes, the big betting shop in town.'

'And how often do you work there?'

'Only part time. Three shifts a week.'

'And Nicholas would have the boys while you were at work?'

'Yes. Well, only Kamran really.'

'Why not Thierry?'

'He goes to nursery and stays at his dad's three nights a week, so it's usually just Kam who needs watching.'

'I see.'

This went on for around two hours. One minute I would be OK, able to answer questions and string a sentence together like nothing had happened. The next, the loss of Kamran would hit me like a train and I would crumble again, unable to speak through my sobs. I was all over the place, behaving erratically, just like I had been at the hospital hours earlier.

At no point did I question why I was there. These women just seemed like nice, normal ladies, making conversation with me. I felt safe. I believed they were on my side, just trying to establish what happened to my boy. But then the atmosphere shifted. One of the women left the room for a few minutes. When she came back, her face had changed. She looked like she was on the verge of tears. Whatever it was she was about to do, I could tell she didn't want to do it.

'I'm sorry,' she said, looking me straight in the eye. 'I'm so sorry to do this, but I have to …

'Sarah Rose, I am arresting you on suspicion of manslaughter by gross negligence and knowing or allowing a child to die.'

CHAPTER TWELVE

I was so confused. *I thought I was helping them. Now they think it was me?* As I realised what the plain clothes officer was saying I felt like the wind had been knocked out of me.

'What? Why am I being arrested? I don't get it. Please, I don't understand!'

My head was spinning again. The tears just didn't want to stop. The women each held one of my hands. They just kept repeating the same word: 'Sorry, sorry.'

The door swung open and Kate and Chris walked in. I realised later that they must have been watching the whole thing on camera. At the time I had no idea I was being filmed, let alone under suspicion of being involved in my baby son's murder.

'You need to come with us now,' Kate said.

I was on my feet. Someone was putting handcuffs on me. I felt heavy, and my mouth felt so dry. I let them guide me back through the station and out into the car park to Chris's car. Another car journey – this time to Stechford Police Station, near Mom's. It was a long drive and Kate was different now. She sat in the back with me again but kept her eyes straight ahead. There were no words of comfort, no hand on my leg. I didn't care. I stared blankly out of the window, lost in my own thoughts. I felt cried out. I had no fight. No energy. No words. All I had was grief. There was a huge empty hole in my heart. It hurt so much that I wondered how a person could be in so much pain and still be alive.

So much was happening. I was with strangers, miles away from Thierry and my family. I'd just been arrested. My wrists were shackled in front of me with metal cuffs. But my brain and my body couldn't cope. There was no room for the present. There was only grief.

An hour later we arrived at Stechford Police Station. I followed Kate and Chris inside. We came to a desk. A man in police uniform was sat behind it, staring at a computer. He turned his head and his eyes met mine.

'Name, please?'

'Sarah Rose.'

As Chris removed my handcuffs, the man returned his gaze to the screen and tapped on his keyboard.

'You are arrested on suspicion of manslaughter by gross negligence and knowing or allowing a child to die. Do you understand the charges against you?'

I shook my head in disbelief.

'No, no, no, no … It wasn't me!' I pleaded. 'It was the hospital's fault! I shouldn't be here! I need to go home! Please!'

Without taking his eyes off the computer screen, the man slid a form across the desk and handed me a pen.

'You need to sign this to say you understand the charges against you.'

'No!' I cried. 'I'm not signing it! I didn't do anything!'

'Sarah, Sarah,' Kate was cutting in now. 'Listen, you have to sign the form to say you understand why you are here. It doesn't mean that you're admitting to anything. OK?'

I looked down at the form, then back at the man behind the desk.

'Sarah?' Kate said again. 'Do you understand? We need you to sign the form.'

This went on for around ten minutes. Then tentatively, I picked up the pen. I'd never been arrested before – I didn't know how it worked. I didn't even know if I could trust Kate any more. She had been so kind to me at the hospital, but now she thought I had something to do with why my son died. They all did.

Finally, I concluded that I had no choice: I had to do what I was told. The biro felt completely alien in my hand as I signed my name. Kate took me by the elbow and guided me through another door.

'We're going to get you to see the doctor,' she said as we walked. 'It's just to check you're OK.'

We went through another door into what looked like a canteen. It was a fairly large, bright room with tables and chairs, a vending machine and a table with tea, coffee and food on it.

'You can sit here,' Kate said, gesturing to a chair. 'Do you want something to eat?'

I wasn't going to answer even if she'd waited for me to. She went over to the table and came back with one of those single-serving plastic pots of Kellogg's Corn Flakes.

'Here,' she said, placing the cereal down in front of me. 'Try and eat something. I'll come and get you as soon as the doctor is free.'

I stared blankly at the pot for a moment then looked up again. On their way out, Chris and Kate stopped to speak to a young policewoman. They spoke briefly and glanced over in my direction. They were obviously talking about me. I sighed heavily and put my head in my hands. Then I sensed someone sitting down next to me. I looked to my left. It was the young policewoman.

'Hi Sarah, I'm Michelle.' She smiled warmly. She was in full uniform and looked no older than I was. Her dark brown hair was scraped back into a neat bun.

'Corn flakes not taking your fancy?' she said.

I shook my head.

'It's my first week here,' she said. 'It's been pretty boring so far. It's nothing like *The Bill*, unfortunately.'

I managed a half smile.

'Are you from Birmingham?' she asked.

I nodded.

'Me too,' she said.

She carried on chatting away for about ten minutes. I was barely listening. She was obviously sent to keep an eye on me, but I was grateful for the small talk. Grateful to not be drowning in this living nightmare, if only for a few moments.

Kate reappeared.

'The doctor can see you now.'

I stood up and followed her back out past the front desk into a corridor. There were doors on both sides. They were big and heavy with small rectangular windows at eye level. I shuddered as it dawned on me they were cells.

The doctor's office was only a few feet away from the prisoners. The door was ajar and a tubby middle-aged man in a suit was sat at his desk.

'Please,' he said to me, 'have a seat.'

I sat down on the chair next to him. Kate pulled the door shut, leaving us alone.

'I'm just going to take your blood pressure and ask you a few questions, OK?'

I nodded. He took my right hand, pushed the short sleeve of my shirt up my arm a little higher then wrapped the blood pressure monitor around it tightly. He pressed the button on the machine and it started to squeeze. I always have a moment of panic that the machine is going to malfunction and keep getting tighter, but it stopped and beeped. The doctor made a note of the result but didn't say a word.

'Are you on any medication?'

'No.'

'And how are you feeling?'

I was crying again. In a barely audible whisper, I croaked desperately, 'I didn't do it. It wasn't me.'

I don't even know why I was saying this to him. I just wanted someone – anyone – to believe me. To know I was innocent. But he didn't react.

'Any bad thoughts, anything like that?'

I wiped my cheeks and shook my head. The doctor stood up and opened the door. Kate was stood outside, waiting for me. He nodded to her. 'She's fine.'

Fine? I thought. *I've never been less fine.*

We walked a few feet then Kate stopped and turned to face me.

'This is you,' she said matter-of-factly. She was stood by the open door of one of the cells. My heart sank to my feet: they were locking me up.

I stepped inside. It was a small room with a high ceiling and concrete walls painted white. There was a large window obscured with white bars that went up and across like a crossword. Below it was the bed – a fitted box with a dark blue blanket. The foot of the bed sat flush against a small wall, which had a toilet the other side of it. Everything about it was grim.

'I'll be back soon,' Kate said. As she walked away, I felt the loneliness and grief bear down on me again. *Why am I in here? Why can't I be in the hospital with Kam Kam? And Thierry, who is looking after my big boy now?* But it was Kamran my mind kept coming round to. I knew Thierry would most probably be safe with my mom by now, but my baby boy was dead. I would never see him again. I sat on the bed, slumped down onto my side and let the tears come.

***

They must have thought I was a suicide risk because there was always a police officer sat on a chair in my doorway. They didn't shut the door once and the guards never said a word to me. If they looked up from their magazines and opened their mouths, it was to chat to each other.

At that point I didn't care that I was in a cell or that I was being watched. I was so consumed with grief for Kamran. I could have been in the biggest bed in the best hotel in the world and I wouldn't have felt any better. I wanted my boys so desperately it hurt.

I'd been lying there less than an hour when my ears tuned in to the sound of another prisoner arriving. With my door wide open I was close enough to the front desk to hear everything that was being said.

First, I heard what sounded like the voice of the man who had checked me in.

'You have been arrested on suspicion of murder.'

Then a man screamed out, 'No! No!'

I recognised the voice. It was Nicholas. He was here. I sat up. The guard looked up from her magazine and our eyes met. She could tell I was listening to what was going on, but still didn't utter a word. When everything went quiet again I lay back down. What was Nicholas doing here? *He must be in the same boat as me,* I thought. *The police are just doing their jobs. They'll question us both, realise this has all been a big misunderstanding and let us go.*

Roughly 20 minutes later there was more noise – doors opening, people running and shouting. I sat up again, my heart pounding. Something was happening and it sounded bad.

I didn't move, even when whatever it was appeared to have settled down. An officer came over to my guard and said, 'He's tried to hang himself with his shoelaces.'

I knew they meant Nicholas – they must have done. He'd just arrived, he'd been charged, put in a cell then tried to harm himself. The staff must have known we were both there as part of the same case, but they didn't care that I could hear everything. They didn't show me an ounce of compassion or consideration. To them I must have been guilty. They must have thought I was a child killer.

I lay back down and tried to hold it all in but I was powerless. The tears just came tumbling out. All I could do was sob as silently as I could manage. *What is happening to us? How could such a normal day end up like this?*

I pictured Kamran's beautiful face. I pictured him saying 'bye-bye' to me that morning. His chubby cheeks, his thick black eyelashes, his gorgeous smile. *How did we get from that to this?* The loss was tearing me apart over and over. The pain would build up inside me until I was rocking, screaming, thumping my fists against my head and pulling at my hair. *My baby is dead. I'm never going to see him again. Never! My life is over. My life is over …*

Eventually I would calm myself down, maybe even drift off to sleep through sheer exhaustion. Then the thoughts would overwhelm me and I'd be hysterical again.

***

The next thing I heard was Kate's voice.

'You need to come and be interviewed,' she said. 'The duty solicitor is waiting for you.'

All concept of time had been lost. I think it was dark outside but I had absolutely no idea what day it was. I didn't care. I dragged myself up onto my feet, wiped my bleary, puffy eyes and followed her. She showed me to the interview room just a few feet away. There was a table with a tape recorder on it and four chairs. In one of them sat a chubby bloke in his fifties hunched over some paperwork. He stood up to shake my hand. His hair was snow white.

'Hi Sarah. I'm Graham Brown, the duty solicitor.'

'Let me know when you're ready,' Kate said, closing the door.

I sat down. The second we were alone, Graham cut right to the chase.

'Tell me the truth,' he said. 'Did you do it?'

I broke down.

'No!' I cried. My head was in my hands again, my fists pulling at the roots of my hair. 'I had nothing to do with this. I've lost my baby! I don't know why I'm here!'

'OK, OK,' he said, handing me some water. 'I'm sorry, Sarah, I had to ask. It's my job.'

I took a deep breath and tried to compose myself.

'Right,' Graham said, picking up his pen. 'I need you to tell me exactly what happened the day your son died.'

I told him how I'd got up that morning, got Kamran out of bed and made him a drink. I told him how I put my uniform on – the same clothes I was still wearing – then went to work, leaving Kam with Nicholas. I don't think it took him long to deduce that I was completely clueless as to why my son was now dead.

'Right,' he said again, 'the police are going to come in and question you now. I want you to tell them exactly what you told me. I want you to answer everything they ask you truthfully and fully. Do you understand, Sarah?'

I nodded. Graham got up, opened the door and told Kate we were ready. He sat back down next to me as Kate came in, closely followed by Chris. They sat down opposite us and Kate turned on the tape recorder.

'It is Friday, 11 May.' She looked at her watch and stated the exact time. Then she went in hard.

'Sarah Louise Rose, did you kill your son, Kamran Rose?'

My jaw fell open.

'No!'

'Do you know who did?'

'He was ill! It was the hospital's fault. I took him there four weeks ago. You need to speak to them!'

'What happened on the morning of Thursday, May 10?'

'I got up and went to work.'

'What time did you get up?'

'7.30am.'

'And who was in the flat?'

'Me, Kamran and my boyfriend.'

'Who is your boyfriend?'

'Nicholas. Nicholas Kirnon.'

'How was Kamran when you left?'

'He was fine. I left him watching TV.'

'Did you harm your son then go to work like nothing happened?'

'What? No! Oh my God, that is sick! Who would do that?'

'Who looked after Kamran when you went to work?'

'Nicholas.'

'So Nicholas killed Kamran?'

'No!'

'Well, if it wasn't Nicholas it must have been you. I'll ask you again – did you harm your son?'

Is she even listening to me? Can she not see I'm just a normal mom who's grieving for her baby? I was sobbing so hard now I could barely talk.

'I would never ...'

'You let Nicholas harm him then went off to work as normal, didn't you?'

'No!' I cried, my face contorted with pain and tears. 'I love Kam! I'm a good mom!'

My head was spinning. I'd never felt so helpless. I felt like I was under attack. Kate was a completely different person to the kind woman I met in the hospital. She was no longer my friend. She was there to do her job.

'How long has Nicholas been your boyfriend?'

I wiped my cheeks with my hands. 'A few months.'

'What's he like?'

'A diamond. He's like a dad to my boys. When I get home from work the flat's tidy and the boys are bathed and ready for bed. He offered to babysit so I could keep my job. I wanted to work. I didn't want to be on benefits forever. I wanted to support me and my kids.'

Graham was still next to me, scribbling notes.

'You said you took Kamran to hospital,' Kate continued. 'What for?'

'It was four weeks ago. I got home from work and noticed his head was swelling. Me and Mom took him to Heartlands. The swelling got worse while we were there. Then his eyes went black. They thought it might be an allergy or a blood disorder or something. They said they were sending us an appointment for a CT scan but I've not had one yet.'

'What about the bruises on Kamran's belly?'

I sat up straighter.

'What bruises?'

'Come on, Sarah, you must have known. You're his mum, you must have seen them.'

I wracked my brain. *Have I seen any bruises? Had he fallen? Am I forgetting something?*

'No, I definitely didn't see any bruises.'

Kate shuffled through her papers.

'Well, we're still waiting on the full post-mortem report but I can tell you that Kamran had bruises all over his abdomen.'

'What?'

'They were all over his belly, Sarah. There were too many bruises to count. You must have known, Sarah. You knew, didn't you?'

'No! No! No!' I was hysterical now. Kate carried on talking but I wasn't listening. She had pushed and pushed. I was screaming, cupping my hands over my ears, desperate to block out this hell I was in.

Graham finally cut in.

'I think that's enough now,' he said.

I was on the floor, practically under the table, rocking, crying and pulling at my hair again. Graham reached out his hand to help me up. Kate and Chris had gone.

'It's OK,' Graham said. 'They've gone now. Calm down.'

I wiped my nose and slumped heavily in my chair.

'You're doing really well,' he continued. 'They will want to speak to you again later. I want you to keep answering their questions truthfully, like you have been doing. Just tell them everything you know.'

I left that room even more broken and confused than I was when I walked in. For two hours Kate had fired question after question at me. I thought I'd been useless. I thought I'd said everything wrong, that I hadn't been able to give them the information they needed – information I, as Kamran's mother, should have known.

***

Now I understand the process, I know that Kate was trying to break me. She wanted me to slip up or confess, but I had nothing to confess to. A liar changes his story, an honest person only has one version of events. All I had in me was the truth. And the truth was that I was a normal mom, who went out to work one day then got a phone call to say her son was dead. I had no idea how or why it happened. The only explanation I had in my mind was that four weeks earlier I'd taken Kamran to hospital because his head was swelling and nothing was done about it. Way down underneath all the loss and pain that was overwhelming me, I clung to the hope that Heartlands Hospital would back up my story and I would be allowed to go home.

CHAPTER THIRTEEN

I could barely hold my head up as I was escorted the few feet across the corridor back to my cell. Physically and mentally drained, I wanted to go to sleep and never wake up.

I realised I needed the loo and turned to the guard already seated in my doorway.

'Can I use the toilet?' I asked. She nodded and I walked behind the small wall that separated the bed from the bathroom. There was no door and the wall provided very little privacy but I was desperate.

As I undid my black work trousers it struck me how disgusting the toilet was. It stunk of wee and there was graffiti scratched all over the walls. My eyes scanned the names and the foul language and it hit me that hundreds, maybe even thousands, of men and women had been here in this cell before me. I hovered shakily over the toilet – I didn't want my skin to make contact with the seat. As I did what I needed to do, my gaze fell upon the guard in the doorway. If she had bothered to look up from her magazine she would be able to see everything. I felt my cheeks burn red with embarrassment. I finished as quickly as I could, straightened up slightly and reached out to the loo roll on my right. As my fingers grabbed the end of the roll, I realised it was the kind you used to get in primary school: the cheap, horrible stuff that was literally like tracing paper. I pulled off a few squares and wiped. There was blood on it. *Great*, I thought. *That's all I need.*

I fastened my trousers, flushed and walked back to my bed. I lay down on my side, facing the wall so the guard couldn't see me cry. Despite knowing Nicholas was in the same building, it was only Thierry and Kamran I longed for. I wanted to feel them both in my arms. I still didn't want to believe that I would never hold Kamran again. Despite being told about the bruising to his stomach, I was completely incapable of taking on any new information, especially something so distressing, something that indicated my baby had been hurt. I couldn't even entertain the thought that he had been harmed somehow. I wasn't ready. Not yet.

Day slipped into night again. I lost count of the times I cried myself to sleep, only to wake up and feel the agony crush me all over again. Eventually, Kate came to get me for my second interview. It was dark outside. As I hauled myself onto my feet and followed her back to the same room, I wondered what fate awaited me this time.

Graham, the duty solicitor, and Kate's colleague Chris were already in their seats. I sat down next to Graham and waited for Kate to launch into me. Only this time she didn't.

'Right, Sarah,' she said. She was firm but not aggressive. 'We've spoken to Heartlands Hospital. They have confirmed you and your mother visited A&E with Kamran last month. They have also confirmed that you have been waiting for a CT scan to determine the cause of the swelling to Kamran's head. In fact, their records indicate that the letter containing your appointment was posted out to you today.'

That stung. *If only it had got to us sooner.*

'Now if you don't mind, we'd just like to go over your movements on the morning of May 10 again.'

I shuffled in my chair and tried to collect my thoughts.

'What time did you get up?' she asked.

'7.30am.'

'And who was in your flat?'

'Me, Nicholas and Kamran.'

'Who got Kamran out of bed?'

'I did.'

'And how was he?'

'Fine. He was smiling, bubbly. I put him on the sofa and put *Milkshake* on for him while I made us both a drink.'

'What was he wearing?'

'Erm, Thierry's vest. The one with *SpongeBob SquarePants* on it.'

'And where was Nicholas?'

'Still in bed.'

'At what point did he get up?'

'After I made me and Kam a drink I went back into the bedroom to get dressed. Nicholas got up, used the loo, I think, then went in the living room to sit with Kam.'

'And you say you left the house just after 8.30am, is that correct?'

'Yes.'

'How was Kamran when you left?'

'I stuck my head around the living-room door and said, "Bye, Kam Kam." He waved at me and said, "Bye-bye, Mommy." He was smiling.'

The memory caused me to break down again. That was it – my last memory of my baby boy. *I'm never going to see him again ...*

'Where was Nicholas when you left?'

I took a breath to try and pull myself together.

'He was in the kitchen, making Kam's breakfast. He always made his Weetabix if I was working.'

'How did you get to work?'

'I got the bus into town.'

'You work at Ladbrokes, is that correct?'

'Yes.'

'What time did you start?'

'I got there just before 10am.'

'What happened at work?'

'I was working on the tills. It was a normal morning. Then I got the call from Nicholas.'

'What time was this?'

'Around 11am when I checked my phone.'

'Did you have your phone on you at work?'

'No, it was in the staff room.'

'What made you check it?'

'I was going to the toilet and just checked to see if anyone had called or messaged me. As I got it out of my bag I realised it was ringing.'

'Who was calling you?'

'Nicholas.'

'And what did he say?'

'The police are coming to get you. You need to get to the hospital.'

'How did he sound?'

'Upset. It scared me.'

'What else did he say?'

'I don't know. The signal went.'

'So what did you do?'

'I tried calling him back, but it just went straight to answerphone.'

'Then what?'

'I tried his mom's landline.'

'Why her?'

'I don't know. I couldn't think what else to do.'

'Did anyone answer?'

'Yeah, his mom was there.'

'What did she say to you?'

'I think she was saying sorry.'

I broke down again.

'Anything else?' Kate pressed.

'She said, "Kamran's dead."'

We went over everything with a fine-tooth comb – Chantelle and Nabeel arriving at Ladbrokes and the three of us getting a black cab to Heartlands. Then I explained again how I had taken Kamran to the very same hospital four weeks earlier but no one could tell me what was wrong with him.

This interview was shorter than the first. It still wasn't easy, but Kate was much gentler on me. I think she must have realised that the bad cop tactics weren't the way to go. When we were finished, she briefly explained that I was being taken to Birmingham Magistrates' Court for a Saturday morning hearing. I wilted at the thought of that huge gothic building

I'd been so scared of a few years before. Was I really going back there – suspected of being involved in the murder of my own son?

'Here,' Kate said, handing me a small plastic bag. It had a flannel, a toothbrush and toothpaste in it. Then I remembered the blood.

'Do you have any sanitary pads?' I asked quietly. Without answering she went and got one. She handed it to me then walked me over to my cell. I realised there was a small wash area next to it. There were no mirrors, just a couple of sinks.

'Freshen up,' she said. 'We'll be leaving soon.'

I wondered what I must look like. I was still in my uniform and I realised I could smell myself. I wanted to cry. I ripped open the sanitary towel and quickly shoved it into my knickers. I turned on the hot tap, pulled the flannel from the plastic wrapper and soaked it in the water. I loosened a few of the buttons on my shirt and wiped under my arms. I rinsed the flannel again, then pressed it against my face. My eyes were so red from all the crying that the warm water stung.

I wondered if my family would be allowed to come to court on a Saturday. I wondered if any of them would even want to. I had no idea what they were thinking, what they were going through. I wondered if *they* thought I was guilty. Everyone else seemed to think I had something to do with it.

I brushed my teeth, pulled out my hair band and redid my ponytail. Then I heard a voice behind me.

'The van's here. Let's get you outside.'

It was a uniformed policeman I hadn't seen before. He was holding cuffs.

'Hands out in front, please,' he said.

I held my hands out to him and he clicked them on. I followed him down a corridor and out of what looked like a fire exit. A prison van was parked a few feet away. As we walked towards it I could see the back doors were already open.

Holding on gently to my elbow, the officer helped me up onto the van. There was a small walkway up the centre and three or four doors on either side. He opened one of the doors and gestured me inside. I found out some time later that they call this type of prison van a sweat box. It's not hard to see why: the plastic-clad cubicles where the prisoners sit are tiny. I'm five foot seven and medium build and there was just enough room for me. If you were tall or even a tiny bit overweight, it would be horrendous. There was a small window so I could see outside. Underneath it, the plastic cladding curved outwards to create a seat.

I sat down. The officer removed my cuffs and shut the door. I heard his key turn in the lock. I leant my head against the back wall and closed my eyes. *All I've got to do,* I thought, *is get through this court hearing. Then I can go home.*

I felt the van start up and pull away. We hadn't been driving for long when I realised we were stopping again. I peered out of the window – there was no way we were at Birmingham Magistrates' Court yet. I was right: we were at another police station and more people were getting on. I leant back again and sat in silence, feeling the slight wobble of the van, listening to the footsteps, the muffled voices, then doors being shut. Then I heard something else – a voice. Someone was shouting my name. It was Nicholas.

'Sarah? Sarah!'

I sat bolt upright. He was in the van too.

'I didn't do it, Sarah! I didn't do it!'

'I know,' I shouted back. 'It's the hospital's fault!'

'I love you, Sarah,' he shouted. 'You know I love you.'

He sounded like he was crying.

'I know,' I said again. 'Don't worry, it will all work out. Everything will be OK. The truth will come out, it always does.'

The rest of the journey was silent. Staring out of my tiny window, eventually I started to recognise Birmingham city centre. As we navigated our way through the traffic, I looked out at the buildings, the cars, the people making their way to the shops. My life was over, but for everyone else it was just another day. The world was still ticking along as usual, like absolutely nothing had happened.

It's hard to articulate exactly what I was feeling. I *did* care what was happening to me, but I'd lost my son. There was such a huge gaping hole inside of me, there was no room to feel or make sense of anything else. Plus, I knew I was innocent. I believed that if I carried on telling the truth and co-operating with the police, we would get to the bottom of this and everything would be fine. It had to be. All I had to do was get through this one, tiny court hearing.

CHAPTER FOURTEEN

The prison van came to a stop inside an indoor car park. After a few moments I heard the doors open and the sound of people getting out. Eventually, my door opened. The guard put my cuffs back on and escorted me off. As I stepped down from the van and onto the tarmac, I glanced nervously at the other prisoners. Nicholas wasn't there – they must have left him till last. The others were all stood quietly in a line, handcuffs on, looking worse for wear. I was the only woman. As it was a Saturday, it was likely that most of the guys had been thrown in the cells for being drunk and disorderly the night before.

The officer walked me straight past them all and through a door into the court building. We didn't have to walk far. The officer stopped at a door, took off my cuffs and let me inside. It was a holding cell – a big square room with bare concrete walls painted white. It had a window with bars on, just like the one in my cell at the police station. The only difference was the block of concrete that ran around the edge of the room, providing a place to sit. And there were women in there.

'Wait here to be called,' the officer said, closing the door behind me.

I froze. Three pairs of dark, nonchalant eyes looked me up and down. They all looked about my age, but skinny and scruffy. Two of them were white, the third was mixed race and wearing a crop top that exposed the bottom of her ribs. They had the glazed, frayed-around-the-edges look of people who took hard drugs. As I sat down between them, the girls carried on with their conversation.

'I can't believe I got picked up *again*, man,' said one.

'I'll be going back to Eastwood for sure,' said another.

I stared at the floor straight in front of me and prayed they wouldn't talk to me. But I was too late.

'Hey, you.'

I looked up. One of the white girls was looking right at me.

'What you in here for?' she asked. I couldn't help but feel on edge. Everything from the tone of their voices to their body language felt confrontational.

'They think I killed my son,' I said.

None of them batted an eyelid.

'Where you from?' the mixed race girl asked, standing up.

'Kitts Green,' I said.

'I'm from Handsworth.'

I nodded. I figured they were all local, I could tell by the accents. She plonked herself down next to me. My heart was hammering in my chest. I had friends who were a bit rough and ready, but around these girls I felt like a hapless kitten. I wasn't used to any of this – police, courts, criminals. I was just a normal mom, frightened and alone. They were acting like they'd done this a hundred times before. They were the kind of girls that had no fear and a nothing-to-lose attitude.

The white girl was talking again now.

'I had a kid too,' she said. 'A daughter. She got taken off me.'

'That'll be the smack, then,' the other said, and they all cackled with laughter. I couldn't tell if they knew each other or not. All I knew was that I was the odd one out. I didn't belong here and I didn't want to.

The mixed-race girl moved closer to me. She yawned loudly, stretching her arms skyward and exposing more of her ribcage. Then she lay down on her side and put her head on my lap. I froze again. I didn't know what the hell to do. I wanted to ask her to get off me, but I was terrified. I genuinely thought that if I put a foot wrong they would turn on me.

'You wanna watch her,' one of the white girls said. 'She's a lesbian.'

They all cackled again. I felt my cheeks go bright red. I wanted the ground to swallow me up. Then the door swung open.

'Sarah Rose? You're up.'

I was first out and I was so relieved. I was on my feet and out the door in a heartbeat. It was a different guard now and the handcuffs he put on me were chained to him. He led me through the building – all high ceilings and bare brick walls. Everything was eerily silent. We had to climb a winding spiral staircase, and at the top was an empty room. The guard undid the cuffs, then walked over to a door and opened it for me.

'In here,' he said.

* * *

I walked through the door and suddenly there I was, in a packed courtroom. The low hum of people noise dropped to a whisper. Everyone's eyes were on me. But the only eyes I saw were those of my family. Mom, Dad and Stacey were there, Chantelle too – all just a few feet in front of me. I wondered where Thierry was, but of course, they wouldn't bring him to court. He must have been with his dad. I managed a weak smile. It was a mix of happiness and relief at the sight of my family's faces. I also wanted them to be reassured, to think I was OK, even if I wasn't. We all burst into tears.

I saw Nabeel sitting close to my family with his uncle. When our eyes met, he started shaking his head. *Does he think I had something to do with all this? Does he blame me for the death of our son?*

I was so overwhelmed to see everyone it took a moment to realise I was stood next to Nicholas. He was dressed in one of those white paper suits with a zip up the front. I presume it was because his clothes were taken off him when he tried to hang himself in the police cells. We were in a box behind a Perspex screen flanked by two prison guards. And Nicholas was speaking to me.

'I didn't do it, Sarah,' he said again. His eyes looked as puffy as mine felt.

'I know,' I said, quietly.

'I mean it, I didn't do it. I loved him. I loved him like my own. I love you.'

One of the guards cut in.

'Pipe down, young man.'

The whole room rose to their feet as the three magistrates walked in. They were clutching huge folders of paperwork as they took their seats at the very front. Their desk was high up and overlooked the whole room.

Surely this is it now, I thought. *They will adjourn the case and let me go home to my family. To Thierry, who needs me. To let me grieve.* I truly believed that Nicholas and I were at the centre of a huge mix-up. The nightmare had to be almost over now.

The magistrate sat in the centre was first to speak.

'Nicholas Kirnon, of 10 Dixon Close, Castle Vale. Is that correct?'

'Yes,' he replied.

'And Sarah Louise Rose of Flat 6, Kempson Road, Bromford. Is that correct?'

'Yes.'

Graham, the duty solicitor I met at Stechford Police Station, was sat in front of me. He stood up to speak.

'I would like to make an application for bail on behalf of Sarah.'

Their conversation went on for a few minutes. I tried my hardest to follow what was being said but there was a lot of court jargon I didn't understand. The one thing I did understand was: 'Application refused'. I wasn't getting bail. I found out later it was not only because the charge was so serious, but because almost everyone close to me – Mom, Stacey, Chantelle – had given statements to the police. If I talked to any of them I would be in contempt of court.

So now what? I thought. *Back to the police station?*

'The defendant will be remanded in custody until May 21 when the case will reconvene at Birmingham Crown.'

I was being sent to prison. For nine days. *No way!* I thought. *I can't go to prison! I've done nothing wrong!* My ears were ringing. I felt like I couldn't breathe, like I was going to collapse. My shoulders caved and my head dipped forward. Tears fell onto the thin brown carpet beneath my feet. I'm sure I could hear my family sobbing too but I couldn't bear to look back up at them. It was all too painful.

I really believed I was going to court as a formality and at the end of it I would be going home to be with Thierry and grieve with my family. I was innocent. I'd done everything I could to co-operate with the police. All I'd done was tell the truth, yet they were sending me to prison – a mother who had just lost her baby. I thought back to the girls in the holding cell and imagined that was probably what everyone in prison was going to be like. But I had no choice: I was going, whether I liked it or not.

***

When the guard escorted me back out the door by the elbow I didn't put up a fight. What was the point? There was no point to anything anymore. My baby was dead and I was being punished. My life was over. I let him cuff me and walk me back down the spiral stairs to a smaller holding cell. I felt relieved that it was empty – I just wanted to be alone. I sat down and sobbed my heart out. I sobbed so hard I could barely breathe. *What is happening to me?*

It wasn't long before Graham appeared at the door.

'You OK?' he asked.

I didn't answer. He sat down next to me.

'They're taking you to Eastwood Park in Gloucester. When we go to Crown Court on May 21, you'll be able to get bail so hang in there. You'll be fine. It's not for long, just nine days, that's all. It's really important that you don't discuss the court case with any of the people who have given statements to the police. That list includes your mother and your sister, so just be warned – if you talk about the case with them, you could all be in serious trouble. Do you understand?'

I nodded.

'Oh, one last thing – your mom and dad told me to tell you that Thierry is fine, and they're going to visit you at Eastwood as soon as they can.'

To some people, nine days in prison must seem like nothing. To someone like me, it was the most frightening thing I could ever imagine. I knew it wasn't a life sentence, but just the thought of setting foot in there was enough to tip me over the edge.

When they were ready for me I was cuffed again and marched back to the prison van. They closed the door of the sweat box and a few moments later the van shuddered to life. As we started to pull away I fell to pieces. The sobs overwhelmed me. My heart was pounding, I was shaking. My chest felt so tight I couldn't breathe. Up until today I hadn't been scared. I'd been devastated, emotional and erratic at times but at no point had I been scared. Now, I was without a doubt the most terrified I had ever been in my whole life.

CHAPTER FIFTEEN

The journey to Eastwood Park prison in Gloucester was an hour and a half. I had barely managed to pull myself together as the van ground to a halt. Staring blankly at the plastic-clad wall in front of me, I sat waiting for the door to open. I was still – almost paralysed with fear. All I could think of was every prison drama I'd ever seen on TV – the hard-as-nails women, the violence, the drugs. I was freaking out; I wasn't cut out for this.

Come on, Sarah, I thought. *You've got to get a grip.*

The guard helped me down from the van onto the tarmac of the prison car park. For a second, I was almost too terrified to look at the building in front of me but there was no hiding from it now. I looked up, blinking as my sore eyes did battle with the daylight. In my head it had been a huge brick fortress, all tall, intimidating walls topped with evil-looking barbed wire. To my relief, I'd let my imagination run away with me. The reality was a small, low-rise building surrounded by open fields. If it wasn't for the HMP sign hammered into the grass outside, it could have been a run-of-the-mill business or council office.

There were guards and other prisoners around me but I didn't acknowledge any of them. I was too preoccupied with trying to put one foot in front of the other as we moved towards the entrance. I don't know why but I was the first one inside. There was a waiting area and a front desk with a small lady in her fifties behind it. She had short brown hair and glasses on.

'Name, please,' she asked, peering over her specs.

'Sarah Rose,' I said. My voice sounded so small.

'Your prison number is TG6315. You need to remember it. That is what you are known as now. Do you understand?'

I nodded my head. She tapped away on her keyboard for a few seconds then looked straight at me.

'Don't tell anyone why you are here,' she said. 'They won't like it.'

Her words hung in the air as a female guard led me away. I wanted to turn back and ask her what she meant but I realised I already knew. She meant the prisoners. I'd heard before that paedophiles and child killers are considered the lowest of the low, even among the most hardened criminals. If anyone found out I was there on suspicion of being involved in the murder of a child, let alone my own son, they'd be gunning for me. Until that stark warning it hadn't even crossed my mind. I was innocent. It didn't matter who knew why I was locked up because I hadn't done anything wrong. But if I was going to survive in here, I needed a cover story. The panic set in again as I grappled for an idea that sounded believable. As if I wasn't scared enough already – now I had to make up lies.

We hadn't walked far when we arrived in a large open-plan room. It had white walls, thin carpet on the floor and painfully bright lighting. There was a row of hooks and a bench on one wall – the kind that reminded me of the PE changing rooms at high school – and three or four large brown cardboard boxes on the floor. Another female guard was already in there, waiting.

'Right,' she said. 'We need everything off. You can go behind there.'

Near the clothes hooks there was a large hospital-style curtain hanging from the ceiling. I walked over and she pulled it across so I could get undressed behind it. My hands trembled as I undid the buttons on my shirt and dropped it onto the floor. I unzipped my black trousers and took my legs out one by one. Then I remembered the sanitary towel.

'I'm on my period,' I said. 'Do I still have to take my pants off?'

'Yes,' came the curt reply. 'Everything has to come off.'

My face crumpled. I tried my hardest not to make any noise. I didn't want them to hear me cry. I unhooked the clasp on my bra and let it fall, then hooked my thumbs into the sides of my knickers and pushed them down to my feet. The towel was sodden with what was now dry blood. Without taking it out, I stepped out of my pants, placed them on top of my trousers and bunched the material up in an effort to conceal the pad.

Just as I stood up straight the curtain flew back and the officers moved towards me. I automatically lifted my right arm across my bare breasts and placed my left hand over my private parts. I was so embarrassed. But there was worse to come.

'I want you to place your feet hip width apart and squat,' said the woman to my right.

Crossing both arms over my chest, I bent my knees and lowered myself to the floor. My legs were trembling.

'Now I need you to cough,' she said as I crouched at her feet. Again, I obeyed.

I found out later this is the way they check whether people are hiding anything in their body. Apparently it's really common for both men and women to smuggle drugs or even mobile phones by putting them inside themselves. I can't even begin to imagine the physical discomfort, let alone the fear of being caught.

For the final part of the strip search I had to lift my arms and do a full turn, then open my mouth so they could check inside. The second it was over, I scrabbled for my bra while one of the women started rooting through the cardboard boxes. She pulled out a pair of navy blue jogging bottoms, a white T-shirt and a pair of black flip-flops. She must have guessed my size because she didn't ask.

'Do you smoke?' she asked, as she handed me the clothes.

I shook my head. From one of the other boxes she pulled out a plastic bag. In it, there was some instant coffee, a tea bag and some sugar sachets. There was also a small toothbrush, a miniature tube of toothpaste, a tiny bar of soap, a face cloth and a phone card.

'Here you go,' she said, throwing something else into my hands. I caught it and looked down. It was a clean sanitary towel. They stood over me, watching, as I removed the used one from my knickers and put the new one in. The whole thing was so humiliating. I felt so dirty, so degraded. I wouldn't wish it on my worst enemy.

They gave me a large clear bag for the clothes I arrived in. I stuffed in my shirt, trousers and shoes then slipped my feet into the flip-flops. Clutching the bag and my welcome pack, I followed the two officers out of a side door and down a long corridor. We came to a large metal gate. Beyond that was the wing.

This was more like the prison I'd imagined. A long, narrow corridor with cell doors on both sides stretched out in front of me as far as I could see. There was a row on the ground and stairs leading up to an identical floor above. I can't remember if the lighting was bad or if it's more down to how I was feeling, but when I picture that moment it was dark. It was also eerily quiet, apart from the occasional sound of prisoners shouting to each other.

We were met by the female guard who was manning the wing.

'Sarah Rose, prison number TG6315, is that correct?'

I nodded.

The two guards who searched me turned on their heels and left. The officer then got up out of her chair and led me to a cell a few feet away. The heavy door was already ajar. She pushed it with both hands and all her body weight. I stepped inside. To my relief it was empty. After my experience of the girls in the holding cell at court, the thought of having to share with strangers was one of the things I had been dreading the most. I was still a wreck, still devastated and frightened beyond belief, but at least now I could be all of those things in private.

Without saying a word, the guard pulled the door shut and locked it behind her. I dropped my arms to my sides and stood still for a moment, holding my bag of clothes in one hand and my pack of basic essentials in the other. I looked around. There was a single bed with one limp-looking pillow. At the end of the bed was a table with a small, black portable TV on it. There was a toilet – actually in the room this time. It was in the corner with a little metal sink next to it. And there was a window, but it was so high up, tiny and thick with metal bars, that it would have been pointless to try and look out of it.

I dropped my bag on the floor and placed my tea and coffee pack by the TV. On the bed there was a fleece blanket and a clean white sheet that had been neatly folded up and left there for me to put on myself. I shook out the sheet then tucked it under the pillow and around the paper-thin mattress. I lay the blanket on top and climbed wearily onto the hard, uncomfortable bed.

How on earth did I end up here? I wondered. *Two days ago I was at home with my boyfriend and children. Now my son is dead and I'm in prison?* It was utterly incomprehensible. The world as I knew it had collapsed in a heartbeat. I felt like I was in a film – a harrowing drama being played out around me and dragging me along with it. My heart and mind were so locked in grief I was unable to process or make sense of anything else.

I lay on my left side, facing the wall. The tears quickly began to soak the pillow beneath my cheek. I ached for my children. I wanted to kiss them and hold them tight. But something terrible had forced us apart. Thierry was miles away and Kamran was gone forever. *Why? Why him? Why us?* I curled up into a ball and cried until I had nothing left.

***

Everything seemed so quiet when I first arrived at Eastwood Park. It felt like a place where time stood still. There was none of the music, laughter or daily hustle and bustle I was used to. No kids, no Kam, just doors slamming and prisoners shouting. There was always something being discussed through the walls.

'Are you watching this on BBC1?'

'Nah, put Channel 4 on!'

'What is this crap?'

'Are you having a laugh?'

It went on and on. I lay there, broken, half-listening to the mundane exchanges and cackles of laughter. They sounded so ... alive. I couldn't imagine ever feeling alive again.

Then, out of nowhere, one of the women shouted something that pierced through the air like a dart.

'She's a filthy baby killer!'

My heart leapt. I lifted my head off the pillow so I could hear more clearly. *Baby killer? Is that what she said?*

'She murdered her own babies, the sick fuck!'

I rolled onto my back, heart pounding in my ears. *They don't mean me, do they?*

'You're gonna get smothered, just like your kids!'

It didn't take long to talk myself down from the ceiling. The snippets of detail – that there was more than one baby; the smothering – were just enough to reassure me that they were goading someone else. Still, it was a terrifying taste of what I'd be in for if anyone found out why I was there.

I rolled back onto my side and thought about my cover story. *What can I say that is believable?* Then I remembered a report I'd seen on the news about benefit fraud. They were saying how serious it is to deliberately claim benefits that you're not entitled to and if you get caught you're likely to get a prison sentence. So it was serious enough to land you in prison, but not so serious that you got beaten up when you got there. I quickly decided to tell people I'd been working and claiming benefits at the same time. I'd claimed Housing Benefit before, plus I had my job. I figured merging a couple of truths would be easier and more convincing than one big lie.

With that settled my thoughts quickly slipped back to Kamran; the moment we said goodbye replayed in my mind over and over again. If I'd known it was going to be goodbye forever I would have put my arms around him and never let go. The loss was like a huge weight bearing down on me. I wanted to scream and shout. I wanted people to know I'd lost my baby boy. I wanted to tell everyone how much I loved him and how much it hurt that I couldn't hold him. But I had to keep it in.

As night fell I thought about Thierry; my darling boy. I wondered if he was OK and who was looking after him. I told myself he would most likely be with Mark or my parents, but I knew he would be missing me and his little brother. He needed me, he needed his mom. I wondered what on earth must be going through his little head. He was only three years old – did he know his little brother was dead? Would anyone have told him? If anyone was going to do it, I hoped it would be my mom.

I wondered what Nicholas was doing. I wondered where he was and if he was OK. I wondered if he was thinking about Kamran. I pulled my arms and legs into my body as the blackness tightened its grip around me. *Kamran – I'm never going to see him again. I can't cope with this pain. I can't carry on without him. What's the point of anything now?* If I didn't have Thierry waiting for me – my one reason to fight to be free – I'm sure I would have been tempted to do something stupid.

***

I must have drifted off to sleep because when I opened my eyes it was getting light. I lay still for a while, staring blankly at the wall and listening to the unfamiliar sound of a prison waking up. I felt cried out and numb. I wasn't completely aware of it yet, but somewhere underneath all that there was a niggling sense of dread, too.

When the urge to pee got so strong I couldn't ignore it, I heaved myself up into a sitting position. I rubbed my eyes and looked around at the empty cell. It looked even more drab than I remembered. I lifted my legs round and planted my bare feet on the cold concrete floor. I couldn't think of anything I wanted to do less than use the manky old toilet in my cell. But this was it for the next nine days; I had to get used to it.

I walked the few steps to my makeshift bathroom and scanned the loo. It looked clean enough and there was toilet paper at least. I pulled down my jogging bottoms and sat down. As I did my business, I remembered the pad in my knickers. I took it out and quickly swapped it for a bit of rolled-up tissue. I remember feeling terrified that the cell door might open at any second.

I rinsed my hands in the sink then splashed some water onto my face. I used the toothbrush and toothpaste in my welcome pack then climbed back onto the bed. I sat with my back against the wall, staring at my cell door. I didn't want to see anyone. I didn't want to mix with anyone. I tried to tell myself I was going to be OK. I tried to mentally prepare for whatever was going to happen that day. But I was scared: scared of who and what was the other side of that door. If it was down to me, it would have stayed shut until it was time to leave. But it wasn't long before I heard movement outside – the low hum of voices, then the jangle of keys. Then clear as day I heard a woman say, 'Wish me luck. I'm going in.'

The lock clicked and my door swung open. She was talking about me. *Wish me luck?* I thought, horrified. *What does she think I am, some sort of psychopath?* She hadn't met me, I hadn't even been convicted, yet she clearly thought I was guilty. I inhaled deeply. As much as I wanted to, I couldn't cry now. I had to be strong. I had to hold it together and look after myself.

'Right then, young lady,' the prison officer snapped. 'It's time for breakfast.'

'I'm not hungry,' I said.

'Don't be silly,' she replied. 'You have to eat.'

'No,' I said firmly, shaking my head. 'My son is dead. I don't feel like eating.'

'Suit yourself,' she shrugged. 'No skin off my nose. But I'll be back in a minute. You've got two inductions to do – one for prison protocol and one for the gym.'

'The gym?'

'Yes, love,' she said, almost rolling her eyes. 'The gym.'

'I don't think so,' I snapped. 'I lost my baby three days ago and you want me to do a fucking gym induction?'

My reaction startled me. It's not like me to swear at a complete stranger, never mind one in authority. But I was tired and suddenly really angry with her attitude towards me. I couldn't hold my tongue. I stared straight back at her, waiting for her response. I wasn't backing down.

'Alright,' she said, raising her palms in surrender. 'I'll see what I can do.'

She turned and left, leaving my door ajar. I took a breath and tried to get a handle on my temper but I was fuming.

She reappeared a few minutes later and said I was off the hook with the gym induction, but still had to watch a video about the prison rules. I decided I was prepared to accept the compromise and followed her out onto the wing. We walked down a corridor then she held open a door and ushered me into a room. There was a table with a TV and a video player on it and several plastic chairs scattered about. There was another girl already in there. I sat down a few chairs away from her. She looked about my age. She was blonde, skinny and dressed like me in jogging bottoms and a T-shirt. She never said a word; she never even looked at me. She just sat with her legs crossed and arms folded, staring straight ahead at the TV. She must have been new, too. I sensed she was as scared as me.

The guard walked over to the TV, pressed 'play' on the video player then took a seat behind us at the very back of the room. I can't remember much about the video other than it being really basic. It told us when meal times were, that there was a library and a common room, what to do in the event of a fire. I didn't pay attention. I was only going to be there for just over a week. I didn't need to know any of this. I didn't care. All I wanted was my son.

The video only lasted around ten minutes. When it was finished, the guard turned off the TV and walked me back to the wing.

'You're in here now,' she said. For some reason they had moved my things to a different cell. It looked identical to the first one. The only difference was that it was almost next door to the staff room that the prison officers used. Again, I didn't care. It really didn't matter to me where I was, as long as I didn't have to share. I opened out the clean sheet and made the bed. Then I kicked off my flip-flops, lay down facing the wall and closed my eyes. I was so tired. I wanted to switch my brain off. I wanted to sleep, to get away from all the pain.

Then I wanted to wake up in my flat with my boys and find this had all been a horrible dream.

***

The prison noise had picked up slightly when I heard a man's voice at my door.

'Time for lunch,' he said as I sat up to look at him.

'I don't want anything,' I said.

'Come on,' he encouraged. 'You've got to eat something.'

I didn't have it in me to fight. Dejectedly, I got off the bed.

'The canteen is just down here,' he said. When I got to my door, several other prisoners were already walking in the direction he was pointing.

'I'll show you,' he said. I followed him down the wing, through the metal gate and into a large open-plan hall. There were rows and rows of tables and chairs, about half of them already full. Then at the far end, there was a long, silver hot food counter, like the kind you get your school dinners from. It was fairly quiet in there. The low hum of people talking was punctured by the sound of food being spooned onto trays and the odd chair scraping along the floor. There was a queue for the food. I saw a pile of cream plastic trays, picked one up and joined the line. I wasn't hungry. I didn't want to be there. I was just going through the motions.

As the queue inched along with other prisoners joining it behind me, I turned my head and gazed idly across the hall.

Then my eyes fell on someone. A girl – she had got her food and was now turning with her tray in her hands, walking to sit at a table. I felt my skin flush and my temperature spike as I recognised the long dark ringlets. She was mixed race and skinny with a jumper tied around her waist. It was the girl from the holding cell. *She knows me. She knows why I'm here.*

My instinct was to run. I pushed past the girls now stood behind me, dropped my tray and bolted to the gate. It was shut. The guy who walked me there was stood next to it, supervising.

'I need to go back,' I told him, glancing back over my shoulder. He could see I was panicking.

'Why? You haven't even eaten yet. What's wrong?'

'Nothing,' I said. 'I just really need to go back. Please,' I pleaded. 'Can you let me through? Please!'

He took pity on me and unlocked the gate. Keeping my head down I walked the few hundred feet to my cell as fast as I could. When I got there I pushed the door shut and sat down on the bed. My heart was thumping so hard. I tried to catch my breath.

Then the door opened. It was the male guard again. He was holding a tray with some food and a plastic glass of water on it. 'What was all that about?' he asked, sitting down next to me.

'Nothing,' I mumbled.

'Didn't look like nothing. Here,' he said, placing the tray on the bed between us. 'I brought this for you.'

'Thanks, but I'm not hungry.'

'You must be,' he insisted. 'Come on. Eat this.' He picked up an apple off the tray and handed it to me. 'Just an apple. For me.'

I relented and took the apple.

'So are you going to tell me what happened back there?'

'Someone in there knows why I'm here and it scared me. I didn't do it, you know? I haven't done anything wrong. But they told me not to tell anyone.' I was looking down at the apple. Tears were dripping onto my jogging bottoms.

'Listen,' the guard said. 'There are people you can speak to in here. Why don't I start by getting you an appointment with the doctor? Does that sound like a good plan?'

'Yeah, OK,' I nodded, wiping my nose on the back of my hand.

'And there's a group called Stepping Stones that you can go to. That might help, too. I'll get someone to come and tell you a bit more about it.'

He got up off my bed and walked over to the cell door.

'Try and eat some more,' he said, turning back to look at me. Then in the style of a gentle, mock telling-off he pointed a finger at me and added, 'This is the one and only time you're getting room service.'

As he left, I placed the apple back on the tray and lay down. He was the first person at Eastwood Park to be nice to me. As grateful as I was for his kindness, I had absolutely no intention of eating the food. I didn't even give it a second thought. I lay on my back, staring up at the ceiling, and decided there was no way I was going back to the canteen again. If that girl saw me I was done for. I was going to stay in my cell as much as I could. *It's only nine days,* I told myself. *You can do this.*

***

The guard was true to his word – a short while later I was taken to see the doctor. The waiting room was surprisingly typical. It had a reception desk, chairs against the walls and coffee tables with piles of out-of-date women's magazines. There was one other prisoner waiting to be seen. She looked up and acknowledged me with a smile, hands resting on her huge, pregnant belly.

The doctor I saw that day must have grown hardened to emotional women because I didn't get an ounce of sympathy.

'How can I help you today?' she asked.

'My baby is dead. He died on Wednesday. They think I had something to do with it but I didn't.'

I broke down. I told her how much I loved my kids and how much I missed them. All she wanted to know was whether I was eating and sleeping.

She prescribed me two lots of medication – an antidepressant in the morning and a sleeping tablet at night.

'Someone will come and get you when it's time for you to take them,' she said. 'If you suffer any side effects or you think they've made you feel unwell, tell someone you need to come back and see me.'

I liked the idea of the sleeping tablets. Sleep would give me a break; a break from the pain constantly tearing at my heart. A break from being stuck here in prison so far away from my family. I wanted to sleep. I wanted to sleep forever.

***

That dinner time I refused to leave my cell for fear of seeing the girl from court. The call for medication, however, couldn't come soon enough. I stepped out onto the wing and quickly scanned my surroundings. There was a queue forming a few feet away. A guard pointed me towards it then turned to speak to a colleague. There were about 15 prisoners making up the line. Most of them were white. They were all skinny, around my age. And they were loud. They were chatting, laughing and bubbling with excitement. They were almost bouncing off the walls, like kids about to get on the coach for a school trip. I joined the back of the queue and stood still with my arms folded around my middle. No one acknowledged me. I felt invisible – which is exactly what I wanted.

My eyes darted from floor to prisoner, checking each one as inconspicuously as I could. They all looked like fearless tomboys in their jeans, joggers and T-shirts. The amount of noise they were making was overwhelming. I couldn't see the girl from court. Not yet at least. I relaxed slightly. In among the line of jostling women, I spotted an old lady in a wheel-chair. She must have been well into her 60s. Chubby and fully grey with glasses, she looked like a typical nan and too old to be in here, especially compared to the rest of us. But it was like everyone knew her. All the girls were buzzing around her. I couldn't hear exactly what they were saying but I could tell by their body language they considered her to be someone important, someone to be respected.

Slowly, the line moved along. One by one the girl at the front would get her medication from a female guard stood inside what was essentially a large square box with a window in it. From the constant chatter fizzing around me, I soon realised why they were all so excited. The majority of them were getting methadone – a substitute for heroin. No wonder they were all so skinny. Most of them were heroin addicts and this was their legal fix, the highlight of their day. The feeling that I didn't belong gripped me again. I just wanted to get my sleeping tablet and get out of there.

After a few minutes I found myself at the front of the line. I stepped up to the window and waited for the guard to speak.

'Prison number?' she snapped. I hadn't memorised it.

'Erm, I can't remember,' I said quietly. 'It's Sarah Rose. I got here yesterday.'

She looked really annoyed. She turned to the shelf behind her, where there were lots of little plastic cups. She turned back to me, holding one of the cups in one hand and a cup of water in the other, and placed them on the ledge between us.

'Here,' she said. 'Take this.'

I picked up the cup that had a small round tablet in it and tipped it into my mouth. Then I picked up the water and took two big gulps to wash it down. I had to open my mouth so she could check it was gone.

'Next time,' she added, 'if you don't remember your prison number, you don't get your medication. Do you understand?'

I nodded and scuttled back to my cell.

I decided to switch my telly on, hoping it might kill some time before the tablet kicked in. We had the five main channels, plus channel 6 for when the guards put a DVD on for us at night. I settled for something on BBC1 and lay down on the bed. I stared at the ceiling for a while, trying hard to remember my prison number. *TG6215? No, TG6135. Or was it 6315? Yeah, that's it, TG6315.*

I wondered what Thierry would be doing now. I hoped he was with Mom and Dad, having his tea. I hoped he was missing me, but I hoped he wasn't sad. *But he must be,* I thought. *His baby brother is dead, his mom is gone. He must be so confused.*

I rolled onto my side and felt the tears slide from the corners of my eyes onto the pillow. I closed my eyes and thought about Kamran again. I pictured every inch and crinkle of his smiling face and winced under the weight of the thoughts still hammering away in my head: *He's gone forever. I'm never going to see him again. I can't live without him. I wish I was dead.*

That night, everyone in the prison cheered because they'd put *There's Something About Mary* on for us. I pulled the brown blanket up to my chin and watched it for a while but it wasn't long before my whole body felt heavy, like it was sinking. The tablet was working. I could finally switch off from all this pain. The dark thoughts that had been cluttering up my brain suddenly seemed quieter and further away. I took a deep breath, and slipped into a deep sleep.

CHAPTER SIXTEEN

The TV was still on when I opened my eyes. It was light and I was still underneath the blanket. I had slept all night. I couldn't remember a single toss or turn. I stretched out my arms and legs. I still felt woozy but on the whole I felt better. My body and mind felt recharged.

I got out of bed and used the loo. Then I ran the tap, splashed my face with water and brushed my teeth. I turned the TV back to BBC1. *BBC Breakfast* was on. I sat back on my bed and tried to watch but my mind soon started ticking over. I wondered what was going to happen today. Was I going to have to use my cover story? I was scared again. I was scared about having to lie and scared of being found out.

My door opened. It was one of the guards doing the morning call for the canteen. Thankfully all she did was say, 'Breakfast,' before moving on to the next cell. I stayed sat on my bed. I still wasn't hungry. And even if I was, I wasn't going to risk another run in with the drug addict from court who could tell everyone I was a child killer.

I sat, staring blankly at the TV, until the next guard appeared at my door. 'Medication,' she said, flicking her head to gesture me out onto the wing. I got up and stepped outside. There was a queue for the morning drugs, but it wasn't quite as busy as the night-time one. I joined the back and waited patiently, repeating my prison number in my head until it was my turn. When I got to the front it was a different woman dishing the tablets out.

'Number?'

'TG6315.'

She handed me the two cups – one with a tablet in, the other half full with water. I took it and went back to my cell, wondering whether a tiny pill was really capable of lifting the darkness I was drowning in.

The TV was still on. I picked up the welcome pack that was still lying on the table next to it. I sat on the bed and tipped out the contents. There was the unused tea bag, the packet of instant coffee and the sugars. Then I saw the phone card. I decided I was going to phone Stacey sometime that day. I knew the court case was strictly off limits, I just wanted to hear her voice.

I sensed I wasn't alone and looked up to see a girl had appeared at my door. She was about 27, slim and about the same height as me but with short, dark, poker-straight hair.

'Hiya,' she said. She seemed to gauge my reaction for a second before stepping inside.

'I'm Dawn. You're new, right? I just thought I'd say hi.'

I shuffled nervously and sat up a little straighter. My heart was thumping. *She's a prisoner. What does she want? Does she know why I'm here?*

'What's your name?' she asked.

'Sarah,' I said, wondering whether I should have lied about that.

'Well, like I said, I'm Dawn. And this is Kat.' There was another girl stood leaning against the frame of my door with her hands in her pockets. She was tall and thin with blonde hair cut into a short, boyish crop. They didn't look like the majority of the girls in here. They were nice-looking. They had clear, healthy-looking skin. They didn't look like druggies.

'So what you in here for then?' Dawn asked, walking towards me. She had her hands on her hips and was scanning my room.

'Erm, benefit fraud,' I stuttered.

'Us too!' she laughed.

I panicked. *She's going to rumble me. I'm a terrible liar.*

'So what did you do?'

'I, er, got a job but carried on claiming benefits.'

She nodded to say she understood.

'We got done claiming disability for our kids. It was about 20 grand altogether.'

'What's up with your kids?' I asked.

'Nothing!' Dawn said, looking back at Kat and laughing. 'We just claimed it and blew the lot. See Kat's tits? Some of it went on those. We had a nice holiday. Then we got busted by *The Sun*. We were in the paper and everything. So how long you got?' she asked.

'Only nine days, I think,' I said.

'Ahh, lucky you,' she said. 'You'll be fine. Have you got kids?'

I nodded and my stomach twisted.

'Girls or boys?'

'Two boys,' I said. 'I'm really missing them.'

'Yeah,' Dawn went on, sitting down next to me on the bed. 'It's shit. But you get through it. How old are they?'

'Three and 15 months.'

'Still little then. They probably won't even remember,' she said, trying to reassure me.

I was suddenly overwhelmed by the urge to open up, to blurt out this awful thing that was happening to me. I wanted to tell her my youngest son had been ill and now he was dead and I didn't understand any of it. I wanted to tell her I had nothing to do with it, that I was innocent and didn't belong here. I wanted to talk. I wanted to burst. But I had to keep it all in. I felt the tears start to run down my cheeks.

'Hey!' Dawn said, catching sight of my face. 'Don't be upset! You've got to be strong in here, it's not for long.'

She had her hand on my knee. She was reassuring me. But she didn't understand. She didn't know my tears were for my baby boy. I looked up and caught her eyeing the packet of coffee between us.

'Have it if you want,' I said, picking it up and handing it to her. 'I won't drink it.'

'You sure?' she said, surprised. 'You can sell it in here, you know.'

'Honestly,' I said, thrusting it closer to her. 'You have it.'

She took the packet and stood up. 'Thanks,' she smiled, walking off. I realised Kat had already gone. I sat up straighter again, wiped my eyes and took a deep breath. *That wasn't so bad*, I thought. Dawn seemed nice and didn't appear to have any suspicions about my benefit fraud story. I wasn't sure about Kat, but then she hadn't said a word.

Dawn reappeared with a bit of paper in her hand.

'Here,' she said, handing it to me. 'That's me and Kat.'

It was a newspaper cutting. The story had a large photograph of two girls lying on sun loungers in sunglasses and bikinis. It was the article *The Sun* ran after catching them abroad, on a holiday they'd paid for with the money they claimed illegally.

'Hilarious, right?' Dawn said, taking the cutting off me and looking at it. She was smiling now. 'It was very naughty but we had a bloody good time.'

A slim woman in plain clothes walked in and Dawn stuffed the piece of paper into the pocket of her jogging bottoms.

'Sarah?' the woman said, looking at me. 'I'm Philippa. Do you want to come with me?'

'See you later,' Dawn said, disappearing out the door. Once she was out of earshot, Philippa turned to me and smiled warmly.

'I heard you might like to come to our support group. It's called Stepping Stones and we meet every other day. It's just a place to relax and there are ladies you can talk to, if you need it.'

We walked through an office and came to what looked like a big classroom. There were lots of round tables with piles of arts and crafts materials on them – things like coloured paper and the rounded scissors young children use. The walls were covered in colourful pictures the prisoners from the group had made.

'Take a seat,' Philippa said. 'If you have any questions, just ask.'

There were two or three staff and quite a few prisoners. Some were stood up talking, most were sat at the tables cutting out shapes and chatting to each other. I made a beeline for an empty table, picked up a pair of scissors and some paper and tried to look like I was doing something. One of the first conversations I overheard really sticks in my mind.

'I'm tellin' ya now right,' the girl said in her heavy Birmingham accent. 'All four of my kids died of cot death, yeah. But they're blaming *me*. It's a fucking joke.'

She was small, five foot four and probably about my age, although she had the face of a teenager. She didn't seem to be talking to anyone in particular. In fact, everyone seemed to be actively ignoring her. But she carried on regardless.

'Looks like they're gonna take *this* baby off me now,' she went on, patting her stomach.

I remembered my first night and the girls shouting about the 'filthy baby killer'. *Maybe this is her,* I thought. She shrugged off the grey hoodie she was wearing and hung it on the back of a chair. My mouth almost hit the floor when I saw them – the scars on her neck; the slash marks all the way up her pale, skinny arms. I looked down at the paper I was cutting and tried to compose myself. I didn't want anyone to see the shock on my face. But as my eyes flitted to the other girls, I realised they all had them. Some only had one or two. Others had them covering every inch of flesh that was visible. Most of them looked like old scars – pale and slightly raised. But there were a few that looked red, angry and fresh. I'd never seen anything like it. I tried really hard not to stare, but I couldn't help it. When I arrived at Eastwood Park I had felt like such

an outcast. But this was something else. I never thought I'd
say it, but I felt more at home in the main prison than in
here. I wondered what kind of lives these girls must have had.
Whatever they'd been through, I knew it was a million miles
away from my life.

One of the counsellors pulled me aside for some one-to-one
time. I followed her into the office and she arranged two chairs
so they were facing each other. She sat in one and gestured
for me to take the other.

'Right,' she said brightly. 'Tell me what's going on with
you. How are you feeling today?'

I could feel the tears rising to the surface.

'Pretty down,' I said, staring at the floor.

'If you could pinpoint one thing, what would you say is
upsetting you the most?'

'My son died on Wednesday. He's the only thing I can
think about.'

'OK,' she said, unfazed. My head sunk down to my chest
and I started to cry.

'What was your son's name?'

'Kamran.'

'That's a lovely name,' she smiled. 'How old was he?'

'Fifteen months.'

'Do you have any other children?'

'Yes,' I replied. 'Another son. Thierry. He's three now.'

'And where is he?'

'With my family, I think. I'm not sure.'

'Are you close to your family?'

'Yes. My mom is like a mom to my kids.'

'And are they supporting you while you're here?'

'I think so,' I said, unsure. 'I'm not supposed to talk to them because of the court case but I think they're coming to visit.'

'I see,' she nodded. Then she sat forward, resting her elbows on her knees. 'Losing a child is a very difficult thing to go through, Sarah. It is very normal to be upset. Are you having any bad thoughts?'

'Not really,' I lied. I was nowhere near ready to tell a stranger that I was hurting so bad I wished I was dead. Plus, I imagined admitting to suicidal thoughts would trigger all kinds of attention. Attention I wanted to avoid at all costs.

'Well,' she went on, 'you are welcome to join us here at Stepping Stones any time you like. We're here every other day and you can just sit and chat in the main room or have some one-to-one time if you need it.'

She was nice and I appreciated the friendly talk but I found it hard to open up to a complete stranger, especially after having my fingers burned by the police. Besides, all I wanted was Kamran. No amount of talking was going to bring him back.

I re-joined the group and watched the girls share trays of sandwiches and fruit, grabbing for their next helping before they'd even swallowed the first. I still didn't feel like eating. I spent the rest of the afternoon cutting out shapes, deep in thought about Kam and my family. I kept my head down and no one bothered me. Then we were walked back to our cells in groups of two or three. When I saw the phone card on my bed I decided it was a good time to go and phone Stacey. I slipped it into the pocket of my jogging bottoms and walked back to my cell door. I had a quick look around before I stepped out and made a beeline for the three phones on the wall at the end of the wing. There was a girl using one of them. She was having a heated argument with her boyfriend. As I got to her, she slammed the phone down and shouted, 'Black bastard!'

'Are you OK?' I asked.

'Men!' she laughed. She told me she was from Handsworth. It felt like everyone was.

I stuck my card into the phone, dialled the number and waited. It rang two or three times before Stacey answered.

'Hello?'

'Stacey, it's me.'

I broke down, covering my eyes with my free hand as all the pain of the last few days came pouring out.

'Sarah? Is that you?'

'Yes.'

'Are you OK?'

I was crying too hard to answer.

'Don't worry, Sarah,' she said. 'Everything is going to be OK. We all love you. I promise everything will be OK.'

She sounded so strong. I wished I could believe her.

'Thierry is here. Do you want to speak to him?'

Before I could answer she was putting him on.

'Mommy?' His little voice shattered my heart into a million pieces all over again.

'Hello, baby,' I said, desperately trying to pull myself together. 'Are you OK? Are you being a good boy?'

'Yes,' he replied. 'Are you coming home soon?'

I broke down again. It was too much. Even if I'd had an answer for him, I couldn't speak for crying. Stacey must have sensed I was struggling and quickly came back on the phone.

'Are you OK?' she asked, concerned. I still couldn't speak. 'Oh God, Sarah. I hate hearing you like this. Please be strong. We all love you. It's going to be OK.'

I heard beeps and realised my time was almost up.

'It's saying I've only got 15 seconds,' I told her. 'I've got to go.'

'OK, be strong, we love you. We'll see you really soon.'

And then she was gone.

I replaced the handset, buried my face in my hands and sobbed my heart out. I had wanted so badly to speak to someone, yet hearing their voices had broken me in two. I hadn't expected to talk to Thierry. I certainly wasn't prepared for how difficult it was.

I took a deep breath and hurried back down the wing to my cell. Thankfully, there were only a few people about and if any of them had noticed the crazy girl with the puffy eyes sobbing into the phone they didn't let on. I climbed onto my bed and sobbed into my pillow to try and stifle the noise. When I refused another evening meal, someone came in with a tray of food and left it on my bed. But I didn't want it. I just wanted the ground to swallow me up. I wanted the pain to stop. I wished I was dead.

* * *

The evening call for medication was the only thing to pull me out of my distress. I joined the queue. Everyone was jostling around me, on a high about getting their methadone while I was in my own little bubble of darkness. I remember thinking it was a good job they dished out the tablets one at a time. I was so low I would gladly have swallowed the whole lot.

I took my tablet, got straight into bed and cried myself to sleep.

CHAPTER SEVENTEEN

Waking up in prison is like Groundhog Day. You're in the same, soulless cell. You hear the same voices shouting and the same doors slamming. And you're still alone.

I lay on my side, staring at the wall until someone came and got me for my morning medication. The sleeping tablets were knocking me out cold for several hours, which was exactly what I wanted. I was still unsure about the antidepressants, but was happy to keep taking them. They couldn't make me feel any worse. So that morning I got my tablet, went straight back to my room and got back into bed. If I could have stayed there all day I would have done.

I refused to get up for breakfast, only to get another tray of food brought in to me. Every time they said it was the last time. I lay there with my eyes closed, replaying the last time I saw Kamran. I pictured his smile and his wave as he said goodbye. Then I thought about the phone call from Nicholas. *What was it he said? 'The police are coming, you need to get to the hospital.' Yeah, that was it. And he was crying. His mom was crying too. Why was he at his mom's?* I wondered. *If Kam was ill, why didn't he just take him to the doctor's opposite the flat?*

The sound of something sliding under my door broke off my train of thought. I sat up. There were three white envelopes on the floor; one from my solicitor – a charge sheet outlining the charges against me, and a letter confirming my next court hearing on 21 May. I recognised the handwriting on the other two. There was one from Mom and one from Nan. I perched on the bed and tore them open.

Hello Sarah,

Just writing to let you know that everyone is thinking of you and trying to be strong. I know it's hard. We're all going through the same thing, hoping each day will be a little easier. We are missing you loads. We are looking after Thierry. I talk to him about you but he is still very clingy. You know what I mean. I hope to God I can see you soon and give you the biggest hug ever.

Nabeel phones every day and came to see me with his dad. They said they were sorry about Kamran and have offered to help pay for the funeral. Mark and Matthew have been great too.

Sarah, if you feel low or think your OCD is getting bad again, please tell someone straight away. There are people there who can help.

Signing off now, so God bless. Love you loads,

Mom xx

PS Dad sends all his love and kisses. He is trying to be strong for all of us xxx

Dear Sarah,

Just a line to let you know I am thinking about you. Please look after yourself. I am really worried about you.

As for what happened, I would never turn my back on you – you know that. I love you. You were a great mother to your babies.

I am really taking it bad about Kamran. I loved him so much.

Go to mass if you can and say a few prayers for you and the baby.

Keep your chin up, Sarah. Please eat. For me.

I will write again, I promise. If you need anything let me know. I love you. God bless you babe.

Love Nan xx

Some of the blue biro was smudged with tear stains. I felt so awful that the people I loved were suffering too. I sat and cried, re-reading the letters over and over. I was upset, but felt so touched by their words. Nan always loved a letter, and now I understood why. Those few words on an old piece of lined paper reinforced the fact that my family loved and supported me. I always knew this deep down, but the separation made it easy for the doubt to creep in. Now here it was in black and white – they believed I was innocent. And Thierry was OK. He was with his nanny; with his second mom in his home from home. I knew he would be getting all the love and attention he needed. I wished I could be the one to hug him and kiss him and tell him everything would be OK, but this was the next best thing.

I couldn't help but feel angry that Nabeel had taken his dad round to Wash Lane. So Kamran had to die for him to finally tell his parents? That hurt. It sounded like Nabeel's dad was actually a nice person after all. And it just confirmed my feelings that if Nabeel had come clean to his mom and dad, we could have been a family.

When Dawn stuck her head round my door and the legal papers were still strewn all over the bed I nearly had heart failure.

'How's it going?' she asked. I sat up and placed my letters on top of the charge sheet as inconspicuously as I could.

'Yeah, OK thanks,' I said, trying to act normal.

'So how come you went to Stepping Stones yesterday? I thought it was for the messed-up ones.'

'Erm, they thought it might help me, you know, cos I'm missing my kids.'

'Oh right,' she said, ''course. Did you meet little miss baby killer up there?'

'Do you mean the girl who says her kids died of cot death?'

'Yep, that's her. She's a nutter. She smothered them all, you know. She says it was cot death but *she* done it. And she's pregnant again, the evil bitch. Those poor kids.'

I didn't reply. *What would she think of me if she knew why I was really here?*

The second Dawn left I stuffed the papers from my solicitor back in their envelope and hid them under my mattress. If anyone saw them now, I would be vilified. Not only for what they would assume I'd done, but for lying about it too.

* * *

I was at Eastwood Park Prison in Gloucestershire from Saturday, 12, to Monday, 21 May. Beyond those first few days,

I can remember very little about my time there. Writing this book has made me realise there is a great deal from this traumatic time of my life that I have blocked out. But I think my poor memory of those nine days inside is most likely a side effect of the drugs I was on.

I was never really aware of the antidepressants working. But when I think back to how I was when I arrived at Eastwood Park and how I was once I started the medication, there is definitely a difference. I didn't feel quite so low, but I didn't feel happy either. I was just zoned out somewhere in the middle, not really feeling anything. And the fact that all I can remember is feeling like a zombie makes me think the drugs must have been strong.

The things I do remember are the letters. I got one from Stacey. 'I'm with you all the way,' she said. 'No matter what.'

She said she was working hard to keep Thierry's spirits up and had been listening to 'Glamorous' because it reminded her of me and Kam. She also said Nabeel, Mark and Matthew were continuing to show their support with regular phone calls and visits.

I replied to Mom, telling her I was OK – even though I wasn't. I didn't want anyone to worry. When she wrote back she said she had been to see Kamran's body at the chapel of rest.

'He is at peace now,' she said.

I was never given the option of seeing Kamran's body. I think I would have gone if I could, but I'm not sure it would have given me any comfort.

Nan sent more letters – each one contained her tearstains and a postal order. The money was put in an account for me so it was there if I wanted to buy anything. Towards the end of the week we were given a sheet listing all the things that were available to buy. We just had to tick the little boxes beside the items we wanted. I bought deodorant, sanitary towels, paper, envelopes and stamps. I remember buying crisps too – one of the few things I ate in there. I never set foot in the canteen again after what happened the first time. The guards or the women from Stepping Stones continued to bring me snacks, despite always warning it was the last time.

I have no memory of showering, only washing in my sink. I have no memory of going outside. I only left my cell for medication or Stepping Stones. Despite my initial shock at the girls and their scars, I felt safe there and it helped break up the days.

The only other prisoners I saw were Dawn and Kat. I think Dawn could sense I was struggling so she called in on me most days. She would talk to me about her kids and I would talk about mine as if Kamran was still alive. It was agony holding in the truth. Sometimes she would tell me funny stories about blowing the money they stole. I remember laughing, only for the shame and guilt to bring me crashing back down. *How can I laugh when my son is dead?*

Thierry was my strength, but Kamran was always at the front of my mind. I started to feel angry – angry at the hospital for not doing more to investigate the swelling and angry at myself for not making them. *But what had happened the day he died? How did he go from waving bye-bye to me that morning to being dead in the hospital?* The questions were piling up in my head. I realised Nicholas was the one with all the answers. He was with Kamran so he must know. I wanted to ask him how Kamran had been that day. *Was he still being needy? Did he want his mommy?* And what had actually happened that morning? *Had Kam had an accident? Maybe Nicholas had done something? No,* I told myself, *it was the hospital's fault. Kam was sick and they didn't do enough to find out why.* I remembered the moment I forgot my keys and phone, *Was that a sign for me not to leave that day?*

All I could really do was focus on my court date. My solicitor had assured me I would get bail so all I had to do was get to that hearing then I would be going home to my family. I washed my Ladbrokes shirt in my sink with the bar of soap. It was the only smart thing I had. There was no way I was turning up to court in jogging bottoms.

Birmingham was a good hour-and-a-half away so when Monday, 21 May arrived, I was woken up early. It was still dark, so it must have been about 6.30am. I had a wash, put on my uniform and tied my hair back. I was sat on the bed ready to go when they came for me. A guard walked me to a waiting room near the entrance. There were several other girls already in there. Most of them were going to court like me, but there were two who were being released. They had struck up a romantic relationship and were saying how difficult it was going to be for them to see each other on the outside. The other girls were reassuring them.

'Don't worry!' they said, 'You'll be back soon anyway!'

I stared straight ahead, anxious to get going and hoping I would never set foot in there ever again.

Around ten minutes later a guard came. He cuffed me and walked me out to the van. Once I was in the sweat box, he freed my wrists and locked the door. I took a deep breath. *All I've got to do is get through this hearing then I can go home.*

The journey seemed to take longer this time. My eyes were fixed on the window the whole time, searching for anything that would tell me I was in Birmingham and almost there. Eventually I started to recognise the roads, then the city centre. It was a busy Monday morning so we crawled through the traffic. Just as I started to think we were never going to get there, the court building came into view. There were people everywhere but I was drawn to two girls walking away from the court. It was Stacey and Chantelle. Before I knew what I was doing my fist was banging at the window and I was shouting their names. But the roads were so noisy they couldn't hear me.

The van went through a barrier and down into an underground car park. One by one, the doors of the sweat boxes were opened and each prisoner escorted into the building. We were all put in holding cells, exactly like the one at Magistrates' Court. When I got to mine there were already women in there, but all I remember is the anxious wait for someone to call my name and take me up to the courtroom. I wanted to see my family. I wanted to be with them as soon as I could. I kept reminding myself, *Just one little hearing then you can go home. You can do this.*

It felt like a good couple of hours before a big bald guy in uniform came for me. He cuffed me again and we walked up to the court. I didn't know for sure if Nicholas was going to be there, but it wasn't a complete shock when the guard opened the door and he was. He was already stood in the Perspex box with handcuffs on and a guard next to him. I sensed him become animated as I took my spot a few feet to his left, but I didn't look at him. I couldn't quite put my finger on it but something didn't feel right. He knew what happened that day. He knew why Kam died. So why were we here? Why were we both under suspicion? All I knew for sure was that *I* was innocent. And as every pair of eyes in the courtroom fell on me, I realised I had to look out for myself.

Mom, Dad, Stacey and Nan were in the gallery to my left. Aunty Maggie and Chantelle were there too, sitting close to Nabeel and some of his family. *Right,* I thought, gathering all my strength, *let's get this done.*

The court clerk cleared his throat.

'All rise,' he said.

As the whole room rose to their feet, the judge appeared and took his seat on the platform directly in front of me.

'Please be seated,' said the clerk.

There was no sign of the duty solicitor who represented me last time, just men in suits. One of them had a turban. He was in his early thirties and probably one of the youngest there. After a few brief conversations the judge looked up to address me and Nicholas directly.

'Nicholas Kirnon, of Dixon Close, Castle Vale. You are charged with the murder of Kamran Rose. How do you plead?'

'Not guilty.'

'Sarah Louise Rose of Kempson Road, Bromford, you are charged with manslaughter by gross negligence and knowing or allowing a child to die. How do you plead?'

'Not guilty.'

The conversations started again. I tried hard to pay attention but it was like they were speaking in a foreign language. I looked at the solicitors, then at my mom and dad, who smiled at me supportively. *You can do this, you can do this. It will all be over soon and you can go home.*

Then suddenly Nicholas was whispering my name.

'Sarah. Sarah.'

I turned my head to look at him for the first time. He was trying to hand me something. It looked like a tiny bit of paper.

Without thinking, I reached out to take it. But before I could, the guard snatched it away.

'Quiet,' he snapped.

I turned my attention back to the courtroom as the subject of bail was being discussed. Nicholas was refused again. The charge was too serious and he was going to remain in custody. When it came to me, however, I couldn't quite get to grips with what they were saying.

I was taken back downstairs to an empty holding cell with no idea what was happening to me. It didn't sound like I was going back to prison. But I didn't dare get my hopes up until it was crystal clear.

After a few minutes my cell door opened and the guy with the turban came in.

'Hi Sarah,' he said, holding out his right hand. 'I'm Mr Bhomra. Good to meet you properly.'

'What's going on?' I asked, confused.

'You've got bail. But because so many of your family and friends have given statements to the police, they don't want you to stay in Birmingham.'

'So where do I go?'

'Gloucester.'

'Gloucester?'

'Your ex-boyfriend, Mark, has arranged for you to stay with his cousin's girlfriend. Her name is Janette. We are just waiting for her to get here. The judge wants to see her before they let you go.'

'Right,' I said, still baffled. 'So I'm not going back to prison?'

'No, you're going to stay with Janette. She should be here soon. You will be called back up to court to hear your bail conditions then you will get the train to Gloucester. Everything is going to be fine. Did you get the paperwork I sent you?'

'Yes.'

'Right,' he said again, standing up. 'See you in there. I'll speak to you again before you go.'

To hear I wasn't going back to prison was an enormous relief, but I was devastated I couldn't go home to Mom, Dad and Thierry. And although now I'm eternally grateful for everything Mark did for me, at the time the idea of staying with a stranger in Gloucester only filled me with more dread.

***

Back in the courtroom, a good hour later, there was a black woman stood in the witness stand. She was medium build, with big short black curly hair. She was dressed in a black coat and black boots. *That must be Janette,* I thought. We were too far away to make eye contact.

The judge came back in and she was asked to swear on the Bible.

'I want you to understand that you are responsible for Miss Rose,' the judge told her.

'I understand,' she nodded.

I had to reside at Janette's house on Woodway Drive, Gloucester, until Nicholas and I stood trial. I had a curfew which meant I had to be in the house from seven at night until seven in the morning and I wasn't allowed contact with children under four. Thierry was exempt, although I was only allowed supervised visits. A family member who wasn't involved in the case would always have to be there. This was particularly painful.

When they released me from the defendant's box, Mr Bhomra went over the bail conditions again to make sure I understood them. I had to go straight to Janette's, then sign in at the police station the next morning as proof I was there. Mom and Stacey had given statements so I was banned from talking to them, but Dad hadn't.

'Good luck settling in,' Mr Bhomra added. 'I'll be in touch. I think your dad is waiting for you.'

I was flying out of the courtroom before he'd even finished his sentence. Dad was stood in the hallway. I burst into tears as we ran towards each other. It was like a scene from a film. I flung my arms around him and he squeezed me so tight he lifted me off my feet. It couldn't have been more different to all those times I shrugged him off as a kid. I've never been hugged so tightly. And I'd never needed that hug more.

When he finally put me down and looked me in the eye, he was crying too.

'Sarah, we love you so much. We know you had nothing to do with this. We know you would never hurt Kam.'

I nodded through a flood of tears.

'How come you didn't give a statement?' I asked.

'We decided there was no point. I've got no information that can help the police. And we agreed that one of us needed to be free to support you.'

'Thanks, Dad,' I whispered.

'Matthew's here too. He's going to take you to Gloucester and help you get settled. Then, next weekend, I'm going to come and see you. I'll bring Thierry. OK?'

I nodded and he pulled me close again.

'We love you, Sarah,' he whispered. 'We love you so much. Everything is going to be OK, I promise.'

He gave me my coat, some cash and my bank card. It suddenly occurred to me that I wouldn't be able to pay my rent and bills.

'The flat,' I stammered.

Dad looked like he had something he didn't really want to tell me.

'What is it?'

'It's been burgled, love,' he said. 'We went as soon as we could but they'd already ransacked the place. They took everything, except ...' His voice trailed off.

'Everything except what?' I asked, confused.

'They left Kam's room untouched. There wasn't a single thing out of place.'

It was a cruel turn of events, but in all honesty, I had too much going on to dwell on it. I didn't care about my things. I knew Thierry was being looked after and wouldn't want for anything. Dad said he'd cleared Kam's room and now had everything stored safely at theirs. That was all I needed to know.

Dad wrapped his arm tightly around my shoulders as we walked through the court lobby and out of the exit. As we stepped out into the afternoon light, I saw the rest of my family stood together on the other side of the road. They were crying, waving and blowing kisses. When Mom's eyes met mine I just wanted to run over and throw my arms around her. She smiled lovingly and I knew she wanted to do the same. I'll never forget the anguish written all over her face. My heart ached, imagining what they must all be going through. I felt so responsible for their pain. And I felt for Mom the most. I knew she felt the same pain I did, like she'd lost a son too.

Matthew appeared out of nowhere and put his arms around me.

'Hello stranger,' he said. 'I'm coming to keep you company.'

I couldn't speak for crying but it was so amazing to see his smile. And I was so grateful he was coming to Gloucester with me – I don't know how I would have made the journey on my own. I gave Dad one last squeeze then turned and waved to everyone else.

'We'll see you next weekend,' he said. 'Call me when you can.'

***

Matthew and I walked across town to New Street Station. He kept asking if I was OK but I was crying too much to speak. I'd been so happy to see my family, but I had truly believed I'd be going home with them. Being wrenched away again had brought me crashing back down.

New Street was getting busy when we arrived. Matthew bought the tickets and got us to the right platform. I could barely see for the tears. God knows what I must have looked like.

We boarded the train and Matthew chucked his sports bag in the overhead compartment while I slunk into the window seat. I closed my eyes and rested my head on the window.

'I should have packed some tissues,' Matthew teased gently.

I turned my head to look at him.

'I'm so glad you're here,' I said, wiping my eyes. 'I didn't think I would be allowed to see anyone.'

'She speaks!' he smiled. 'Yeah, well, lucky for you I didn't give a statement to the police.'

'Did they ask you to?'

'Yeah, and I thought about it. But I couldn't think of anything I knew that would help them. Plus, if I did, it meant I wouldn't be allowed to talk to you. So it was a no-brainer, really.'

'Thank you,' I croaked.

'No problem,' he smiled kindly.

I felt the train judder to life and start to pull forward.

'So, yeah,' he went on, 'you've got me for the whole week.'

'What about work?' I asked.

'I took it as holiday so you better start showing me a good time, yeah?'

He was smiling again. His face was like a ray of sunshine.

I cried the whole way to Gloucester. The train took an hour then we got in one of the cabs lined up outside the station. Matthew had Janette's address written on a piece of paper. The driver said it wasn't far. Everything felt so surreal – being out of prison and around normal people doing normal things. Now here we were in a strange city on our way to stay at a stranger's house. My nerves were jangling as we pulled up outside the house.

Janette was staying in Birmingham for the night so it was her 18-year-old daughter Dionne who welcomed us in. She showed us around their home – a neat new build with plain magnolia walls throughout. It had a large square kitchen and a good-sized living room with a huge brown corner sofa and matching chair. Dionne's room reminded me of my own – wardrobe, chest of drawers and clothes all over the place. She had a double bed that I would be sharing with her. I said I didn't mind, but I would be lying if I said I didn't feel awkward. I wondered how Dionne must feel about having to share with *me* – not just a stranger, but a stranger on bail and grieving for her dead son. I felt like such an inconvenience.

Dionne had a friend with her that night – Hannah, a skinny girl with ginger hair. Hannah lived in Gloucester with her mother, but they didn't get on. So with Jannette in Birmingham all the time, the girls were free to spend their spare time hanging out here.

The four of us sat on the big sofa watching *MTV Cribs*. Matthew suggested getting fish and chips and Hannah offered to show him where the local takeaway was. As I watched them leave, the loneliness struck me. Matthew was my lifeline – my friend and protector. Already I was dreading the goodbye on Sunday.

Me and Dionne carried on watching *Cribs* while we waited for them to come back. She got me a glass of squash and made small talk about whichever celebrity home was on the TV. She never asked about me or Kamran or the court case. She seemed like a nice girl but I couldn't help but feel like the elephant in the room.

I felt myself relax when I heard the sound of the front door opening and Matthew's voice. 'Dinner is served,' he smiled, walking in holding two carrier bags aloft.

The smell of fish and chips quickly overwhelmed the living room. He dished out the portions and for the first time in almost two weeks I ate a meal. We sat in front of the telly, eating straight out of the paper. Matthew went out of his way to make sure there were no awkward silences, chatting to the girls and making them laugh. I didn't join in the banter like the old Sarah would have done, but I was grateful to be in the same room as one of my very best mates. For the first time since Kam died I felt safe. I think that's why I ate.

I slunk off to bed about nine o'clock, flagging under the weight of the day's events and my unusually full stomach. Matthew, Dionne and Hannah had all been lovely to me, but

I needed to be on my own. I changed into a pair of pyjamas Dionne lent me and climbed into her double bed, pulling the duvet right up to my ears. The tears came almost immediately. It was the first time I'd cried since we'd arrived. But to be honest, even when I wasn't crying, I was only holding it back. I was glad to be out of prison, but I was missing both my boys. I was so devastated about Kamran it was hard to feel positive about anything. And I was still so confused. *How did he die? Why did the police think I had something to do with it? And why was I here, away from my family, being made to suffer even more?*

***

I must have cried myself to sleep again because I don't remember Dionne coming up to bed. When I woke up the house was silent, apart from the sound of her breathing next to me. I got up as quietly as I could and went into the bathroom. It must have been early as it was only just starting to get light. I used the loo and decided to have a shower. I stood under the hot running water and thought back to my last shower at the flat, the night before Kamran died, before me and Nicholas had sex. I wondered for the millionth time how on earth we had got from that to this.

Matthew must have brought clothes for me because I remember changing into clean underwear, jeans and a top. Downstairs, the TV was still on. Matthew was spark out underneath a sleeping bag on one end of the sofa and Hannah was wrapped in a duvet on the other. It was so huge there was probably enough room for me in-between, but I didn't want to wake them, so I killed some time in the kitchen by making myself a bowl of cereal then doing the washing up. Then I went back to the living room and sat down next to Matthew. He stirred and opened his eyes.

'What time is it?' he said, his voice still rough.

'Dunno,' I said. 'Early, I think. Dionne isn't up yet.'

'You sleep OK?' he asked, yawning then sitting up. I shrugged and tried hard not to cry.

'Hey,' he said, seeing the look on my face. 'I'm here now, Sarah. You're gonna be OK.'

I nodded, but I didn't believe him.

Hannah woke up and we watched TV until Dionne came down, dressed and ready for work. She said Gloucester Central Police Station was close to her office, so when Matthew had changed into some clean clothes, the three of us headed into town together. It was a bus ride and a short walk to Dionne's place, then she explained where we needed to go.

The police station was a busy place. All I had to do was fill in a form with my name, the address I was staying at in Gloucester and my signature. We must have been in there all of five minutes.

Matthew decided we might as well have a walk around the town to help me get my bearings. The streets were mostly pedestrianised, with brick paving and two-storey terraced buildings occupied by all the usual shops – Boots and Superdrug, New Look, River Island. Compared to the noise and high-rises of Birmingham it felt small and quiet. Matthew pointed out the cathedral and a park that would be good for Thierry. Then he spotted a jacket potato stand and bought us both one. We sat on a bench to eat, then wandered around a bit more. We came across a branch of Ladbrokes. It reminded me of work and getting the phone call from Nicholas.

When we felt like we'd seen all there was to see, we headed back to the house. The bus journey had been a straight road, so we walked, and it took about 40 minutes. Matthew chatted away about work and what he'd been up to while I felt the fresh air in my lungs. It felt good to be outside, but the loss of Kamran still weighed heavily on my shoulders. I imagined it always would.

Back at the house, Hannah had gone so we had the place to ourselves. We sat side by side on the sofa, drinking squash and watching MTV. For a while we didn't say a word. I was just starting to drown in my thoughts of Kam when Matthew spoke.

'I miss him too, you know?'

I started to cry. Matthew turned to look at me. His face was angry now, snarling almost.

'I could kill him, Sarah, I swear.'

'Who?' I asked, wiping my cheeks with my hand.

'Nicholas. I hate him, Sarah. I mean it – I *hate* him. If I could see him now ...' His voice trailed off as he closed his eyes and took a breath. It was the first time I'd heard anyone express anger towards Nicholas over Kamran's death. His reaction didn't seem inconceivable, but I couldn't join the dots. In my head there *was* a question mark over Nicholas because he must know what happened. But I always came back to the hospital. *Kam was sick and they didn't help him in time.* I didn't realise it at the time but I had so little information beyond that. I was in the dark and in constant turmoil because of it.

I assumed Matthew must be thinking the same as me – that I was innocent and Nicholas must know something. But I didn't share his anger. Not yet. *Nicholas was good to me,* I thought. *No one knows him as well as I do.* Something stopped me from saying it aloud, though. I didn't want Matthew to think I was sticking up for him.

***

That afternoon, shortly after Dionne got home from work, Janette arrived back from Birmingham.

'Everyone alright?' she asked loudly. 'Has Dionne been looking after you? Sorry I wasn't here to welcome you, but I figured you kids would have more fun without me anyway.'

She disappeared into the kitchen and started cooking dinner. When she called us in and I saw what it was, I panicked. It was Spaghetti Bolognaise. Can you believe it? Twenty-one years old and scared of Spaghetti bloody Bolognaise! It sounds so daft now, but I was a creature of habit. I knew where I was with a Sunday roast or chips, eggs and beans. But Bolognaise? I didn't want it, but Janette was loading a huge portion onto my plate and I was too polite to refuse.

There was no dining table so we all sat on the sofa with the plates on our laps. Everyone tucked in while I pushed mine around. Every now and again I would lift the fork to my mouth and take a tiny mouthful, but I really couldn't bear the taste. Bit by bit I hid the meat under the pasta like a child. Then before anyone else could finish, I seized my moment. Keeping my plate up by my chest so no one could see it was still full, I rose to my feet, flew into the kitchen and scraped my dinner into the bin. Then in a final flurry of paranoia, I put rubbish on top of the uneaten food to disguise it. My cheeks burned with embarrassment at the thought of being found out. The last thing I wanted was Janette to think I was rude or ungrateful. If she noticed I was being weird she didn't let on. She collected the rest of the plates then disappeared upstairs to watch TV in her room. I stuck it out with Matthew and Dionne for a little while longer, but was counting down the minutes until it felt like an acceptable time to go to bed. Once I was alone, I cried as quietly as I could manage. I thought about how angry Matthew was and wondered if my parents felt the same. *Do they want to kill Nicholas too?*

I was still awake when Dionne climbed into bed next to me. I stayed on my side with my back to her. Once I knew she was asleep I cried some more. I lay awake for what felt like an eternity, my head buzzing and my heart aching. Then all too soon the daylight was creeping in through the curtains.

***

I was first up again. Dionne went off to work then eventually Janette surfaced and told me and Matthew she was off out. When she wasn't in Birmingham she had family nearby who she called in on nearly every day. As well as Dionne she had a son and a young grandson, although I never met them.

When Matthew got hungry we walked to the local McDonald's for chicken nuggets. Then we meandered back to the house and watched more TV. That was pretty much our routine for the whole week – watching back-to-back *Cribs* and *My Super Sweet 16*. We left the house when Matthew wanted food, or if I needed to sign in at the police station. Then every night I was the first one in bed crying myself to sleep.

I had a mobile phone, although I can't quite remember where it came from now. I phoned home almost every night. I would wait until seven o'clock when I knew Dad would be home from work. The conversations were short. He would ask how I was and I'd tell him I was fine. I would ask how Thierry was and he would tell me *he* was fine. I think it was about the third time we spoke when I got a glimpse of what was really going on at home.

'Mom's been to the hospital today,' said Dad. 'She's not doing too well.'

'How do you mean?' I asked.

'She's not eating, not sleeping. Just overdoing things a bit, you know? They've given her some medication.'

I felt so guilty. She'd lost a grandson – a grandson that was like a son to her. And now I was gone too. I knew she was hurting just as bad as I was, if not worse. And there was nothing I could do about it.

***

Even though I always knew it was temporary, I couldn't help but get used to having Matthew around. It meant the world to have a friend there with me. I don't know what I would have done without him. So when Sunday came I started falling to pieces. Matthew spent the morning on the sofa with me, then around lunchtime Dionne offered to walk us to the train station. I think she could tell I wouldn't be in a fit state to get back on my own. And she was right: I wanted to throw myself on the train tracks to stop him going. We stood under the departure boards hugging and I didn't want to let go.

'Keep your chin up,' he smiled, flashing his gold tooth. 'You're gonna be fine. I'll see you soon.'

I managed to hold back the tears as he walked off to find his platform and I followed Dionne back outside. We had something to eat in a nearby fried chicken shop, then caught the bus back to hers. I went straight upstairs – I had to have a good cry in the bedroom before I could go down and face Janette. I felt so lost and alone without Matthew. How was I going to cope on my own?

CHAPTER EIGHTEEN

When you've got kids, you get used to living with noise and chaos. There's always someone pestering you for something. There's always housework to do, a nose to wipe, a nappy to change and food to prepare. Your children's needs naturally become your sole focus. They suck up all your attention, almost without you realising. When you're in the thick of it you fantasise about having time to yourself, being able to go out when you want and lie in when you need it. All you want is a tidy house and a bit of peace and quiet. Now here I was in a tidy house with all the time, peace and quiet in the world. And it was hell.

The silence was deafening. I didn't know what to do with myself. Prison had been about survival. All I had to do was get through those nine days. *But what now?* There was no support group, no drugs to numb the pain. The court case was months away. Matthew was gone. I had no routine, no focus. All I had was grief, closing in on me like a black cloud.

That first Monday in Gloucester without Matthew, I got up early and caught the bus into town with Dionne. I walked with her to her office before signing in at the police station, then walking home alone. Back at the house, Janette was out so I wandered aimlessly into the kitchen and started doing the washing up. I worked through each item slowly and methodically – washing, rinsing and placing everything carefully on the draining board. My hands were busy, but my mind was stuck on one thing – Kamran.

It was still so difficult to come to terms with the fact my precious baby boy was gone. I knew it was true but I didn't want to believe it. I wanted to hear his giggle. I wanted to see him running towards me, smiling, with his arms outstretched. I couldn't accept that I had already experienced all those things for the last time. I didn't want to let him go. Not now, not ever.

I looked down as I felt the weight of the large wet kitchen knife in my hand. The blade glistened as the bubbles slid off. The ache in my heart overwhelmed me again. There was no escape. If Kam had really gone forever, then surely this pain would last forever, too.

I turned and sank to the floor. With my back against the cupboards, I wiped the last of the bubbles onto the leg of my jeans. I was calm, but the pain inside me was at bursting point. I just wanted it to stop. I lifted my left wrist and pressed the side of the knife against it. The metal was still warm. *Just end it*, whispered the voice in my head. *Kam's gone. There's no point being here anymore. You're not strong enough for all this.*

Slowly, I turned the knife so the blade was against my skin. I held it there for a few moments. *Do it*, said the voice. *This pain won't go away unless you make it.* For several minutes I sat there in complete limbo. Eventually, I crumbled. The knife clattered to the floor. I dropped my forehead to my knees, wrapped my arms around my legs and sobbed. With no one in the house to hear me cry, I let it all out. I cried and wailed, like I was trying to set the pain inside me free.

I don't know how long I spent on the kitchen floor that morning, but when I came round I was curled up on my side. I saw the knife next to me. My mind flashed back to it being in my hand and all the bad thoughts that had been running through my head. I realised I was scared – scared I was losing my mind and scared of what I might be capable of.

Standing up, I grabbed the knife and threw it into the sink. Then I went to the hallway, grabbed my coat and walked straight out the front door. I'd seen a GP's surgery on the next street. Maybe I could get help there.

I told the receptionist I wanted to register as a new patient. She said I could fill in the forms but they had no appointments until the following day. I booked the earliest they had and was back there, the next morning, with time to spare.

'Good morning, Sarah,' said the female GP, welcoming me into her office. 'You're a new patient, is that correct?'

I nodded.

'How can I help you today?'

I sat down and took a breath.

'My son died two weeks ago. I'm here on bail.'

Her friendly expression faded as she stiffened in her seat.

'I'm having bad thoughts,' I went on. 'I'm either crying myself to sleep or lying awake all night. Yesterday I had a knife in my hand. I don't know what I was going to do, but it really frightened me, so I came here.'

She stared straight at me as she settled on the right words.

'Have you harmed yourself at all?'

'No,' I said. 'I just thought about it.'

'Would you like me to prescribe you some antidepressants?'

I thought about it for a moment. They had helped in prison, but I didn't want to be a complete zombie now.

'Is there anything else I can do?'

She frowned.

'You mean like counselling?' she asked.

'Yeah,' I said hopefully.

'I'm sorry, but there's a six-month waiting list.'

Her words were like a door slamming in my face.

'If you don't want any medication I'm afraid there's not a lot else I can do.'

In that moment it dawned on me that I was completely on my own. My only choice was to pull myself together and get on with things as best I could. I wanted to get to the bottom of what happened to Kam. I wanted to prove my innocence and get back to Thierry. I had to focus. But there was no way I could sit around the house all day. I was already going crazy.

As I walked back to the house I felt the mobile phone in my pocket and had a lightbulb moment. There was a Ladbrokes in Gloucester. Maybe I could get a job there. I called Tracey, my old area manager, hoping she could help. She sounded shocked to hear from me.

'Oh my God, Sarah! Are you OK?'

'Yeah, I'm OK, thanks. Listen, I'm sorry for walking out on Charles the other day.'

'Don't you dare,' she cut in. 'Chantelle told us everything. You don't need to apologise.'

'OK, thanks … Can I ask a favour?'

'Anything, my love.'

'There's a branch of Ladbrokes in Gloucester. Do you know if they need any staff?'

'I know the regional manager,' she said. 'I'll give him a call now.'

A few hours later Tracey called back with good news.

'There's a full-time job going. I've set up a meeting for you this Thursday. Is that OK?'

'Oh my God, Tracey, that's brilliant! Thank you so much.'

'You're welcome, sweetheart. I'll text you the address so you've got it.'

When I think back to everything that was going on and the state my head was in, the idea of going back to work seems crazy. But all I knew was if I sat around in Janette's house all day on my own I was going to do something stupid. A job would fill my time and give me routine. I would be able to pay my way and save some cash for when I got home to Thierry. It felt right.

For my meeting on Thursday, Dionne lent me a shirt to wear with my black trousers. I had to go to the Ladbrokes in Cheltenham, and I must have arrived about three hours early because I found the branch then walked anxiously round the town centre for what felt like ages.

I needn't have been nervous. Tracey had obviously put a good word in for me. The guy said the job was mine, I could start on Monday and I was fine to take time off when I needed to see my solicitor, provided I gave them as much notice as possible. To this day I can't believe how lucky I was to have so much support from Ladbrokes. They could have easily cut all ties and I wouldn't have blamed them, but they really stuck their necks out for me. Having a job lined up gave me some-thing to focus on. And I had something positive to tell Dad when he brought Thierry that Saturday.

* * *

The morning they came I was already up and dressed when Dad called to say they were leaving Birmingham. I sat staring out the front window, twirling my hair around my fingers, desperate to set eyes on them as soon as I possibly could. I didn't recognise the car when it pulled up outside. When I realised it was Dad getting out of the driver's seat and looking expectantly at the house, I ran outside straight into his arms.

'How are you doing?' he asked.

I shrugged.

'New car?' I asked.

'Nah, it's your Uncle Martin's. I didn't think mine would make the journey!'

We both smiled. I glanced over Dad's shoulder to get a look at Thierry. He was in the back, strapped into his car seat. You would think I'd have been running up to him for a huge hug, but something was holding me back. I felt awkward and scared. *Does Thierry blame me for his brother dying? Does he still love me?*

'Come on,' Dad said. 'Get in.'

I took a deep breath and walked round to the passenger side of the car. But before I opened my door, I opened Thierry's.

'Hello angel!' I smiled. 'Can I have a kiss?'

He looked at me and said, 'Are you coming home with us, Mommy?'

It knocked the wind right out of my sails.

'I wish I could, sweetheart,' I said, kissing his head. 'I've missed you.'

Before the tears could start, I shut the door and climbed into the seat next to Dad. I closed my eyes and took another deep breath. Dad gave my knee a reassuring squeeze.

'So, where to then?' he asked.

I directed him into town. We parked the car and took a slow walk through the shops towards the park. Dad had his arm around my shoulders while Thierry walked alongside us, holding Dad's hand. It was a sunny Saturday so there were a lot of people about, especially around the shops. I pointed out the Ladbrokes. Dad agreed it would be good for me to work and keep busy.

At the park, Dad hung back, leaving me to push Thierry on the swings and help him on the slide. He seemed a little shy around me at first. It hurt, but I understood. The hardest thing was seeing him without Kamran. Don't get me wrong – I was so happy to see him and spend time with him. But seeing him on his own made me even more painfully aware that Kamran wasn't there. At one point, it all got too much. I turned my back on Thierry and flew over to Dad in tears.

'I can't do this, I can't do this!'

I don't even know what I meant, but I didn't want Thierry to see me cry.

'Look at him,' Dad said, putting his arm around me again. 'He's fine, I promise you. He's got the same routine, he's still the same healthy, happy kid.'

'But he hasn't got Kam anymore,' I said, the tears still streaming. 'Or me.'

'Kids are resilient little things,' Dad assured me. 'We're going to get through this, Sarah – together, as a family.'

When I'd pulled myself together and Thierry had had enough of the park, we walked back into town and took him to McDonald's for a Happy Meal. Dad tried to keep the conversation light. He told me Mom was doing OK, but I knew he was only saying that so I wouldn't worry. I don't remember talking about Kamran. It didn't seem right in front of Thierry and I would only get upset. There was no talk of the court case or Nicholas, either. Neither of us dared put a foot wrong when it came to that.

After we'd eaten we walked back to the car and Dad dropped me home. My stomach was already in knots about the goodbye. At the house, I opened Thierry's door and leaned in for a hug and a kiss.

'Bye, baby,' I said. 'See you soon.'

He smiled, kicked his legs and carried on playing with his Happy Meal toy. I walked round to Dad and he put his arms around me.

'Good to see you,' he said. 'We all miss you so much.'

'I miss you too.'

'We'll come see you again soon.'

'OK,' I nodded. 'Drive safe.'

Waving them off felt like watching my heart being driven away. I felt abandoned. I know they only left me there because they had no choice, but it was still a bitter blow. I went into the empty house, up to the bedroom and collapsed on the bed in despair.

CHAPTER NINETEEN

The visit from Dad and Thierry was bittersweet. I wanted to see them both – I needed it, I had looked forward to it and cherished it. But it was hard to hold on to the comfort it brought because it was so devastating when they left.

My first day back at Ladbrokes couldn't come soon enough. The day before, I got Dionne to show me how to use their washing machine so I could get my uniform clean. When it was washed and dried, I carefully ran the iron over my green shirt, wishing I could wash away all the things that had happened to me while I'd been wearing it.

That Monday I was up early enough to do the 35-minute walk into town and still get to work in plenty of time for the 9am start. The Gloucester branch of Ladbrokes was in an old terraced building on Southgate Street – one of the main pedestrian shopping drags – sandwiched between a recruitment agency and an NHS drop-in centre. As I pushed open the heavy glass door, a blonde lady clocked my shirt, came over and shook my hand.

'Hi, you must be Sarah,' she smiled. 'I'm Cara, the manager. So, you're from Birmingham?'

'Yeah.'

'And you worked at the big city centre branch for a few months?'

'Yeah.'

'Well, it's exactly the same computer system here, so I'm sure you'll be fine. If you have any questions just let me know.'

The branch was nowhere near as busy as Birmingham, but there was a chatty till operative called Michael and a steady enough trickle of customers to keep it from getting too boring. Work-wise, it was like riding a bike. When my shift was over, I picked up some cereal and a few microwave meals from the supermarket then walked home in the warm summer air. Part of me was worried about how my decision to go back to work would look to other people. *Does it make me look like a bad mother? Will they think I didn't care about Kam?* But that night I had the best night's sleep I'd had since prison.

***

That week, as well as starting work, I took Wednesday off for my first meeting with my solicitor. The police gave me a permission slip that both excused me from signing in that day and allowed me to travel to Birmingham.

Mr Bhomra – a devout Sikh – works from a converted block of terraces on Soho Road. The row of bright white buildings is directly opposite a large mosque and when I arrived for my appointment, the receptionist told me he would be a few minutes late because he was at prayer.

When he finally arrived, Mr Bhomra shook my hand and took me through to his office. The room was dominated by a huge wooden table. It must have been big enough to seat at least ten people. Against one of the walls he had a large bookcase that looked like it was groaning under the weight of all his legal books. He told me to take a seat as he scooped up his files and put them on the table in front of us. Then he looked me square in the eye and started talking.

'Someone did this, Sarah. Someone killed your son. Was it you?'

I wasn't expecting such a brutal start.

'No,' I said, desperately. 'I loved him.'

'Well,' Mr Bhomra went on, 'It must have been him. It must have been Nicholas.'

'I don't understand,' I said, my head in my hands.

'Listen, Sarah. Do you remember the duty solicitor from the police station? When he gave me your case file, he said "This girl is innocent." He believed it, and now I believe it.

'I'm going to show you this,' he said, pulling out a piece of paper. 'You need to see it, but it's not going to be pleasant.'

I looked at the paper. Mr Bhomra started talking me slowly and methodically through a list. I realised it was Kamran's post-mortem; a gruesome roll call of what the doctors had found after he had died. There was the bruising to his abdomen – too many bruises to count. There was a slow bleed on his brain and both his liver and spleen had been ruptured. By the end of it I was wailing with my head on the desk. *What had happened to my poor baby?* I sobbed uncontrollably, completely traumatised, imagining how much pain he must have been in. I cry when I hurt my finger so to think of his tiny little body feeling all those awful, horrible, painful things was absolutely unbearable. The worst thing was imagining how much he must have cried. And knowing he would have been crying for me.

For those few moments, as all this new information sunk in, I was completely consumed. But I was still missing the point. What Mr Bhomra was trying to tell me was that it wasn't the hospital's fault. Kamran wasn't ill. Someone had done this to him.

It was there in that office that the denial finally started to fall away. I knew Kam had died. I knew the police had been saying the word murder and I knew Nicholas must have known something that I didn't. But my mind had been too preoccupied with the loss to make the leap. It was only now, with this harrowing list of injuries in front of me, that I was forced to fill in the blanks. Kamran had been murdered and all the fingers were pointing at Nicholas.

I have no memory of the rest of the meeting. Mr Bhomra wrote down three more appointments on a bit of paper so I wouldn't forget them, then I got the train back to Gloucester. I couldn't get the list of injuries out of my head. I couldn't stop picturing my baby boy screaming in pain, screaming for his mommy.

My mind was finally starting to see Nicholas in a different light, but it was still hard to imagine him doing anything to hurt Kamran. *What exactly did he do to cause all those injuries? Did he hit him? Punch him?* I couldn't understand why anyone would harm a child. I couldn't understand why Nicholas would harm *my* child. Kamran was a sweet, loving, affectionate little boy; a defenceless baby. And the Nicholas I knew was a good guy. I thought about how he'd cried at Stacey's party and how I'd never once seen him lose his temper. *Was he really capable of this?*

And if Kamran was dead because of Nicholas, then it was all my fault. *I let Nicholas into our lives. I trusted him to look after my kids.* The guilt started creeping in. I started to feel angry and dirty. This was the man I loved, the man I shared my bed with. The man I'd made love to the night before Kamran died. I started thinking awful, violent things. Things I'd never even thought before let alone wished on another human being. Nicholas was the guilty one and I wanted him to suffer.

***

I didn't think it was possible to get any lower. Yet here I was, alone in Gloucester, trying to process everything I'd learned from my solicitor. My son was dead and all the evidence seemed to be saying that my boyfriend had not only hurt my child, but hurt him so badly it had ended his life.

Dad and I spoke briefly every other night and I continued to exchange weekly letters with Nan. But even if I hadn't been terrified of affecting the court case, there was no way I could tell my grieving family the horror that was really going on in my head. I wouldn't have known where to start.

Work helped a lot. No one knew who I really was or why I was there. It didn't stop me thinking or feeling, but it stopped me from losing my mind completely. When I was at my desk, having to deal with staff and customers, I was forced to put a brave face on. I still had plenty of dark days; days where the slightest thing would tip me over the edge and I'd have to lock myself in the toilet for a while. But I became good at putting on a mask. In private, however, the grief and anger were all-consuming. Unless I was utterly exhausted, I would lie awake at night, wanting to scream the house down and rip Nicholas to shreds.

One evening, when I'd been working for a couple of weeks, I arrived back at Janette's after a shift. Almost as soon as I shut the front door behind me, I heard the sound of someone knocking. I opened the door to see a middle-aged man in a navy jacket.

'Sarah Rose?' he asked.

'Yes?' I replied.

He handed me an envelope, turned on his heels and walked away. *What the hell is this?* I thought, tearing open the envelope. My stomach lurched as I realised what it was – court papers, filed by Mark. He had taken out a Residential Order for custody of Thierry.

I sat alone in the house and sobbed my heart out. Mark had been so good to me, organising a place to stay in Gloucester, but now he wanted to take my son away? Eventually, I pulled myself together and phoned Dad.

'Do you know about this?' I asked. 'I've had a letter saying Mark wants custody.'

'It's not as bad as it sounds,' he said. 'We've agreed that Thierry will stay with us one week and his dad the next.'

Dad's words gave me little comfort. It felt like my whole world was slipping through my fingers.

'But he's my son! What if I never get him back?'

'Your mom and I really tried,' Dad said. 'Honestly, love, we did. But Mark's Thierry's dad. There was nothing we could do. Try not to worry. No one is trying to take Thierry away, I think Mark just wants to make sure he's protected.'

For the next week I barely slept, all the 'what ifs' running through my mind. *What if Mark runs away with Thierry? What if social services never let me have him back?* Having the authorities come between me and my boy was absolutely insufferable. I was terrified I would never see him again. When I wasn't a complete wreck I just tried to focus on the court case. It wouldn't bring Kamran back but I had to get justice.

I saw Mr Bhomra every week. He was confident that the manslaughter charge would be dropped but said the charge of knowing or allowing a child to die would be more difficult to prove in my favour. Both Chantelle and my Aunty Maggie had given statements to the police. Chantelle told them about the day she erupted at Nicholas when he was vacuuming, and Maggie told them how she had challenged us about it at Stacey's party. It was becoming clear that what Chantelle saw at the flat that day was a lot more serious than I thought. She said she witnessed Nicholas throw Kam onto the sofa and it was the *way* he did it that had shocked and upset her so much. In the heat of the moment I had reasoned that Kam was unharmed and tried to diffuse an argument but in light of what happened to Kam less than two weeks later, could this have been a glimpse of how Nicholas was treating him when no one was around?

I felt no anger towards Chantelle and Maggie because all they'd done was tell the truth but the prosecution, Mr Bhomra said, would use their statements against me. They would say

I was warned about Nicholas and argue that I ignored the warnings because I was covering for a child abuser.

Knowing or allowing a child to die was a relatively new charge at the time. If found guilty I would be looking at a four-year prison sentence. I didn't care. They could do whatever they wanted to me, as long as Nicholas got what he deserved. I thought about how scared I'd been in prison and how vile the inmates were to the girl who had killed her children. On my angry days, I hoped Nicholas was being terrorised like she was.

Meanwhile, my poor mom was organising her grandson's funeral. Dad told me the date so I could make sure I was off work. We agreed it would be best for Thierry to spend the day with his dad, Mark. It's a decision I've often regretted, but I know in my heart he was too young to be there.

We accepted the kind offer of financial help from Nabeel's parents, but in terms of all the arrangements, Mom did everything herself. I knew she would make sure it was the best it could be, but I found it really difficult not being involved in the process. Kamran was my baby. If anyone had to organise his funeral it should have been me. Dad said Mom and Stacey had written poems to read out at the service so I consoled myself by writing a few words too.

***

On 26 June 2007 I left Gloucester early. I didn't say a word to Dionne or Janette about where I was going. It was just easier to let them assume I was out at work. I wore my black trousers and a shirt with a black blazer I'd bought from New Look one lunchtime. I remember my palms were sweating. I felt anxious, but the enormity of the day wasn't even close to hitting me yet.

I got the train to New Street, a bus to Wash Lane and let myself in. The house felt strange. There were already several people congregated in the living room, but Mom's tired, broken face was the first one I saw. She burst into tears at the sight of me. Apart from seeing each other at court, it was the first time we'd had any proper contact. She walked towards me with her arms outstretched. We embraced and she kissed my head over and over again. Dad, Stacey and my nan and grandad were there too. Then I saw Matthew and my Uncle Martin. Gemma's mom arrived a few minutes after me and gave me the biggest, warmest hug. I hadn't seen her in years yet here she was supporting me. Despite the sadness, I felt a lot of love that morning.

Nabeel turned up at the house too. He was going to ride in one of the funeral cars with us and some of his family were expected at the church. He looked thinner, tired and pale. We shared an awkward hug, but didn't speak.

When Stacey said the carriage was outside, I was the first one out the front door. I heard the clip-clop of the horses' hooves on the road. Then I saw all the neighbours stood outside their houses with their heads bowed. It all felt so strange and surreal. But I was touched that they would pay their respects.

A man in a full black suit and top hat passed me and started talking to Mom. It was the funeral director she had been liaising with.

'This is Sarah,' she said, turning to me and introducing us. 'She's Kamran's mom.'

He took my hand and said sincerely, 'My deepest condolences. I'm so sorry for your loss.'

I followed him across the grass verge outside the house with everyone else a few steps behind. It wasn't long before the carriage came into view. I'd never seen anything like it. I thought a horse and carriage was something people had at weddings but here it was – a fairy tale black carriage with two beautiful black horses stood side by side. I saw the flowers spelling out 'Kamran', 'son' and 'brother', then the tiny white coffin placed among them. That's when it hit me. This was it – Kamran's funeral. It was like facing up to his death all over again.

I shared a car with Mom, Dad, Stacey, Nan and Nabeel. We drove in silence with some of us holding hands. The service was at Corpus Christi Roman Catholic Church – the church where Nan and Grandad married and where Kamran was christened at two months old, just like his big brother before him. When we pulled up outside, a crowd of people had already gathered. I spotted the police officers Kate and Chris almost immediately.

'Why are *they* here?' I cried, turning to Mom and Dad. 'There's no need for them to be here!'

Uncle Martin marched over to confront them. They told him they only wanted to pay their respects. I wanted to believe this was true, but I couldn't help thinking it might be an opportunity for them to observe who was there and how I behaved.

Chantelle came over and hugged me tightly. Then Grace with her boyfriend and her sister, Eve. There were so many people, some I hadn't seen in years. I watched as Kam's coffin was taken out of the carriage and my dad, Grandad, Nabeel and Matthew lifted it onto their shoulders. It looked so tiny and light. My heart ached. I didn't want this; I wanted him back. No child should end up in a box.

Mom linked my arm and we walked slowly behind the coffin into the church. We sat together holding hands at the front as everyone else filtered in and took their seats. I remember clutching the piece of paper I'd written my speech on as the coffin was placed on a stand a few feet away from us. I didn't take my eyes off it for the whole service. A few months ago Kamran had been here, a baby in my arms. Now I was sat there staring at a box. I started sobbing and couldn't stop. I'd been in pain for weeks now, but this was something else. It all felt so final. I wasn't ready to say goodbye – I would never be ready.

The priest conducted his service and there was a reading by a local nun. Then it was our turn. Stacey was the first one on the mic.

Happy, jolly, sad too
My little man, why did he take you?
My twinkle, my baby, my little star
You were here, but now so far.

God took you to become a big part,
But he doesn't know how much he broke my heart.
Mommy, Daddy, Nanny and Grandad too,
We're all so sad and really miss you.

You were so special and so dear too,
We don't understand why he took you.
You became the little angel that you are,
Up in the sky, shining like a twinkle star.

Writing this poem to say goodbye
We will be strong, well, we'll try.
This poem is filled with kisses and hugs
We miss you, Kam Kam, we love you so much.

So goodnight for now, my little man
We'll see you as soon as we can.

She was so brave and strong. I don't think her voice wobbled once. Mom went next.

Those brown eyes I loved so well
Those brown eyes I long to see
How I miss those brown eyes
Strangers they have grown to be.

Many weeks ago today
Those brown eyes went away
Up in heaven I long to be
Where my brown-eyed angel is waiting for me.

I'll see you soon, my brown-eyed boy
So save me a place in that big blue sky
Until then, look down on me
With those brown eyes that shine with glee.

The time has come to say goodbye
So God bless Kam, my brown-eyed boy.

When Mom finished, I stepped up to the microphone and began my speech.

Kamran was my little star. He meant everything to me and from the moment I saw him, I loved him so much. I was his protector, the one who was supposed to have looked after him. I wish I could turn back time. We were so happy. He was such a good baby. I was convinced he was going to be a dancer – the way he used to wiggle his hips made me laugh so much. Words can't explain how much I miss him. God gave me an angel then took that angel back. I hope Kamran is watching over me and Thierry, and everyone else that loved him. Kamran, I will always love you and never forget you.

Love from Mommy.

People told me afterwards that they couldn't understand a word I was saying. I knew I was crying – the kind of cry when you can't catch your breath – but I was determined to finish. Standing up and saying something was my one contribution to the day. I didn't care that no one understood – I was only saying it to Kamran anyway.

I sat with Mom and Stacey's arms wrapped around me and we all cried together. They played Puff Daddy's 'I'll Be Missing You' as we followed the coffin back out and got straight in the car. As we pulled away from the church, it started raining. I remember the raindrops on the roof and the scrape of the windscreen wipers as we crawled behind the carriage to the cemetery, where the coffin was going to be buried. The driver pulled up right next to the grave and we all got out.

'Look,' Stacey said. It had stopped raining and the sun was out. 'Kam's here with us.'

As I felt the warm sun on my face, I believed he was too.

We crossed a grass bank to where the coffin was being positioned over a large hole in the ground. Me and Nabeel stood side by side at one end and the priest stood at the other as everyone else gathered round. Not everyone who was at the church came to the burial, but there were still 20 or 30 people there. I remained fixated on the coffin, crippled with longing for my little boy.

The service was brief. The only thing I remember clearly was his coffin being lowered into the ground. I remember because that was the worst part. We all threw single-stem roses as it sank down – a beautiful idea of my mom's. They looked so pretty, but he was going, he was leaving me. This was it. This was goodbye.

Everyone started to trickle away, leaving me rooted to the spot, looking down at the white box until I was the only one left. I didn't want to leave my baby. To leave him here in a hole went against every instinct. *This isn't right, this shouldn't be happening.* My legs buckled and I came crashing down to my knees. It was all too much: I wanted to be with him so bad.

A moment later I felt my grandad's hands underneath my arms. He lifted me onto my feet and practically threw me into the car.

'Chrissie,' he growled at Mom, 'Get her home, now.'

***

It still hurts that my goodbye that day was cut short. I never said anything to Grandad because I wouldn't want to upset him, but I wasn't ready to leave. I found out some months later that he'd been to a funeral where the grieving widow threw herself into the grave, so when he saw me collapse he was frightened I was about to do the same.

A small wake was held back at Mom's but I barely stayed an hour. I had to be out of Birmingham by four o'clock and, to be honest, I'd reached the limit of what I could cope with. As I left, my cousin Sam came over to say goodbye. She was heavily pregnant and had been struggling with a bit of pain so Nan was taking her home to rest.

I couldn't face the train so I ordered a taxi. It set me back £75, but I really didn't care. I wasn't sure how I was going to explain the black suit and puffy eyes so when I arrived back in Gloucester I was relieved to find the house empty. I got changed, picked at some food, then cried myself to sleep. The next day, I got up, put my green shirt on and went to work like nothing had happened.

CHAPTER TWENTY

The funeral was such a huge blow to me, both physically and emotionally, that I don't know how I kept going after that. I felt hollow, like a robot on autopilot. Work became my sanctuary – the one thing getting me out of bed in the morning. I went to work every day simply because I was terrified of what would happen if I didn't. I worked all the hours I possibly could – anything to avoid being at home with all the grief and anger.

It helped that the place had quite a motherly atmosphere. As well as chatty Michael, I worked with a woman in her fifties. She was always bringing in a cake that she'd made and loved to talk about her children and grandchildren. Some days I enjoyed her stories, on others it would trigger memories and I'd have to run to the loo for a cry. Although the area managers knew I was on bail, I didn't breathe a word of my situation to any of my colleagues. Michael was the only one who asked why I'd moved from Birmingham to Gloucester. I shrugged it off, saying I just needed to get away for a while.

Dionne and Janette had busy lives so with me working at least five shifts a week I didn't see them much. Janette spent at least half the week in Birmingham, if not more, and Dionne was out with her mates most weekends. She and Hannah were always inviting me on nights out, but even if I'd wanted to go, I was too much of a worrier to risk breaking my curfew. A couple of times, I let Hannah twist my arm into wasting a few hours at the local bowling complex during the day. Another weekend, Dionne talked me into going to a friend's house with her.

'Come on,' she said. 'It's only for the afternoon. It'll do you good.'

She meant well, but I spent the whole time feeling like an alien in the corner, listening to them chatting about people I didn't know and wanting to go home.

The police never phoned or came to the house to check I was sticking to my curfew. The only official visit I had was from a pair of social workers, worried I might have contact with Janette's grandson.

'I've never even met him,' I told them. 'He doesn't come round here. And I haven't done anything wrong anyway.'

'Well,' one of them scoffed patronisingly, 'you haven't proved it yet.'

They were pretty unpleasant. I felt so embarrassed and ashamed. Janette thought they were being heavy-handed and ridiculous. They didn't have a leg to stand on anyway, because he was five and my bail conditions only prohibited contact with under-fours. I think they just wanted to frighten me – and it worked. Sometimes it felt like the whole world thought I was guilty.

Every pay day I made sure I gave Janette £150. I don't think she expected it, but I've been brought up to pay my way so it was always my intention to give her board. Besides, I was earning over £1,000 a month and had nothing to spend it on. The tiny amount of food I was eating and the odd splurge on phone credit or a cheap top from New Look barely put a dent in my account.

Dionne and Janette never once asked how I was or what was going on. Not because they were rude or uncaring, I think it was just easier not to even go there. Dionne caught me crying a few times. She would hug me and tell me everything would be OK, but that's as far as it went. And to be honest, I preferred it that way. I'm not the kind of person who likes fuss or attention. I'm a mom and a big sister – I'm used to being the comforter, not the one who needs comforting. So even on the nights I wanted to scream into my pillow, I kept everything bottled up. As a result, my OCD flared up again. When I walked to work, I obsessed over not stepping on the cracks in the pavement. If I dropped a crisp, I had to drop another one to make it even. When I used the bathroom I had to pull the cord on the light switch ten times, and if it didn't work properly, I would have to start again. I would get so angry with myself – I knew it was crazy but I couldn't stop.

My weekly visits to Mr Bhomra helped keep me focussed. I had been a little nervous of him to begin with, but as he began navigating me through the complicated legal mess I'd found myself in I started to see him as a friend. He had copies of all the police statements made by my friends and family and we went over each one with a fine-tooth comb. He would read them out slowly and clearly and if there was anything I disagreed with, we would stop and make notes in the margins.

It was really strange to be hearing other people's accounts of Kamran's death, especially in this way. For instance, in

Stacey's statement, I learned that Nicholas had spoken to her the morning Kamran died. She was at home with Mom, getting ready for a job interview, when he rang them on the house phone. She said the call took place around 10am, which meant he contacted them before me.

'Kamran's not breathing,' he told her. 'He's lifeless.'

The first thing she asked was, 'Have you called an ambulance?'

'No,' he said.

The phone went dead. Stacey shouted for Mom, who tripped and fell as she was going up the stairs. Nicholas called them back to say an ambulance was on its way. Then he spoke to Mom.

'What's happened?' she asked.

'He's banged the back of his head. He's not breathing properly.'

According to Mom's statement, the first thing she did – the first thing she always did when she was worried – was speak to Grandad. He said he had a bad feeling and advised her to make her way to the hospital. At this point Stacey didn't share their concern, but decided to abandon her job interview and go too. This explained why they were already at Heartlands when I got there. In all the commotion that morning, staff took them to Kam's body before anyone told them he was dead.

While we poured over the statements, it struck me that Mom and Stacey didn't have a bad word to say about Nicholas. They were telling the truth, but would it work against me? Mr Bhomra assured me it was all good back-up: if Nicholas the nice guy was an act, then I wasn't the only one to fall for it.

The sticking points were the statements from Chantelle and my Aunty Maggie. Chantelle's centred around the day she saw Nicholas throw Kam onto the sofa while he was vacuuming. Again, it was strange to read everything from her perspective. To me it had been such a minor incident, yet for her it set alarms bells ringing. It was the same for Maggie. It was painful to read her perception of me – that I often left the boys with Stacey to go out partying. Stacey was round at the flat most days, but to spend time with us, not to babysit every night. You could count the amount of times I went out on one hand. I was worried that Maggie's evidence made me sound like a terrible mom but she loved Kamran and even though she couldn't have foreseen he would end up dead, she obviously had a bad feeling about the situation. The confrontation at Stacey's birthday party was her way of trying to warn me. If only I had listened.

Grace told the police I was a good mom. As far as I was aware she always got on with Nicholas, but she said that while she was in the flat one evening, she saw Nicholas snatch Kam's dummy from his mouth and tell him he wasn't a baby anymore. She made out it had upset her, but never once mentioned it to me.

* * *

Certain pieces of information threw up more questions than they did answers. But nothing confused and angered me more than the things Mr Bhomra told me about Nicholas. Our solicitors knew each other, so there were things we were able to keep tabs on. Things like Nicholas changing his statement; one minute he was telling police I was a good mom, then he made out I was a terrible one, who only fed the kids beans on toast and let them do whatever they wanted.

'Did you know about this?' Mr Bhomra asked one day, handing me some paperwork. 'Please tell me if you did, it's really important.'

I was stunned at what I saw: Nicholas had a string of previous convictions. I told Mr Bhomra that I knew about one robbery. But the minor-sounding incident Nicholas told me about on our first date was only the tip of the iceberg. There was more than one and he had been to prison too.

In 2004 Nicholas was convicted of two robberies and an attempted robbery, which landed him a 30-month jail sentence. He only served half, but that meant he was in prison for the whole of 2005 and never once mentioned it to me. Six months after his release he tried to rob someone else. So when he met me in December 2006, he was still under supervision from the probation service. That's why he was living at his mom's – his supervision order stipulated that he had to reside at her address. He shouldn't even have been sleeping at my flat.

It hit me all over again that I'd fallen for someone I knew nothing about. I took him at face value. I didn't question his past because I had no reason to suspect he had one worth worrying about. No wonder he was jobless and always disappearing back to Mommy. How could I have been so naive?

I thought I'd heard it all, but Mr Bhomra had another bombshell.

'Nicholas has been advised to plead guilty but has so far refused.'

'So how will he explain Kamran's injuries?' I asked.

'His story is that your son fell off the sofa.'

Have you ever heard anything so insane? Toddlers fall off the sofa all the time. When was the last time falling off a sofa gave a child ruptured organs? I'd been angry before, but now my blood was boiling. I thought back to Gloucester and my conversation with Matthew – finally I understood why he felt so strongly. I hated Nicholas too but it was nothing compared to how much I hated myself.

The more I learned and understood about the situation, the more difficult it was not being able to discuss it with anyone. I found myself calling Dad less and less. He brought Thierry to visit me in Gloucester a couple more times. We always did the same thing – a walk round the park, then a treat at McDonald's. It was reassuring to see Thierry. He always looked so happy, like he'd barely been affected. But every time they left, I would hit rock bottom. It sounds backwards, but I found it easier to cope if I didn't see them. I knew Thierry was being loved and cared for. Backing away from him was my way of protecting us both.

My cousin Sam – one of the few people I was allowed to talk to – started keeping in touch with the occasional text. I was grateful, but when I found out she had given birth to a baby boy the night of Kam's funeral, it opened a whole new can of worms for me emotionally. Some Catholics believe in transmigration – that when a person dies, their soul and spirit are re-born into a foetus or newborn. I couldn't help but feel strange that her son, Akeal, arrived two weeks early, on the very day we buried mine. I didn't want to see him or hold him; it would have been too difficult.

Thankfully, the first time Sam came to Gloucester she left Akeal with Maggie. She brought Thierry and her daughter Shereen, who was 18 months old at the time. It was the weekend of the annual Gloucester carnival and the weather was beautiful. There was music, stalls and a fair on all day in the park. We sat on the grass and had a picnic and watched the kids running around. If Thierry wanted an ice cream or a drink, it was me he came to. It gave me a lot of comfort to know he still saw me as his mommy.

That day was easily the best one I had in Gloucester but like always, the high was followed by a huge, crushing low. When I waved off their train at the end of the day, it absolutely broke me that Sam was going home with *my* son.

***

As summer faded into autumn, I grew painfully tired. Putting the mask on for work became harder and harder. And as lovely as Dionne and Janette were, I was tired of living in someone else's space, so far away from my family. With the trial still a few months away, Mr Bhomra suggested I look at moving closer to Birmingham.

I can't remember who came up with the idea of Wolverhampton, but it seemed like an obvious choice. Nabeel was still in regular contact with my parents and when he found out I was looking to move he found me a flat and paid the first month's rent. I left Gloucester without saying goodbye to anyone. I packed my stuff while Dionne and Janette were out, leaving them a thank you note and a month's board money. Dionne phoned me later that day.

'Why didn't you say you were leaving?' she asked, confused.

'I'm sorry,' I said. 'I just didn't want a fuss.'

I didn't even hand in my notice at work, I just didn't go back in. Stuff like that really hammers home to me how messed-up I was, because it's something I would never dream of doing normally. It was rude and unprofessional, especially after they'd been so good to me. A quick phone call would have been better than nothing. But at the time, it felt easier to just disappear.

***

Dad met me at New Street Station and drove me to my new address in Wolverhampton. The flat was on the ground floor of a two-storey block. It had one bedroom with a double bed in it and a wicker sofa bed in the living room. Mom and Dad must have given it the once over because it was spotless. They had set up a TV and Dad brought a load of fresh bedding and a throw Nan wanted me to have for the sofa.

'I can be here in half an hour if you need me,' Dad said as I waved him off. I was relieved to see the back of Gloucester and to have my own place. It wasn't home, but until the trial was over, it was as close as I was going to get.

Now the court case was on the horizon there didn't seem any point trying to get another job. Wolverhampton city centre was only 30 minutes away on foot, so on the days I had to sign in at the police station, I would walk there, then waste time at the local library, either reading or playing solitaire on the computers. There was a Waitrose near the flat, where I bought my basics – tea and milk, bread and butter, so I could have toast. My eating habits had been so dismal that I'd lost over a stone in weight. I felt like a ghost, floating around another strange place all by myself with no purpose. I went from living at home with my family to sharing my own place with the boys, so I'd never once lived on my own. I found it hardest at night and could only sleep if all the lights were on. Without people around me or a job to give me routine, I was drifting through each day. I have no idea how I got through them. I wasn't living, I was existing because I had to.

Between them, Dad and Sam kept a close eye on me. Dad frequently popped in after work for a cup of tea and every few weeks Sam would stay over. She would sleep in the double bed with me and encourage me to go out for a walk or something to eat. I remember her bringing Thierry and Shereen once because we took them to a local pub with a play area. She brought Akeal a couple of times too. My feelings about him being born on the day of Kam's funeral had started to ease off a little, so although I still felt like there might have been a weird connection, I didn't mind seeing him.

He must have been about six months old because he had just started sitting up. Some music came on and he started bopping to it, just like Kam used to. I burst out crying and had to leave the room.

I probably would have coped a lot better in Wolverhampton if it wasn't for the time of year. I had only been there a month or so when Christmas 2007 started to make itself known. The lights went up in the streets, the trees started appearing in people's windows and shops were taken over with Christmas stock. It made me angry. *How can the whole world just carry on as normal when my son is dead?* I resented all the families walking around with their kids, drinking hot chocolate and shopping for presents. Kam's death had always felt so painfully unfair, but never more so than in December. For the first time in my life, I hated Christmas. I didn't want anything to do with it. But Dad had other ideas.

'I'm going to bring Thierry to see you on Christmas Day,' he said. 'Just for a couple of hours.'

I wanted to tell him not to bother. *I'll only be miserable*, I thought. And I knew I'd be a mess when they left. But I missed Thierry so much I couldn't bring myself to say no. I bought him a small gift, but didn't bother with any decorations – I didn't see the point for just that one day. When they came, it just felt like any other visit. I'm pretty sure Dad only did it to make sure I wasn't on my own for the whole day, but whether they were there or not I just felt completely lost.

New Year was just as difficult. Sam came with her kids and we put them to bed and watched TV. At midnight we stood outside my front door and watched some fireworks that a neighbour was setting off.

Then, come January, I had to face up to what would have been Kamran's second birthday. The dread I felt in the days leading up to 24 January was nothing compared to the blackness that engulfed me on the day itself. I woke up crying and didn't stop. I thought about everything that happened the day Kamran came into my life – when I would have been having contractions; the exact time he was born and I held him for the first time. Then I thought about his first birthday, how happy he had been and how crushing it was, knowing he would never see another one; all because of me. It's hard to explain how it hits you because every day is so painful but for some reason, Christmas and birthdays are especially difficult. The only time I got out of bed that day was to answer the door. Dad had phoned to see how I was and I sounded so distraught he sent Sam to check on me.

'Surprise!' she said as I opened the door. She had pizza in her hand and Akeal on her hip. We never mentioned what day it was, but I was grateful for the company.

***

My meetings with Mr Bhomra slowed down to once a fortnight as he prepared for the trial. One afternoon, I met him outside Birmingham Chambers and he took me inside to meet my barrister, Mr Cook. He was a polite, approachable man, with papers all over his desk. He wore glasses and had hair so black it must have been dyed. They explained how they had been trying to recruit an 'amazing' QC to work with them on the case and he had finally been able to accept. The hold up now was from the prosecution team, who had three experts preparing to give their opinions on Kamran's autopsy.

'Will I have to listen to the medical evidence?' I asked. I didn't know if I could handle it.

'Not if you don't want to,' Mr Cook assured me.

That afternoon Mr Cook and Mr Bhomra explained the structure of the case to me. The Crown Prosecution Service would make the case against me and Nicholas. Then they would call the witnesses they had chosen to back up their story. My team would go second. They had lined up Thierry's dad, Mark, my cousin, Kelly, and my sister, Stacey, as character references. Then I would give evidence.

Between them they spent hours prepping me.

'Nicholas's QC will ask you questions,' Mr Cook warned. 'He will attack you. He will try and twist everything you say and confuse you, hoping you will trip up. All you need to do is keep it together and keep telling the truth.'

I never once thought that I needed a good lawyer to get me off, but it gave me strength to know I was in such good hands. At this point the trial was all I had. If I couldn't bring Kam back, all I could do was fight to clear my name and expose Nicholas for the lying, murdering monster he really was. I was ready for my day in court.

CHAPTER TWENTY-ONE

The thing that terrified me most about going back to court was seeing Nicholas. We were facing trial together which meant standing in the defendant's box, side by side. I'd managed it twice before, of course, but that was before I knew the truth. This time, I knew he was guilty of murder. My blood was pulsing with so much anger and hatred, I had no idea what I might do to him.

The weekend before the trial I barely slept. I remember walking into Wolverhampton and buying a pair of grey trousers and a white blouse with grey flecks from Dorothy Perkins. My barrister, Mr Cook, had advised me to look smart, but I didn't need telling. I wanted to look my best and give the best impression I possibly could. I wanted to look respectable and show the jury I was a good person who was taking things seriously.

On 18 February 2008, the day the trial started, I was up at 5.30am. I had a shower, put on my new clothes and tied my hair back into a neat pony. With just my coat, phone and a bit of cash, I walked into the city centre and caught the tram that took me all the way to Snow Hill station in Birmingham. With my nerves at screeching point, the 15-minute journey seemed to take forever. I walked across town to the court. Once inside, I studied the digital notice boards for my name then made my way to the courtroom we'd been allocated that day. My family and friends were already gathered by the door like a huge welcoming committee. Mr Bhomra was chatting to Mom and Dad. When they saw me, everyone smiled. Mr Bhomra ushered me into a seat a few feet away from them.

'Once they've given evidence,' he said, 'you are free to talk to them.'

'I don't want to do it,' I told him. 'I don't want to go in there and have to sit next to Nicholas.'

'I know, Sarah, but you've got to. You've come this far. You've got to be strong. We're all behind you. Let's do it for Kamran.'

***

I was the first one to be taken into court. A guard escorted me to the defendant's box and I sat down as all my family, friends and the other spectators came in and started to take their seats. Nicholas's mom and stepdad were there. His dad came too, but sat alone. And there was an elderly man I didn't recognise. The jury came in and quietly took their seats. I made eye contact with several of them. I didn't feel intimidated, I felt ready – ready to tell them the truth. But I was on the edge of my seat knowing Nicholas would be brought up from the cells any second. My heart stopped when I finally heard the lock click. I froze. Out of the corner of my eye I saw him come in and sit down. My whole body went hot – a mixture of burning rage and revulsion. This time there were two guards, one sat between us and one stood behind Nicholas. I never looked at him directly, but I could tell he looked rough. He was in joggers and a T-shirt, he hadn't shaved. He looked a mess.

Everyone rose to their feet as the Honourable Mr Justice Treacy entered and took his seat at the head of the room. Just like Mr Cook had explained, Mr Burbridge from the Crown Prosecution Service was first to make his case. His aim was to convince the jury of two things; that Nicholas committed acts of violence towards Kamran and that I knew about it. The stress in the courtroom was palpable. Here is what I remember.

After all the introductions, Mr Burbridge spent the first five days of the trial working his way through a list of prosecution witnesses. First to the stand was Chantelle. She went over the day she saw Nicholas throw Kamran on the sofa and how she told Mom and Aunty Maggie about it afterwards. The CPS hinged their whole case against Nicholas and I on this one incident, claiming Chantelle saw Nicholas's violent side, warned me about it and I turned a blind eye. But when she was quizzed by my QC, Mr Cook, her evidence seemed less strong.

'When you saw Nicholas throw Kamran on the sofa, Kamran didn't cry. He suffered no visible injuries. So what was it that angered you so much about what you saw that day?'

'It was just the way he did it,' she shrugged. 'It annoyed me.'

If Aunty Maggie was nervous when her turn came, it didn't show. From the look on her face and the tone of her voice, she was still angry – not just with Nicholas but with me. She told the court that she didn't agree with me going out so much and leaving the boys with my sister.

'Stacey is a teenager,' Maggie said. 'It's not right.'

Without actually saying it, Mr Burbridge used her perception of me to make it sound like I didn't care about my children. It was nothing I hadn't read in her statement but it still stung to hear it all out loud, when my future was hanging in the balance. Was she turning the jury against me? My stomach was in knots.

'Miss Mannifold,' Mr Burbridge asked, 'is it true that Miss Coggins told you she saw Nicholas Kirnon throw Kamran onto the settee?'

'Yes.'

'Can you tell the court why you then took it upon yourself to confront Mr Kirnon about this incident?'

'Kamran wasn't his son,' she said. 'He had no right to discipline him.'

Mom was next. She looked smart, her hair washed and styled, not frizzy like it usually is. I could tell she wanted to make a good impression. She was the person I was most nervous about. Not because I thought she would let me down, but because I know how much she hates being the centre of attention. I knew she would be dreading having to speak in front of all those people and that any mention of Kamran was going to break her heart. I was right. Her hands shook as she swore on the Bible and even the briefest of eye contact with me made her cry.

Mr Burbridge was patient with her, walking her through what she thought of Nicholas.

'I only met him a few times,' she explained. 'Maybe three or four.'

'And from these brief meetings,' Mr Burbridge went on, 'can you tell the court what kind of man you thought Nicholas was?'

'Erm, I don't know,' she stammered. 'He would say hello, but that was it. I felt he could have made more of an effort.'

Mr Cook stood up.

'Mrs Rose, do you recall the day your sister confronted Nicholas about his behaviour towards Kamran, as described by Miss Coggins?'

'Yes,' she replied.

'Can you please tell the court how you felt about the situation?'

'He cried his eyes out. I felt sorry for him. I thought he was getting a hard time over nothing.'

Nicholas's QC, Mr Thomas, was on his feet with a pile of papers in his hand.

'Mrs Rose,' he said, almost sarcastically, 'One of the main reasons we are all here is because the Crown Prosecution believe your daughter left her son with a man who was violent.'

Mom glanced at me, fearfully.

'Yet from what I understand,' he continued, 'she had absolutely no problem leaving her two sons with you.'

'I don't understand,' Mom said, her voice tiny.

Mr Thomas turned to the jury.

'I have here in my hand,' he said, 'the criminal record of Mrs Christine Rose.'

There were rumbles of dissatisfaction from the gallery as he slapped it down on his desk.

'This woman,' he said, pointing at my mother, who was crumbling before my eyes, 'is no angel herself. She has a criminal record. She has a black mark against her name for a violent offence. She had a fight, no less. A drunken fight outside a pub. A fight, with a man.'

I couldn't believe what I was hearing. I knew about the fight – the guy had started on Mom, but she was only cautioned and she was only in her twenties when it happened. Yet Nicholas's team were using that one isolated incident from over two decades ago to imply that she was a violent person – my lovely, caring, do-anything-for-anyone mom. And she wasn't even the one on trial. It was agony watching her being pulled apart. It was like she'd been thrown to the wolves. I knew she'd think she'd let me down, but I felt guiltier than ever. And there was worse to come.

Out of everyone, my sister Stacey had the toughest grilling. When me and the boys were living in Bromford, she spent more time with us at the flat than anyone. The CPS stabbed her in the back by using her as a key witness. She thought she was there to help me, but their plan was to wear her down.

'According to your statement you visited Sarah's flat on Kempson Road in Bromford several times a week, is that correct?'

'Yes.'

'And you used to babysit for Sarah's children, your nephews, Thierry and Kamran Rose, is that correct?'

'Yes.'

'And how often did your sister Sarah go out exactly? Once a month? Once a week?'

'It wasn't that regular.'

'Can you be specific, please?'

'I don't know. Once a month, if that. She was only in the flat a few months.'

'How would you describe your relationship with Nicholas?'

'We got on really well. I thought of him like a brother.'

'In your statement you said that on two occasions when you were babysitting he came to the flat to keep you company. He brought pizza for you to share and watched television with you until Sarah came home.'

'Yes.'

'Would you say you and Nicholas were close?'

'I thought we were, yes.'

'Did you ever see anything that worried you?'

'Never.'

'Did you ever see Nicholas behaving inappropriately?'

'No.'

'Did you ever see any marks on the children?'

'No.'

'The morning Kamran died, Nicholas spoke to you on the phone.'

'Yes.'

'What did he say?'

'"Kamran's not breathing, he's lifeless." I asked if he'd called an ambulance and he said no.'

'Why did Nicholas ring you first?'

'I don't know.'

'Can I put it to you again, Miss Rose, if you were at your sister's flat so often, how is it possible that you never saw anything out of the ordinary?'

'I don't know,' she said. 'I just didn't.'

'Because if you did, if you knew little Kamran was in danger, then you should be in the defendant's box too, don't you think?'

***

What little strength I'd mustered at the beginning of the trial was slipping away with every witness. My poor family were being torn to pieces while doing everything they could to tell the truth. I was beginning to lose all hope. Then Mr Burbridge called a lady named Anne – the grandmother of Nicholas's daughter. She claimed she had witnessed his temper first-hand.

'Your daughter had a relationship with the defendant, Mr Nicholas Kirnon, is that correct?'

'Yes, it is.'

'And although they are no longer together they share a young daughter, is that correct?'

'Yes.'

'And what did you make of Nicholas when he was your daughter's boyfriend?'

'He was a terrible boyfriend,' she said, shooting Nicholas a dirty look. 'He was vile. They were always arguing. She was always crying.'

'Were you ever frightened of him?'

'Yes,' she nodded. 'He kicked my door in.'

'This was when your daughter still lived at home with you and they were in a relationship?'

'Yes.'

'What happened when Mr Kirnon, as you described it, kicked your door in?'

'I didn't answer the door quick enough. He kicked the door open and ran upstairs to get to my daughter. I heard her screaming and him hitting her.'

Mr Thomas attempted to discredit Anne's story by telling the jury that Nicholas was never charged with assault. But we all knew that wasn't because it never happened, it was because the victim – his girlfriend – was too scared to press charges. It was shocking.

Next we heard from a middle-aged woman who lived on Dixon Close in Castle Vale – the same road Nicholas lived on with his mom. This woman claimed she witnessed Nicholas commit a serious assault on a young woman in the middle of the street.

'Can you tell the jury what you saw?' Mr Burbridge asked.

'I saw Nicholas fighting with a girl on the grass outside his mom's place.'

'He had something in his hand, is that correct?'

'Yes, he was holding a kettle.'

'And what did he do with the kettle?'

'He poured it over the girl. He slapped her across the face, then poured it all over her.'

There were gasps from the gallery. I thought about all the times Nicholas had walked out on me before the bickering could escalate. I'd assumed it was because he didn't want to argue. But was it because he was scared of what he might do?

Mr Cook had just two questions for the neighbour.

'May I ask,' he said, 'have you ever seen the defendant, Sarah Louise Rose, before?'

'Yes,' she said. 'I saw her walk up to the house once. She had the two children with her. She must have been shopping as she was struggling with a few Sainsbury's carrier bags.'

'Did you speak to her?

'We said hello. I remember thinking, "What a polite young lady."'

***

I can't begin to describe how stressful that first week was. The enormity of the situation weighed down on me so heavily I felt like I might break. Every night I travelled back to Wolverhampton, sat alone in the flat with all the lights on and the day's events swimming around my head until I collapsed into bed in tears. By Friday I was at breaking point – I couldn't cope being on my own. I asked Mr Bhomra if there was any chance I could find someone else to stay with. I was allowed contact with Mom now she had given evidence, but the charges still over my head meant I wasn't allowed to live with Thierry. Mr Bhomra discussed it with my parents and it was quickly arranged that I would spend the rest of the trial with my mom's youngest sister, Aunty Joanne, her husband and their daughter, Sinead. I couldn't pack my stuff quick enough. With my rent up-to-date the landlady was happy for me to leave without any notice.

'Just leave the keys on the fireplace and make sure you lock the door,' she said.

Dad came to pick me up. We loaded what little stuff I had into the car and drove to Joanne's.

Being there made a huge difference. For the first time in nine months I was around my own flesh and blood. I had company, a cooked meal every night and hot chocolate before bed. It was a blessing. But there was still a huge amount of work to do.

Week two of the trial started with my defence team building up a more honest picture of the kind of person I was. Thierry's dad Mark gave evidence. He talked about how we met and how good things were between us in the beginning. He talked about how our relationship fell apart while I was pregnant with Thierry. He was honest about the fact that I wouldn't let him see our son at first. Again, I worried about how that made me sound but, on the whole, he only had good things to say about me.

'Before Kamran died,' Mr Cook asked, 'what was your relationship like with Miss Rose?'

'Things were good,' Mark said. 'We shared custody of Thierry. Things were amicable. We were all happy.'

'Did you ever have any concerns about leaving your son in Sarah's care?'

'None whatsoever.'

My cousin Kelly was Mr Cook's next witness. Her evidence was brief. She talked generally about the kind of person I was and how I was with the boys.

'She loved her kids,' she said. 'And they loved her. She would do anything for them.'

'You were there the night Sarah met Nicholas, is that correct?'

'Yes.'

'And what did you make of him?'

'He seemed OK.'

'Just OK?'

'Well, the music was loud, we all had a few drinks. I saw them swap numbers so I thought he must like her. I didn't know they were a couple until Sarah told me a few months later.'

Around halfway through the second week, when Nicholas sat down in the box like he had done every morning, I realised he had a black eye. I assume someone in prison got wind of his charges and attacked him. It was comforting to know there were people as angry as I was.

Poor Stacey had to give evidence a second time as a witness for my defence. Mr Cook used her as an example of someone who believed – just like I had – that Nicholas was a decent guy. But Nicholas's defence ripped into her, just like the CPS had. They wanted to break her; they wanted her to say she had seen me do something untoward so they could hold her up as a liar and completely discredit her evidence. Only she wasn't a liar – all she had said was the truth.

***

When it was my turn Mr Cook gave me the nod and I stood up. I had to walk past Nicholas to be let out of the box. I felt his eyes on me but stared straight ahead. In the witness box, I placed my hand on the Bible and swore to tell the truth, just like I always had. This was my time, my big chance to tell the truth. I couldn't let Kamran down now.

'Sarah,' Mr Cook said, 'can you please tell the jury what kind of boyfriend Nicholas was.'

'He was a good boyfriend,' I said, my voice calm and clear. 'I thought I'd found a good one.'

'Can you give some examples of the kind of things he would do for you?'

'He didn't play games with me. He always called or came round when he said he would. He helped with the housework. He had time for my kids.'

'Did you argue?'

'Just silly bickering, maybe he would want to go out with his mates when I was hoping we could watch a DVD. Stupid stuff.'

'So you never had a heated argument?'

'Not once that I can remember. If it looked like it was going that way he always walked out. Then he would come back later or we would make up on the phone.'

'Were you aware that Mr Kirnon had a volatile relationship with his ex-girlfriend?

'No, I thought they got on. He never had a bad word to say about her. He saw their daughter all the time. I thought he was a good dad.'

'Which is why you had no qualms leaving your children in his care?'

'Yes.'

'Why did you rely on Mr Kirnon to look after your two children?'

'Because I went back to work,' I said. 'Nicholas wasn't working, he was round all the time. He offered to have them for me. The kids liked him. I thought it was a good idea.'

'And why did you want to go back to work? Why not stay at home with the children?'

'Because I didn't want to be a single mom on benefits. I wanted to support myself.'

'What happened the day Kamran died?'

I took a deep breath and more than ever wanted to cry. But I kept my head up and answered the questions.

'I got up and went to work as normal.'

'How was Kamran that morning?'

'He was fine. He was happy, smiling. I left him watching telly while I got dressed. Then when I left I said bye. He waved at me and said, "Bye-bye, Mommy."'

'When did you realise something was wrong?'

'A few hours later. I was at work and Nicholas phoned me in tears. He said, "The police are coming for you, you need to get to the hospital."'

'What did you think had happened?'

'I don't know. Just that something was wrong with Kamran. Something bad.'

Half an hour into my evidence I was managing to hold it together. Part of me was shaking with nerves, but I was determined to tell the jury my side of the story. I steadied my breathing as I sensed the opposing team sharpening their knives. *Bring it on,* I thought. *You've got nothing on me.*

***

'So,' Mr Thomas said, 'twenty-one years old and two children by two different men? That's not an ideal situation, is it?'

I wanted to scream, *So what! Is that all you've got?* It had nothing to do with why Kamran was dead.

'Yes,' I said calmly and clearly. 'I've got two kids by two different dads. I didn't plan it. It just didn't work out.'

'You met Nicholas at a bar on a night out, is that correct?'

'Yes.'

'So you've got two young children at home, being cared for by your teenage sister. And you're out getting drunk and kissing boys you've only just met?'

'It wasn't like that. I wasn't drunk – I hardly drink.'

Mr Thomas cut in.

'And even when you were at home, you didn't really take care of your children, did you? All those people coming and going, boys sleeping over at the flat, the kids eating nothing but cheap beans on toast every night. You were far too preoc-cupied with earning money so you could afford to have a social life, am I right?'

'It wasn't like that.'

I didn't recognise the person they were making me out to be – some selfish slapper who didn't care about her kids. And at the end of the day, does it really matter what kind of person you are? Would I have deserved all this if I *was* that girl? Because that's essentially what they were saying, 'Look at this awful girl and her awful family. They deserved this.'

Mr Thomas went on.

'Do you recall going into Kamran's room the night before he died?'

This was part of Nicholas's story. He was trying to pin this on me, to make out I'd done something to him, something that led to his death.

'No,' I said.

'So you deny getting out of bed at three or four o'clock in the morning and going into Kamran's room?'

'That never happened.'

'Why would you have gone in there, Miss Rose? To check on him? To hurt him, maybe?'

'That never happened. Kam never woke up. Both my kids slept through the night. I had no reason to go in there until it was time to get up.'

Inside I was reeling. *Did the jury believe me?* Mr Burbridge was on his feet now.

'Sarah, did you kill your son?''

'No, I did not.'

'So Nicholas killed him and you went to work like nothing happened, am I right?'

'That did not happen.'

'But you must have known he was in danger?'

'I had no idea. Do you really think I would leave him if I'd known?'

'But everyone warned you about Nicholas. Your best friend, your aunty. Why didn't you listen, Sarah? Why didn't you act? Why did you continue to leave your 15-month-old son with this man? You were covering for him, weren't you? You knew he was hurting your baby boy and you turned a blind eye because you didn't want to rock the boat. You didn't want to lose Nicholas. You were a vulnerable, naive single mom who didn't want to be on her own. Am I right?'

'I believed he was a good guy. I would never be with someone who hurt my kids.'

***

I was on the stand for around 45 minutes – the longest of all the witnesses. I left feeling proud of how I'd handled myself. Mr Cook had prepared me well. But I still couldn't be sure which way the jury were going to go. Did they believe me? Or were they falling for the prosecution's distortion of me?

I remember Chris – the policeman who had me arrested – giving evidence. He talked about how Nicholas and I had behaved during those initial interviews and I started to understand why I had been put through all of this. Chris was highly experienced in child protection. He was acting in Kamran's interests and it was better to arrest two people and use them to nail down the truth than to arrest no one at all.

'This was, without a doubt, one of the worst cases I have ever seen,' he said.

***

The medical evidence dragged on for several days. I wanted to listen because I wanted to know what happened to my son. If he was being discussed I wanted to be there and to understand. But when it came to it, it was just too difficult. A young paramedic, who tended to Kam when the ambulance was called, gave evidence. When he started discussing the bruises on Kamran's body – bruises that were already there, he said, not caused by CPR as Nicholas was trying to claim – I was on my feet begging to be let out of the defendant's box. I was allowed outside the courtroom, where I sat down and took a few moments to compose myself. There were two policemen stood outside because they'd had a tip-off Nicholas was going to try and make a run for it.

'Don't worry, love,' one of them said. 'He'll get what's coming to him when he's sent down.'

It was reassuring to know that even people who didn't know me were on my side and despised Nicholas as much as I did.

Once I'd calmed down I went back in, only to find the jury looking through copies of a book that contained detailed photographs of Kamran's body and his injuries. My stomach lurched up to my mouth. The junior solicitor on Nicholas's team, who was sat just a few feet away from us, had one of the books open on the table in front of her. I watched in horror as she turned the book so I could see it. Before I could register what the picture was I was back on my feet and out the door, convinced I was about to throw up.

After that I opted to sit in the lobby outside the courtroom every day until the medical evidence was over. During this time, our stay at Heartlands Hospital when Kamran's head swelled was discussed at length. They now knew the swelling was the result of the bleed on his brain, most probably caused by trauma to the head. The bald patches Kamran had after the swelling went down were alopecia. When I found out about this later, I had to Google what alopecia was and when I saw that it was hair loss caused by stress it was another dagger in my heart. Kam wasn't sick, he'd had a serious head injury. It was highly likely Nicholas seriously assaulted Kamran at least once before the fatal attack.

There were also two old bruises on Kam's back that I never saw because Nicholas had been bathing him and getting him ready for bed. When I found out, I remembered the smashed vase and wondered whether that had anything to do with what had been going on. I racked my brain trying to think of any other signs that I might have missed. To know that there was a catalogue of systematic abuse going on right under my nose was almost too much to bear; it still is. His brain was bleeding and I shooed him away for being clingy. I had no idea what he was going through, but even so, how can a mother not hate herself for that?

It became clear that if the hospital had done the CT scan they would have found the bleed and he could have been saved. It transpired that some of the nurses were concerned Kam had suffered an injury that wasn't an accident, but the doctors we saw rejected those concerns because they weren't suspicious of *me*. They saw how worried I was, how much I cared and how clingy Kam was. They had no reason to suspect I was lying. So important questions – such as, 'Does anyone else care for this child?' – questions that might have set off alarm bells about Nicholas, were never asked.

***

On Monday, 3 March we all assembled back in court for the judge's summing up. We were into our third week now. The hearing was essentially over, but I couldn't relax yet. We had been warned that the jury could take days to reach a decision so when we all took our seats that day we were expecting things to drag on for a little while yet. But then the atmosphere changed. Mr Cook stood up and addressed the judge. From what I could understand, he was explaining that he wanted my manslaughter charge dropped. A hush fell over the court as Mr Justice Treacy began his response. It was a lengthy speech, full of language I struggled to understand. I took very little of it in at the time, but was later able to read the whole judgement in a copy of the court transcript. He said:

> In my judgement, the evidence adduced by the Crown is not evidence of the sort which a jury, properly directed, could use in order to come to the safe, just and proper conclusion that Sarah Rose is guilty of the manslaughter of her child. There is simply a dearth of evidence to show that in the circumstances there was a risk of death being caused to Kamran and that the mother failed in her duty of care by ignoring that risk.
>
> The evidence here shows that she was a good mother to the child. She was a mother who did not herself chastise

the child and if anything was too soft with the children. There had undoubtedly been problems with Kamran which lead to his hospitalisation in April. There is nothing to show that she misled the doctors or failed to cooperate with them. The doctors considered and rejected the possibility of non-accidental injury being caused.

I conclude that the evidence adduced by the Crown has simply not achieved a level of quality or cogence which would, which could or should permit this case, on either count, to go forward for the jury's consideration in relation to Sarah Rose. That is my ruling.

Mr Cook was smiling at me. Mr Bhomra gave me a thumbs up, then came over to the box.

'That's it,' he smiled. 'It's over. They've dropped all the charges against you.'

'What do you mean?' I asked, confused.

'You're free to go.'

CHAPTER TWENTY-TWO

I don't think I ever really expected a jury to throw me in prison. As low as I was, deep down I clung to the hope that doing the right thing, telling the truth and playing by the rules, would pay off eventually. But I never expected to be acquitted either. What happened that day was like a bolt out of the blue: Mr Justice Treacy quite simply saved my life.

I ran out of the defendant's box into the arms of my family. We hugged and cried with relief. It was over, for me at least.

We were stood outside the courtroom when the police investigators, Chris and Kate, came over. They wanted to congratulate me, but they also had something serious to ask.

'Nicholas will be tried on his own now,' Chris explained. 'We need you to give evidence for the CPS.'

Hearing those words brought me crashing back down to earth. Yes, I was free, but this nightmare was far from finished. To get Nicholas convicted, there would have to be a whole new trial and they wanted to use me as a key witness. I couldn't believe it. *The police want me to help them? After everything they put me through?* I wanted to tell them to stick it where the sun doesn't shine.

'No,' I said. 'I've had enough. There's nothing I can say that makes him sound bad anyway.'

'We understand what you're saying,' Kate said. 'But telling the court what a good boyfriend he was will help expose his Jekyll and Hyde character.'

I slumped onto a chair with my face in my hands. It didn't take me long to think about what they were saying. Nicholas needed to be convicted. If they needed my help I couldn't say no.

'OK,' I said.

'Thank you,' Chris replied. 'We'll be in touch. And congratulations again.'

Mr Cook and Mr Bhomra said we all deserved a big drink so a crowd of us agreed to head to the pub over the road. Mom and Dad had their arms around me as we got into the lift with Stacey. The doors were about to close when Nicholas's solicitor and his junior got in too. As the lift sank to the ground floor, the junior turned her head to look at me.

'Well done,' she said. 'You should get an Oscar for that.'

The lift pinged and the doors opened. We were all too stunned to reply.

At the pub, Mr Cook got the drinks in. We clinked glasses and shared a moment of muted celebration. Then I said my thank yous and goodbyes, got into Dad's car and went home with my family. That night, I slept properly for the first time in months.

***

Unfortunately, because of Mark's residential order, I couldn't be reunited with Thierry until we'd attended a case review with social services. So, a week after my court case ended, me, Mark and my mom sat round a huge table with a selection of social workers, health visitors, police and Thierry's teachers. I went in there all guns blazing: I wanted full custody, I wanted my son back.

'As far as we are concerned,' the police said, 'Sarah has been acquitted of all charges. Therefore, she should be allowed to resume caring for her son.'

Social services were more wary. They felt we should approach things cautiously, given a child in my care had been murdered. Their attitude made me mad.

'I never did anything wrong,' I told them. 'I've been cleared of all blame, and you're still blaming me? He's my son! It shouldn't be up to you to decide!'

Mom told me to calm down. But it was so hard to keep my cool. I was angry at everything – all the people who wrongly accused me, all the people who looked down on me and thought I was something I'm not. And I was scared; scared that I would always have to answer to someone and scared I might never be allowed to have Thierry back. It felt like I would never be in charge of my life again. When I realised one of the social workers was doodling on her paperwork, I lost it again.

'Look!' I screamed. 'She's doodling pictures of diamonds! Are any of you even taking this seriously? This is my life!'

'Listen,' Mark said, 'Sarah's understandably upset about everything but I've got no problem with her seeing Thierry. I've never had a problem with her. I just wanted something in place to protect him while everything was going on. It's over now. I'm happy for Sarah to see our son.'

The panel decided I was allowed back at Mom's. Mark would continue to have Thierry every other week, and Mom and I would share care on the weeks he was with us, just until I got back on my feet.

***

When Kam died, all I wanted was to be able to go home to Mom, Dad and Thierry. Yet when I finally got there, nothing was like I thought it would be. None of us knew what to do or say. Mom was a shell of a woman. There was no big sit down, no big talk or emotional reunion with Thierry. He was so settled it made no difference to him whether I was there or not. We were finally back together but I had never felt so far apart.

I remember Kate, the police officer, turning up at the house. She had a few things to return, like the *SpongeBob SquarePants* vest of Thierry's that Kamran had been wearing when he died. I couldn't bring myself to look at any of it, but I did tell Kate what I thought of her.

'You put me through hell,' I told her. 'You stopped me from seeing my family. You looked me in the face and called me a murderer.'

'I'm sorry,' she said, her eyes filling up.

'I want to see him,' I told her. 'I want to see Nicholas. I've got things I need to ask him.'

She was shaking her head at me.

'Please don't, Sarah,' she said quietly. 'Please. It won't help you.'

***

Over the next few weeks I tried to claw back some routine by walking Thierry to and from school every day. Some days I felt like we were getting close again then something would happen to knock me back. If he wanted a drink, he would ask my mom. If he hurt himself, it was her he ran to. I was so sensitive to it all the slightest thing was like a knife through my heart.

Me and Mom started arguing.

'He's my son!' I would scream. 'You're taking over again, just like you always do!'

I was jealous of her relationship with Thierry. I felt pushed out and more like Thierry's sister than his mother. I tried to fit back into his life – at least I thought I tried. Maybe I didn't try hard enough. And when he didn't accept me back I started to resent him too. One day, a few weeks after the trial, I woke up and thought, *Forget it.* I was done fighting. Kam was gone, Thierry didn't need me. I figured I might as well just do whatever the hell I wanted.

I started spending more and more time with my cousins, Sam and Kelly. Their mate had a car, so we would drive around listening to music, eating sweets and having a laugh. At the weekend we would buy cheap vodka and sit in the car and drink. I had never been much of a drinker before, but now I didn't want to stop. Kelly knew someone who was setting up a new estate agent so she got us both a job there. It was only part time and doing the basics like photocopying and filing, but it kept me busy, helped me avoid being at home, and gave me money for booze. With cash in my pocket the drinking soon spread from weekends to weeknights. My cousins' friend would pick me and Kelly up from work, we would buy something to eat, and either vodka or WKD, and stay out until God knows what time. I didn't care if I had to get up in the morning. If anyone wanted to go home, I would be the one who teased and moaned at them to stay out a bit longer. Everyone thought I was the life and soul and I think I believed it too for a while. It never occurred to me that I was scared to death of being on my own.

At the weekend we started going to the Digbeth area of Birmingham. We liked it because there were several backstreet pubs that played garage music and stayed open until the early hours of the morning. I think we were in the Hen and Chickens the first time we were offered cocaine. A guy just came over and asked if we wanted to buy some.

'Shall we?' I suggested, excited.

Twenty minutes later we were all huddled in a filthy toilet cubicle, rubbing white powder on our gums.

'It tastes disgusting!' I said, spitting into a tissue.

'No!' Kelly said, 'You make it into a line and sniff it!'

Sam and I watched her take some, then copied her. I always say it didn't really affect me, but it must have done something because I immediately wanted more.

Cocaine became a big part of our social lives. There was always someone who knew someone who knew a dealer we could call. Every weekend we would chip in a tenner each and buy a gram to last us the night. I loved it because it helped us stay up later and drink more, which was all I wanted to do. On the weeks we were short of cash, we got creative by stealing from Asda. We would stuff whatever we could into our jackets, then drive to the next Asda to get a refund. Because we didn't have receipts, they would give us store credit, which we would use to buy alcohol. We thought it was hilarious. And we didn't stop there. If the car was low on petrol, we would fill up the tank and just drive off. We did it several times. I would be in the back with a coat over my head and we would all cheer as we made our getaway. I don't know how we got away with it, but we did.

***

By this time I was leaving the house on a Friday and not going back until Sunday. During the week I was at work in the day, then staying out drinking as late as I possibly could. I barely saw Thierry. Mom and Dad bit their tongues at first. They probably thought I needed to let my hair down and get it all out of my system. But the truth was, 18 months on from Kam's murder, I still hadn't dealt with it. All I'd done was learn how to block it out.

One day I ran into an old friend from school. His nickname was Beaver on account of his two front teeth being quite large. He was going to a house party and, even though I had work the next day, me and the girls invited ourselves. We followed Beaver's car to Yardley, where he picked up his mates, Noel and Stephen, then we spent an hour trying to find the party. No one had Sat Navs back then and the host wasn't answering her phone, so eventually we gave up and went back to Noel's. He was 20 and lived with his dad, but had the place to himself for the night. We got the music on and cracked open the vodka. Every so often me and the girls would sneak off to the bathroom to perk ourselves up with a line.

At some point that night, Stephen and I realised we'd met before. I'd been walking down the Coventry Road one afternoon with Thierry and Kamran, when we saw police closing the road. I found out later that a pregnant woman had been hit by a car and killed. Stephen had been walking past too, and we'd spoken.

'Small world!' he said. 'How are your two boys?'

'My eldest is fine,' I said, 'but my youngest was murdered by my ex.'

I'd blurted it out before my brain had time to stop me. There was an awkward silence then I moved away to compose myself. I was completely unprepared for that kind of question. I was so busy blocking everything out with people and drink and drugs that having it brought up was a real slap in the face. Thankfully, chatting to Noel helped smooth things over. He told me his family were from South America. Slim and athletic, he didn't drink much, he said, because he was training to become a fireman and in the middle of football trials for Birmingham and Leeds.

We all crashed out at his then I got up and went straight to work. At some point during my shift, I got a text from Noel saying he was going to pick me up. *Great,* I thought. *A free lift!* He must have fancied me to do that, but my head was too all over the place to notice. We went for a drive then back to his. That night we ended up in bed together. It's not something I planned. I promise you, it's not even in my character to jump into bed with someone

I've just met. But I wasn't thinking straight. With me avoiding life at home and Nicholas's court case coming up soon, I was doing absolutely everything in my power *not* to think.

***

The second trial began to weigh on my shoulders just as heavily as the first. Even though I wasn't in the dock this time, I still had to stand up and give evidence. I still had to face Nicholas again and rake over all the awful things that happened to Kamran. Emotionally, it was going to be like opening Pandora's Box.

I coped by continuing to bury my head in the sand, drinking and partying and barely eating or sleeping. Noel stayed in touch, even though – if I'm being completely honest – I couldn't have cared less if he did or not. I didn't have the headspace to think about anyone but myself. I'm ashamed to say I probably even used him a bit. If me and my mates had nowhere else to go, I'd call Noel and ask if we could go to his. He didn't seem to mind. We were silly drunks and I think he found us entertaining.

I barely noticed, but the number of people congregating at his house got fewer and fewer until one day it was just us. I was too blind to see it at the time, but he'd become my safe place. I needed him, and I think he could tell I needed someone to look out for me.

'So what happened?' he asked. 'What happened to your kid?'

He sat and listened while it all came pouring out – Nicholas, Kam's murder, the court cases. It was the first time I'd opened up to anyone. He was shocked, but I think he finally understood why I was so haywire.

Mom must have been stressed about the case too because she started nagging me to stay home more.

'You need to spend more time with Thierry,' she snapped. 'And what's this about you sleeping at some guy's house?'

It had got back to her through my cousins and she wasn't happy.

'It's way too soon,' she said.

'I don't care what you think,' I shrugged. 'I'm an adult, I can do what I want.'

She was right, it was too soon. And I fell for a murderer when I was happy. She must have been going out of her mind wondering what kind of man I was going to attract now.

***

I quit my job at the estate agent's so I would be able to attend court every day. I knew there would be a lot of waiting around until it was my turn to give evidence but I still wanted to be there.

Being back in court at the end of June 2008 was like horrible déjà vu. All the same faces came out to support me. People came on their days off, used holidays or showed up on their lunch breaks. Most days the hallways were packed with my family and friends and all their kids running around. The support they showed me throughout both trials was incredible. This time, though, we were here for one reason – to see Nicholas put behind bars. And we by no means had a conviction in the bag. Just like before, if the jury weren't satisfied beyond reasonable doubt that Nicholas was guilty of murder, there was no manslaughter charge to fall back on.

I sat outside waiting my turn as one by one, Chantelle, my mom and sister gave evidence, each of them reporting back to me afterwards and claiming the questioning was almost identical to the previous trial. We were three or four days in when I was finally called to say my piece. My hand was steady as I placed it on the Bible and swore to tell the truth. I avoided looking at Nicholas by focussing on the prosecutor, Mr Franck, as he began his questions.

'Miss Rose, can you tell us what kind of boyfriend Nicholas was?'

'He was a good boyfriend,' I said. 'He helped around the house, he was great with the kids. We never argued. I thought he was a keeper.'

We went over how Nicholas and I met that night on Broad Street. I talked about how he naturally became part of our lives and how he had offered to babysit when I was struggling with work. We went over how I'd taken Kamran to hospital when his head swelled and how I'd taken him home believing he was better. Then I talked about the day Kamran died – how I got up and went to work, then received the phone call that changed everything.

Nicholas had a different QC – Mr Sidhu-Bahr. I thought I might get an easier ride this time, but his tactic was the same – to convince the jury I was a horrible person and a terrible mother. It felt like I was watching the same episode of a soap opera all over again.

'Two children by two different men? Your first child at 17? Where did it all go wrong, Miss Rose?'

Again, I was asked why I got up in the night and went into Kamran's room.

'That didn't happen,' I said.

But Mr Sidhu-Bahr was like a dog with a bone.

'Are you sure, Miss Rose? Because my client states categorically that he heard you get up in the night, and then the next day your son ended up dead.'

I couldn't believe they still had the audacity to make out I had something to do with Kamran's death.

'This isn't about me anymore!' I snapped. 'I've had my trial!'

The judge, Mr Justice Butterfield, cut in.

'That's enough, Miss Rose.'

The jury weren't supposed to know there had been another court case, but no one had told me.

The tears started streaming down my face as I finally looked at Nicholas. A wave of sadness washed over me as I opened my mouth to speak.

'I loved him. I don't know why he would do this, not just to my son, but to anyone.'

* * *

Once I'd given evidence, I was allowed to join my family in the gallery. I was sat with Mom and Dad when Nicholas's mom gave evidence. After Nicholas, she was the person I had the most questions for. I hoped I was about to get some answers.

'On the morning Kamran died,' Mr Franck asked, 'why did your son, Nicholas Kirnon, take the little boy to your house?'

'He panicked,' she shrugged. 'Kamran had banged his head, he was lifeless. Nicholas didn't know what to do.'

'There is a doctor's surgery directly opposite the flat where Sarah Rose lived with her children. Why would he not go there? Or phone an ambulance?'

'I don't know,' she said again. 'He panicked.'

'What happened when Nicholas and Kamran got to your house?'

'Kamran was lifeless. I got him out of the pushchair and took him into the garden for some fresh air.'

'But Nicholas had just walked the 10- or 15-minute journey to your house. Do you not think that would have been a sufficient amount of fresh air?'

'I don't know,' she said again. 'I panicked.'

'So you were both panicking, but waited another 15 minutes before calling an ambulance?'

'Yes,' she stammered. 'I mean yes, we were panicking, but he'd only banged his head. We thought Kamran was going to be OK.'

'Can you remember what you said when you telephoned Miss Rose?'

'I told her to get to the hospital.'

'You told Miss Rose her son was dead, did you not?'

'I don't remember saying that.'

Mr Sidu-Bahr asked about the time we met at her house, after I had been to Sainsbury's.

'What did you make of Miss Rose?' he asked.

'She seemed OK,' she said. 'But I didn't think she had much of a bond with Kamran.'

Mr Franck pressed her on that point.

'Can I ask, where was little Kamran sat that day?'

'On Sarah's lap.'

'Did he get off Sarah's lap at all?'

'Not that I remember, no.'

'So a little boy doesn't move from his mother's lap and you say they have no bond?'

'I just didn't see it, no.'

***

Both trials always had an air of hostility about them, but this one got particularly bad. A young guy I knew turned up one day only to be escorted out for standing up and shouting abuse at Nicholas. I had to deal with filthy looks from Nicholas's mom and stepdad, day in, day out. One day, I had to run outside when a piece of evidence upset me and Nicholas's ex-girlfriend – the one he allegedly assaulted – kissed her teeth at me. My cousin Sinead heard and confronted her.

'What's that supposed to mean?' she asked.

'My daughter's going to grow up without her dad because of her,' she said, pointing at me.

'He killed her son!' Sinead shouted.

They squared up to each other and started pushing and shoving. I stood up and tried to break it up but security ran over and intervened.

***

It's only recently I found out Nicholas gave evidence in his trial. Stacey and I think I must have missed it after leaving the court to avoid hearing medical evidence. From what we can piece together, when Nicholas was on the stand he reverted back to his claims that I was a good mom. But he insisted I went into Kamran's room the night before he died and once again explained away Kamran's injuries as being caused by a fall off the sofa.

It took the jury just four hours to reach their decision. There was a huge crowd of us sat all over the floor of a waiting room when the clerk appeared.

'Everyone for Kirnon, please.'

I flew back into court. Although he hadn't been in court much because of work, Nabeel was there for the verdict that day. I sat with him on one side and Mom clinging to my hand on the other. The judge asked the head of the jury to stand. I dropped my head and shut my eyes tight. The court fell silent as we held our breath and waited for that one, tiny statement.

'How do you find the defendant?'

'Guilty.'

The court erupted around me. Everyone was on their feet, cheering, punching the air and screaming with relief.

All I remember is the noise and commotion around me. I sat motionless as I soaked it all in. We had got what we wanted. The truth was out and Nicholas was going to prison.

I was so lost in the moment that I didn't see Nicholas lose his temper. Apparently, when they read out the verdict he lost it, swinging punches and kicking the inside of the defendant's box. When the security guards couldn't restrain him, he was escorted down to the cells.

When everything had settled down, Judge Butterfield closed the case. He said:

Nicholas Kirnon has been convicted of murder. He has chosen, once the verdict was announced, to behave in an angry and aggressive way, whilst being restrained by prison officers.

This is a tragic case and no sentence of mine can restore life to little Kamran. No sentence can reflect the value of that life. Kamran's life was priceless. Nicholas Kirnon took that life from him in what must have been, on medical evidence, a vicious and prolonged assault, committed in anger and temper, inflicting grave internal injuries on a defenceless baby.

Nicholas Kirnon had been trusted to care for Kamran. He grossly abused that trust. But there are no winners here; everyone is a loser. Kamran himself, his older brother, his mother, his grandmother, and Nicholas Kirnon's family too, no doubt all devastated by these terrible events.

Judge Butterfield imposed life imprisonment with a minimum of 15 years. Because Nicholas lost his temper, he decided to increase that to 17 years, which is what he will have to serve before he will even be considered for parole. And even then, the parole board will keep him in custody until they are satisfied he is no longer dangerous.

Judge Butterfield concluded:

This was an act committed, in my judgement, in an explosive rage, in which the defendant repeatedly assaulted the child causing the terrible injuries and consequences of which we have heard. To some extent, the position is made worse by his relatively extensive record of previous convictions, showing that from time to time he is prepared to use violence.

Members of the jury, this is a harrowing case. There is no question about that. It is perhaps easy for the lawyers. They, I am afraid, see this sort of thing day in and day out, but you do not. And it will have left its mark on each of you to some extent. What I propose to do is to direct that you should not be required to sit on a jury again for the next ten years. Our thanks to you for your plainly very careful consideration of this case.

We left court that afternoon, elated. I remember clinging to my family, the sound of triumph still ringing in my ears. Chris, the detective inspector, came over and asked if I could write a statement for the press. Grace's sister, Eve, had a pen and helped me cobble something together which, I believe, Chris then read out on my behalf.

There must have been a high-profile case going on that day because when we left the court building there were armed police outside. I remember seeing Nicholas's family huddled together, his mom in tears. His stepdad turned to me and shouted, 'We're gonna get you for this! This isn't over!'

Before I could think about what I was doing, I broke away from my family, ducked under a policeman's gun and got right in his face.

'The truth's out now,' I snapped. 'Nicholas killed Kamran. Deal with it.'

Dad and one of the armed police grabbed me by the arms and pulled me back.

'Come on, love,' the copper said. 'He's not worth it.'

CHAPTER TWENTY-THREE

Somehow, I mistook the trial for the finish line. I thought seeing Nicholas convicted would give me closure, but the glow of success was short-lived. Now he was locked up, where did it leave me? Kamran was still gone, Thierry didn't want me. I was right back in the pit of emptiness, numbing myself with drink and cocaine. I fell from pub to party to Noel's bed and back again.

Mom was at her wits' end.

'If you want me to bring up Thierry for you,' she said, 'I'll do it.'

I don't know what he saw in me, but for some reason Noel was always there for me. When I told him I was thinking about letting Mom bring up Thierry, he was stunned.

'I don't think so, Sarah,' he said. 'He's *your* son. He needs you.'

He was right, of course. Noel could tell I was running away from things I needed to confront. But my confidence was at rock bottom. I'd let Kamran down so dreadfully, I truly believed Thierry was better off without me.

'I know it's hard,' Noel said, 'but pushing Thierry away isn't the answer. You need each other. You need to rebuild your relationship or the regret will eat away at you.'

'I don't even know where to start,' I said tearfully.

'I do,' he said, looking me in the eye. 'You need to stop taking cocaine and start looking after your son.'

'Why are you saying all this?' I asked.

'Because I can't be with you if you're going to carry on like this.'

***

Noel's words were like a light switch in my brain. Mom had been trying to get through to me for months, but I'd written it off as nagging. Hearing it from Noel was different. I realised that his opinion really mattered to me. Suddenly, I saw myself through his eyes. Drinking myself senseless wasn't solving my problems, it was adding to them. If I didn't pull myself together I was going to lose not only Noel's friendship, but the single most important person in my life – Thierry. I'd been so busy turning my back on the world, I hadn't stopped to think how devastating it would be if he was gone from my life for good. Noel was right – I couldn't be a mom to Kam anymore, but I still had a chance with Thierry. I had to keep going for my son.

I stopped going out as much and quit the cocaine. I thank my lucky stars I was able to stop so easily because the way things were spiralling I have no doubt I would have wound up addicted or dead. Instead of spending all my time out chasing company, I made a conscious effort to spend time with Thierry. I started walking him to and from school again. Then I reinstated the weekly family time just for the two of us. I would let Thierry choose something fun to do, like bowling or the cinema. Sometimes he was just happy having a trip to McDonald's. Slowly, we started talking again. He told me about his school and his friends – all the things I'd been missing out on. And we talked about Kamran – not about his murder, but about the happy things we both remembered. My heart was still broken, but to be Thierry's mom again meant the world to me.

***

From the moment Kamran died I had issues with Heartlands Hospital. Even before I understood that my son had been murdered, I felt strongly that the staff there should have done more to help him. And the trial strengthened my belief. Granted, it wasn't an illness that ended Kam's life, but I believe that if the right things had been done when I took him to hospital in April 2007, he would not have been dead four weeks later.

One night, during the weeks I started to get my focus back, I Googled 'medical negligence' and stumbled across a specialist law firm in Manchester. Before I could talk myself out of it, I picked up the phone and called them. I spoke to their in-house expert Janet Johnson, who sounded confident I had a strong case. 'Leave it with me,' she said. 'It may take a bit of time, but I believe we're in a good position to move things forward.'

Meanwhile, I read in the paper that Nicholas's mom was planning to re-mortgage her house to cover the cost of an appeal. It made my skin crawl – he didn't deserve to be saved. But thankfully, that article was the first and last I heard of it. Twenty-eight days after the trial ended, Kamran's brain and spleen – which had been kept as evidence – were released, meaning there would be no further legal action. I received a letter asking if a piece of Kamran's brain could be kept to help future cases. I agreed they could keep it – it gave me comfort to know it could help a family who have lost a child. But now that I had nothing going on, no court case to hold it together for, it really haunted me that Kam's little body was in pieces. I Googled what a spleen was – it sits behind the stomach and filters the blood – and drove myself mad imaging what they did to him in the post-mortem. I understand that they had to do it, but he went through enough when he was alive.

The Catholic belief is that you have to be buried whole to get into heaven, so I really struggled with the notion that Kam's spirit might be stuck. I asked for his remains to be sent to the funeral directors and we arranged a second burial.

The day of the service, in August 2009, we had one car collect immediate family and another ten or so people met us at the cemetery. Noel came to support me. Nabeel was there too, although we barely spoke.

I carried what was left of Kam from the house to the graveside in a little white box. I can't describe what that felt like, sitting in the car with his brain on my lap. Not even in my deepest darkest nightmares could I ever imagine having to do something so distressing. Inside that box were pieces of the little boy I loved so deeply, but I felt sick to my bones knowing how and why they were taken from him. We gathered around the open grave for a prayer, and then the white box was placed on top of the coffin. It was another goodbye, even more final than the last. I still felt no closure, only darkness and loss.

***

Although it was something I had to do, the second burial was a real setback for me emotionally. I could tell Mom was struggling too. She visited Kam's grave every day without fail, to replace the flowers and make sure it was neat and tidy – her way of still looking after him even though he was gone. I was grateful. I wanted it to look nice but found it too difficult to go myself. All I'd be thinking was, *My baby is in a box in the ground*.

Thank God for Thierry. Fixing his breakfast and getting him to school became my reason for getting out of bed in the morning. When it was Mark's week to have him, I would spend more time with Noel. He was my friend and my comforter, the safe place I could run to when the sadness at home got too much. He talked a lot about helping me find my own home, somewhere nice for me and Thierry.

Exactly two weeks after the burial, Noel fell ill. He said it was only a cold, but when I went round to see him he was slumped on the sofa.

'What's wrong?' I asked.

'I need to take my tablets,' he said.

He was slurring his words. I knew he took medication and he'd mentioned hospital appointments in passing but had never gone into detail. When I managed to find his pills he couldn't swallow them. Then he started gasping for breath.

'What's going on?' I asked. 'I'm scared. Shall I call an ambulance?'

He tried to say no, but I could tell he needed help. I called 999 and within minutes paramedics arrived and rushed him to Heartlands Hospital. I was completely at a loss as to what was going on as he was admitted to intensive care. When his parents arrived, his mom pulled me to one side.

'Noel has got myasthenia gravis,' she explained. 'It's a rare autoimmune condition from the same family as MS. The brain tells the muscles to work but the message doesn't get through and the antibodies that normally fight infection go wrong and attack the body instead.

'His football coach noticed he wasn't well when he was 19,' she continued. 'He was so tired all the time I was scared he was on drugs. Sometimes, he can't hold his arms above his head for more than ten seconds. That's why he has to take steroids.'

Her words knocked me sideways. Noel was such a fit guy; now he was covered in tubes, with a ventilator breathing for him. His airways had started to close up – a sign his body was shutting down. I had never seen anything like it.

'Why didn't he tell me?' I asked.

'He's quite shy about people knowing,' she said. 'He gets embarrassed. Look, Noel mentioned you've been going through a really hard time lately. Are you sure you want to take all this on as well?'

Before I could think of what to say, a doctor took Noel's parents to a private room and told them he might only have 48 hours to live. His mom was in tears when they relayed the news to me. I felt like the whole world was crashing down around me again. I was standing in Heartlands Hospital, feet away from the cubicle where Kamran's body had been, being told that my boyfriend might only have two days to live. It was like a cruel joke. I remember looking at Noel, thinking, *My God, does everything I touch get destroyed?* I was beside myself.

'Please don't die,' I begged him, quietly. 'I need you. I need you to keep helping me.'

I called Mom in tears. She came straight to the hospital and wrapped her arms around me.

'Why is this happening?' I asked. 'I can't cope with losing someone else.'

When I told Mom about Noel's illness she shared the same opinion as his family – that I already had enough on my plate without taking on a seriously ill boyfriend. But Noel had saved my life. I couldn't walk away when he needed me. I spent the next two days at Noel's bedside with his family, fearing the worst. The hospital gave us a little bedsit, so when we couldn't keep our eyes open we had somewhere to sleep close by.

***

We sat there staring at his lifeless body, hour after hour, truly believing he was about to slip away. So when the doctors suddenly told us he had turned a corner, it was a battle to take in the good news. But they were right – after three days, Noel opened his eyes. I hugged him and cried. I think he was shocked to see me. I don't think he expected me to stick around.

For a few days Noel had to communicate by writing on a white board. When we had a moment alone, he wrote: 'Just go. Live your life. You don't need this.'

I shook my head.

'No,' I said, tears streaming down my cheeks. 'I'm not going anywhere.'

And I meant it. I'd been so swamped with stress and grief that it took the shock of nearly losing Noel to make me realise how much he meant to me. I was in love with him. I could have run for the hills when I found out about his condition, but I didn't want to. We needed each other; we made each other stronger.

***

After three weeks in hospital, Noel was allowed home to rest. True to his word, he approached his landlord about rentals and found me and Thierry a two-bed terrace walking distance from Thierry's school. I jumped at the opportunity for a fresh start. I barely had any stuff, so with Mom and Dad's help it didn't take long to pack up and move. It must have been upsetting for them to let us go, but we were only ten minutes away. I'm sure Mom knew we would be round at hers expecting our dinner most nights. I worried Thierry would be upset about leaving his nanny, but he drank in all my enthusiasm about it being a new adventure for us. Noel paid the deposit and the first month's rent for me, then I supported myself by getting a job as a carer that fitted around Thierry's school hours. It felt good to be sorted and busy again. If I was busy I could hold it together, maybe even pretend I was normal. The nights I lay in bed alone I was right back in the black hole. But by day, I was slowly getting back on my feet: I had to for Thierry and Noel.

It probably comes as no surprise that I avoided introducing them for as long as I possibly could. I don't know how many rows Noel and I must have had about it. On a good day, he wholeheartedly understood why I had trust issues of the worst kind but sometimes my unspoken fear that he might harm or even kill my son really got to him.

No matter how much I resisted, their paths had to cross eventually. In the end it happened in dribs and drabs. I think we started by arranging an informal playdate with Noel's little brother because we felt it would be less threatening for Thierry if he had someone his own age to play with. The first time Thierry spent a full day with Noel, the three of us went to Drayton Manor. Thierry was horrible to Noel for pretty much the whole trip. He was rude and snappy and didn't want Noel anywhere near me. I beat myself up, thinking maybe it was too soon. But Noel took it on the chin.

'It's going to take time,' he said. 'I can handle it.'

Noel's health was constantly up and down. In the first year of us being together, he was admitted to intensive care five times. One day he would be fine, the next he would struggle to walk up the stairs. On more than one occasion he got in the bath then needed help to get out again. He was forced to abandon all hope of joining the Fire Service or playing professional football. His weight fluctuated – a combination of comfort eating and being too weak to exercise. I tried my best to keep his spirits up as he went through the humiliating process of claiming disability benefits. Everyone must have thought I was mad to take him on, but my feelings never wavered. I loved Noel unconditionally.

***

When a child dies under suspicious circumstances, it is protocol for the local authority to publish a Serious Case Review. Kam's was released in 2009 and echoed the concerns I had about Heartlands Hospital:

> The possibility of non-accidental injury was raised, but not fully explored as part of the differential diagnosis. It would appear that this may have been an opportunity to identify the abuse of the child, prior to the death.

If they had stopped to consider Kam's head injury might have been caused deliberately either with or without my knowledge, if they had asked me who looked after Kam, maybe I would have suspected Nicholas. At the time I had no experience of child abuse – it wasn't even remotely on my radar. They should have at least asked me the question, but no one ever did. The more I thought about it, the more I felt like they'd got away with something.

Thankfully, after 12 to 18 months of emails and phone calls, the medical negligence lawyer Janet Johnson finally had some news about my case against the hospital.

'I know it's not quite what you wanted,' Janet said, 'but they want to settle out of court. They're offering to donate £10,000 to a charity of your choice.'

Janet advised me to accept the deal on the grounds she thought it unlikely the case would make trial. I never set out to put myself through another court case, I just wanted them to take some of the blame. I know I let Kamran down, but I wanted the staff who saw us to accept *they* let him down too. This was as close to an apology as I was going to get. I had them donate the money to the NSPCC because I read that more people donate to animal charities than charities for children. I'm not saying animals don't deserve help, but that really shocked me.

***

At the beginning of 2010 – nearly three years after Kamran died – me, Thierry and Noel moved in together. By this time they were really close, but I'd be lying if I said I found it easy. The fear that something might happen to Thierry was a daily battle. I'd been with Noel long enough to know in my heart that he was a good man who would never do anything to hurt either of us, but there was always a part of me refusing to let my guard down completely. Noel talked about having kids of our own, but I was so frightened. My confidence and self-esteem were barely off the floor. And I didn't know whether I would be able to handle it emotionally. Surely a new baby would feel like a replacement for Kamran?

Once again, fate stepped in and made the decision for me. In the summer of 2010, I fell pregnant. Noel was over the moon – I'd never seen him so happy. I fretted about telling Thierry, worried he might feel pushed out. But when we told him he thought it was the best news ever. I wished I could share in their excitement but I was all over the place. I didn't know what I was feeling, but it wasn't joy.

I was still struggling to get my head around it when there was a knock at the door.

'Sarah? Hi, I'm Anna from social services. I just need to ask you a few questions. Is that OK?'

I burst into tears and couldn't stop. She sat on the sofa with her arm around me.

'I'm so sorry, Sarah. I promise you, it's nothing to worry about. It's just routine.'

But I was a wreck. I felt dirty, like I was still being treated like a criminal. She went through a never-ending list of questions: how was I feeling? How did I feel about the baby? Then she asked about Noel: how did we meet? What he was like? They were only acting in the baby's interests, but it was another reminder that I was always being watched and judged. On top of all the emotions I was already struggling to deal with, I now thought they were going to take my baby away.

***

We had only been in our house a few months when the land-lord informed us he needed the property back. We found a bigger house in Yardley with a huge kitchen diner, spacious living room and decent garden.

'Fill up all the bedrooms!' the owner smiled as he showed us round. 'Have lots of children!'

When we were all moved in and Thierry was at his dad's, Noel took me into Birmingham for something to eat. Halfway through a meal at Jamie's Italian, he placed a little box on the table in front of me. My jaw dropped when I saw the engagement ring inside.

'Shall we get married?' he smiled.

The ring was stunning. He told me he'd taken Mom and Stacey to the Jewellery Quarter the day before to help him choose it. I cried, of course – overwhelmed by the surprise proposal and touched that he so thoughtfully involved the women who know me best. I felt so lucky to have him in my life and had no doubt Thierry would feel the same. My answer was a big fat blubbery yes.

***

I didn't expect to set a date immediately. I'm not the kind of girl who's always dreamt of her wedding day. But Noel was straight on the case. Within a few weeks he'd booked the church for September 2012 and a marquee at the Meridian Hotel for the reception. He did *everything*, from finding a photographer to organising flowers. He had so many ideas and specific things he wanted that we joked he was the Bridezilla of the relationship. I really didn't mind what cars we had or what the colour scheme was as long as everyone I loved was there. The only thing I would pick was my dress.

In among all the wedding planning, we found out we were having a baby girl. I cried with happiness and relief. I think Thierry was secretly hoping for a baby brother, simply because boys would rather play with boys. But I don't know how I would have coped with another son. Somehow, a girl felt like a fresh start and less likely to take Kamran's place.

* * *

My newfound happiness didn't stop me worrying what people would think, though. By this time Facebook was a part of everyday life. I set up a memorial page for Kamran and, believe it or not, not everyone who posts on it has kind words to say. They write underneath Nicholas's mug shot that he looks like an 'evil monster' and ask me 'how could you not have known?' like I should have spotted a killer a mile off just by looking at his face. I agree – he does look evil in that police photo. When I see it, I want to punch it. But it's easy to pass judgement on someone's photograph when you know they've done something bad. The man in that photo looks nothing like the man I fell in love with. I can't explain it, but he doesn't. I barely recognise him. The man in that photo is a stranger to me.

Knowing how brutally judgemental people are, we didn't shout about the pregnancy. It was difficult enough without feeling the whole world might stick their oar in, look down on me, speculate and assume I was moving on and forgetting about Kam. If anything, carrying a baby the same way I'd carried him made me miss him even more.

***

When you've had two caesarean sections, any natural births after that are considered too risky. So on 4 April 2011, I was admitted to Heartlands Hospital for a planned caesarean. I was a paranoid wreck. Not just about the birth, but about the hospital staff trying to kill me. I convinced myself they would look at my record, see that I'd sued the hospital and finish me off. It sounds laughable now, but I'd had so many unimaginable things happen to me I couldn't help but fear the worst.

Thankfully, our little girl Savannah was born safely that day. After three days in hospital recovering, a very proud Noel drove us both home. He made sure he had the Moses basket set up and a bunch of fresh flowers waiting for me. He invited Mom round too – a conscious effort on his part to make sure she felt involved. It was the first time I'd had a baby and not had her holding my hand during labour and helping out 24/7. I think we both felt a bit sad we weren't sharing the experience like we did with Thierry and Kamran, but I wanted to show her I could do it.

Noel was hands-on from the word go. He took an interest in everything from baby clothes to routines. He wanted to be the best dad he could possibly be. I didn't have to ask him for help, he just got stuck in. Night feeds, nappy changes – you name it, he did it. He read up on the benefits of breastfeeding and encouraged me to try. It was a noble effort, but I couldn't get past my squeamishness, so that was the one thing we disagreed on.

***

When the midwife came to the house for our first check-up, she gave me the usual advice.

'No sex for six weeks,' she said.

You always roll your eyes because it's the last thing you're thinking about. Even when the baby hasn't been born the natural way, you're shattered and have a scar that's still healing. But when Savannah was six weeks old, it happened. And low and behold, just from that one time, I was pregnant again. I broke down, imagining all manner of horrible scenarios; my scar splitting, dying. I didn't even think it was possible to fall pregnant that quickly.

The look on my GP's face didn't make me feel any better. If I was going to have any more children, they wanted me to wait at least a year. And even then, having more than three C-sections in one lifetime is stepping into dangerous territory. But what could I do? I didn't want an abortion so I had no choice but to have another baby. I was due at the end of February 2012, which meant we could still go ahead with our September wedding that autumn. It was a crazy time – so many happy things, but so much fear attached to them all.

Because I was high risk, I saw the midwife almost every week. Despite the emotional rollercoaster, there were no problems and at 20 weeks they told us we were having another little girl. Complications with blood not passing through the placenta properly meant I was given a planned C-section four weeks early, on 30 January 2012. Out of all four births, Porshah's was the most dramatic. When they got her out, she wasn't breathing and had to be resuscitated. Poor Noel could see them pumping her chest. It took several minutes before we heard the cry everyone was holding their breath for. She was tiny – just five pounds four ounces – and needed a week and a half in neo-natal care. It was a stressful time – one baby at home and the other in an incubator. I remember crying as I changed her nappy because her skinny little legs reminded me of a fragile little bird. I was almost scared to touch her in case she broke.

Once she was well enough to come home, having two babies under ten months old was mind-meltingly full on. The weeks flew by in a blur of unsettled nights and hectic days. There was a constant flow of visitors. Noel and I juggled chores and bath times, slept when we could and stepped in whenever the other one was about to snap. It was madness, but we kept going because we were absolutely bowled over with love for our baby girls.

The flipside to that was a lot of guilt about Thierry. For years it had just been him and me. He was only just getting used to Noel and now there were two new babies in the mix, taking up all our time and attention. I didn't want Thierry to feel like second best but there wasn't even a flicker of jealousy. He was a natural – always there to pass me a nappy or feed one of the girls while I dealt with the other. I was blown away by how caring and attentive he was.

There wasn't a moment I didn't think about Kamran, too. Everything baby-related, from the smell of the girls' heads to making up the bottles, reminded me of him. Falling pregnant with Porshah had been such a shock, but I started to feel like everything was happening for a reason – everything from getting Thierry back, supporting Noel through a near-death experience and then having two babies. It all helped stop me from drowning, as if life deliberately bombarded me so I had no choice but to keep swimming.

***

Sadly, as fate would have it, it wasn't quite time for me to be entirely happy. We were still getting to grips with life as a family of five when my beloved nan was diagnosed with Alzheimer's. She had been deteriorating for some time, repeating herself a lot and becoming increasingly disorientated. For example, when Savannah was born, she came to visit us at Heartlands and instead of speaking to the receptionist or trying to find her way to the ward she sat in the waiting room for two hours until one of the family happened to spot her. I blame myself. As the eldest grandchild I've always been her favourite. I'm convinced the stress of what happened to Kamran has been a big factor.

Despite the diagnosis, Grandad refused all offers of help. He was too proud for that. He wanted to keep his marriage vows and care for his wife himself. He took on all the cooking and cleaning – things we'd never seen him do before. But his grand plans were derailed when he was admitted to hospital himself. While receiving treatment for a water infection he developed pneumonia. He was eventually discharged, only to be struck down by a massive heart attack. I still remember the phone call from Dad.

'You need to get to the hospital,' he said. 'We think you need to say your goodbyes.'

When we got there Grandad looked so frail that Stacey and I broke down at the sight of him. He always said that if the worst happened he didn't want to be resuscitated. The prognosis wasn't good. I threw my arms around him.

'Don't go yet,' I begged, 'we need you.'

Life without the rock of the family seemed inconceivable. But a week before the fifth anniversary of Kamran's death, Grandad passed away.

We considered cancelling the wedding. I agonised over it – the loss was so raw it didn't feel right to go ahead without him. But a big part of me had come to view getting married as a chance to finally have some security and peace for me, Noel and the children – especially Thierry. As devastated as I was about Grandad, something was telling me to seize my shot at happiness.

***

In the end, my family assured us the wedding would give everyone something to look forward to. Grandad loved a party – he wouldn't dream of letting us cancel one on his account. So, just as we'd planned, on 15 September 2012 I became Mrs Sarah Rose Edwards.

Thanks to our families, we were able to afford quite a big traditional do. We even got lucky with the weather. I remember being over the moon with my hair and make-up, and thinking, *He better be at the church!*

On the outside, I probably looked like any other bride. But inside, I was still fighting with myself. *You don't deserve this. You're moving on. You're forgetting Kam.*

Thierry, now eight, was the ring bearer and did a beautiful reading. Porshah was still only eight months' old. Savannah was 17 months and had just started walking. I hated being the centre of attention, but there's no getting away from it on your wedding day. My knees were practically knocking as Dad walked me down the aisle. It was a very emotional moment, especially for him.

Noel gave a moving speech saying he was proud to have Thierry as part of his family. Then I stood up and told everyone that Kamran would be happy with the man I've picked to look after me and his brother. The day was bittersweet, like anything good in my life. Kam should have been there with us, running around with his brother and new sisters.

***

That night, the kids ended up in the hotel bridal suite with me and Noel. We all sat snuggled in the king-sized bed together watching TV. People are shocked when I tell them that's what we did on our wedding night, but to us it was perfect. The next day we kissed them all goodbye and left them with Mom and Dad while we had a week's honeymoon in Greece. I missed them all so much I spent the whole time in tears. I kick myself now, but I couldn't wait for the holiday to be over so I could get home and see them. Even now, I just feel better when they're all around me.

After our honeymoon we all sat down to watch the wedding video. The friend who put it together for us told me to make sure I watched right until the very end. I welled up when I saw Thierry on the screen.

'I'm so happy Mom's happy again,' he said.

EPILOGUE

In July 2013 I set up the charity Sharing Kams Cuddles. I felt strongly about spreading awareness of child abuse and wanted to help other victims in any way I could. The statistics are grim. In the UK alone, one in four children are sexually abused and at least one child is murdered every week. A staggering percentage of this abuse is carried out by family members or friends. We are very good at teaching 'stranger danger', but what if the danger is in the home?

Sadly, it's something the public find hard to swallow. I organised a protest in Birmingham during a national awareness campaign, we had placards with the stats emblazoned across them and we chanted, 'Protect our children.' We had people giving us dirty looks and covering the ears of their children, as if *we* were the enemy. How can we stamp this problem out if we don't talk about it?

Every week there are more stories in the press – stories that I would have skimmed over before, but now I pore over every detail, my heart aching for the children who are hurt or killed by the very people who are supposed to love and care for them. It destroys me. I shouldn't read them but I can't help it.

With the help of my family, I started raising money in Kam's name. We held fun days and bingo nights. We did a six-hour Zumbathon, my Uncle Martin did a 10k run and

Stacey did a parachute jump. We use the money when we hear about someone who needs help. For Keanu Williams, the two-year-old Birmingham boy beaten to death by his own mother, we donated some money to help the family pay for a funeral. We bought one little abuse survivor all the gear he needed to take up boxing.

We did an Easter egg appeal for Women's Aid. We collected over 500 eggs and delivered them to children taking refuge with their mothers in local domestic violence shelters. We also donated cash to help the women who find permanent accommodation decorate their children's bedrooms – because when they leave abusive partners, of course they have nothing. These are only small things, but they make a huge difference, not only to the children but to me. If the charity can make one child smile and feel loved then something good has come out of Kamran's death. I think he would be proud that we are using his memory in this way.

It's a relief to finally be able to turn all the grief into something positive. I get Facebook messages from people who have been touched by what happened. I exchange emails with a woman in Texas who is going through an almost identical situation. I wake up to messages she's sent me at four in the morning saying how much she hates herself. I tell her she must not blame herself. I remind her that she loved her son and would never knowingly have put him in danger.

I know I should take my own advice, but it's much easier said than done.

* * *

One of the hardest things is the effect it has had on my friendships. I haven't spoken to Chantelle for a long time. We saw each other at the cemetery a few times but every time we saw each other things got tense and we would end up in tears. I don't harbour any resentment towards her, she just told the truth like the rest of us. After everything we both went through, it is just too upsetting to carry on being friends.

It feels the same for me and Matthew. After he supported me in Gloucester and through both trials, we lost touch. Very recently, we bumped into each other by chance in a Caribbean takeaway. He said he'd become a dad, which is lovely news. I'm happy for him, he's a lovely guy and I wish him the best. I do wonder if people like him blame me. I would completely understand. I still blame myself. To this day I can't help but feel that I *was* guilty of allowing a child to die and that I should have been punished.

The impact on my family is still being felt every day. It's only since writing this book that we've started to talk about the effect Kam's death had on Stacey and Dad. Everyone was so focussed on supporting me and Mom that no one ever asked how they were. There was no place for them to be upset. Stacey still finds it hard to believe Nicholas was capable of such an awful crime. It hurts her that she was reeled in by him too. She was only 16 at the time. She helped collect what was left of my things from the flat and whoever burgled it had scrawled the word 'murderer' on the wall in red paint. As if that wasn't upsetting enough someone then shouted it at Stacey as she left.

Thankfully she is a tough cookie and we are closer than ever now. The age gap seems to have got smaller as we've got older. We tell each other everything. She still smokes and I still tell her she stinks. She lives at Mom and Dad's with her boyfriend Aaron and their daughter Cady, who was born two months after Porshah. We are together almost every day – our girls are so close we always say they're like triplets. Stacey is a great mom – much more independent than I ever was. She had so much practice with mine she was a pro by the time she had her own. Mom moans about the mess that comes with sharing the house with a young family, but I think she'd be lost if they moved out.

Out of everyone, I would say Mom has been affected the most. She lost a grandson she loved like he was her own. And the fact that this has happened to me, the daughter she would walk to the ends of the earth for, tears her apart all over again. It kills her that I've lost a child in such a brutal way. It kills her that she wasn't able to protect me. She hates that she felt so sorry for Nicholas when he cried at the party, and it breaks her heart remembering how desperately upset Kamran was when she was saying goodbye at the flat the day after.

We've never been able to speak in detail about what happened – she's still far too emotional for that. If anyone mentions Kam, even if they're referring to happy times, she will disappear into the kitchen for a cry. It's changed her. She used to be so strong and happy. Now she's a shell of a woman who barely leaves the house, apart from her weekly trips to the cemetery to visit Kamran and Grandad. In 2010 she quit smoking in a bid to get healthy, but as soon as her dad died, she started up again. She has been diagnosed with depression, but has always refused to take any medication.

Occasionally I see glimpses of the Mom I remember. In September 2014, two days after my twenty-ninth birthday, Mom and Dad got re-married. Inspired by me and Noel, they had the big white wedding she'd always wanted. It brought me a lot of comfort to see her smiling again and to know how deeply they still love each other.

* * *

The anniversary of Kamran's death is always a difficult time of year. The events of that day never really leave me, but when 10 May draws in it's even harder to escape them. I imagine my baby boy confused, frightened and in pain, screaming for his mommy. It haunts me like a horror film every time I close my eyes.

We mark the day with a family exodus to the cemetery. We take fresh flowers and set off balloons to try and make it nice for Thierry, Savannah and Porshah. Some people might think it's a bit morbid for the kids, but I want them to remember their brother and still think of him as part of the family. We go roughly once a month, as well as on special days such as Kam's birthday and during the main holidays like Christmas and Easter. Still, it's not easy for me to go. I have to build myself up to it because I know I'll spend the rest of the day wanting to lock myself away and cry. I prefer to remember Kamran as he was – smiling and dancing, giving everyone hugs and kisses. If I close my eyes and clutch my arms tightly enough, sometimes I can still feel him.

***

Kamran would be nine years old now. I find it really hard to see any of my friends who have children the same age because it's a reminder of where Kam should be. I can't help but feel jealous of them living life and reaching milestones. Grace's little boy Kyron gets to me the most because he and Kam were such good buddies. I know that if he were alive they would still be close.

Thierry is ten now and Mark and I still share custody every other week. We never actually got the residential order changed. It doesn't matter to me any more – we are both Thierry's parents and our relationship is fantastic. I'm so grateful for all the support Mark has shown me and that he continues to be such a good dad to his son. He's still single, but he knows that if he does meet someone he will have to be sure she's the right one before introducing her to Thierry. Thankfully, Mark and Noel get on like a house on fire. If Thierry has a football match, they go together. I'm so glad Thierry has them both in his life because he has been through so much – more than most adults. He's a very emotional kid – if his sisters fall over and hurt themselves, he cries too. The other day I asked him to pick his shoes up and he got so angry he was gritting his teeth.

A little while ago we were talking about Kamran and Thierry started to cry.

'Did Savannah replace Kamran?' he asked.

'No,' I said. 'No one can replace your brother.'

'I'm scared,' he said.

'Why?'

'Because I've forgotten my memories of Kam.'

I completely understood what he meant, because I feel the same. The more time passes, the further away Kamran feels. When the memories of a person are no longer fresh in your mind, it can start to feel like they're slipping away altogether.

It was hard to hear Thierry say something like that. He's still so young, yet he's articulating such grown-up feelings.

He had some counselling when he was four and they said he would need more once he hits his teens because he will probably develop feelings he doesn't understand. It scares me to death that he might grow up angry. I dread the day he turns round and tells me I'm a crap mom and that Kam died because of me. What if he decides that he hates me? And what if when he's a grown man he decides to hunt Nicholas down?

If I could freeze him at this age and protect him forever then I would. I'm constantly warning him about drugs because I don't want him doing what I did. I'm lucky that he's so bright and has a good head on his shoulders. He's a credit to me and I don't know what I would do without him.

* * *

Nicholas has served eight years of his 17-year sentence. Every year I get a letter from the Probation Service telling me nothing has changed, and every time I'm scared it will be one saying he has committed suicide. He's a coward and I wouldn't put anything past him. Look how far he was prepared to take his lies, dragging everyone through two court cases instead of just pleading guilty. It riles me, but if he *had* pleaded guilty he would have got a shorter sentence. I try my best to focus on that, but I still hate Nicholas – it's a hate that makes my whole body burn. I know it's unhealthy to hold onto it, but when I have to live with what he has done to me and everyone around me, I don't see how I'm ever going to be able to let go of it. What he did to us is ingrained on everyone's lives forever.

I think part of the reason I've struggled to get closure is because Nicholas has never admitted to Kamran's murder. I used to want to know every detail of what happened to Kamran the day he died, but now I'm at a place where I think I'm better off *not* knowing. What I do want to know is why – why did Nicholas do this? It tears me apart not being able to understand. I would love to get a letter from Nicholas giving me some kind of plausible explanation, but I can't see how there could possibly be one.

I used to want to see Nicholas, to confront him and ask him all the questions that go round and round in my head. But I'm not sure it would help. When I imagine myself seeing him, I go for him. But once, I was walking through Birmingham and saw a man across the street who looked exactly like him. Even though I knew it couldn't possibly be Nicholas, I froze. So it's hard to know how I would even react. I just hope he is suffering. I don't want him dead – I want him to live his life carrying this with him like I do every day.

***

Sadly, we lost my Nan just after Easter 2015 – just before I finished this book. She was 79 and I think she was ready to go. It's always sad losing someone, even when you know they are old and it's probably their time. But with Nan, I still carry a huge amount of guilt that it was Kamran's death that set her health on a downward spiral. My family tell me otherwise, but I know I'll never shake the feeling that she might have lived a healthier, longer life if Kamran hadn't died. I will miss her terribly.

While I've been writing this book Noel has been in and out of hospital again. The doctors are about to try him on a new treatment so we are hopeful he will get his health back on track. He never says it out loud but I know it really hurts him when he's too weak to do little things, like lift up the children when they want a cuddle. The illness can be tough on us all, but I've never regretted standing by him – not for a second. He is a wonderful husband and father – the most thoughtful, caring, supportive man you could ever meet. I feel so lucky that we found each other. After losing Kam, I never even dared imagine I might go on to fulfil my hopes of finding a husband and having a house full of kids, yet thanks to him, here I am.

Savannah is three now and rules the roost at nursery. Porshah was potty trained practically overnight because she just copied her big sister. They are amazing – so cute and funny. When I sit and watch them pottering about together, they remind me so much of how Thierry and Kamran were.

Aunty Maggie is still a big part of our lives. Obviously, it wasn't easy going through the court case when what she was saying about me felt like the difference between freedom and prison. I never confronted her or fell out with her because of it, but I did hold a bit of a grudge for a while. But like Chantelle, all Maggie did was tell *her* truth.

Despite going through more sad times, I would say that as a family we are stronger than ever. I've never been brave enough, but nearly everyone in my immediate family has got a tattoo of Kamran's name. I think it's a lovely marker of how much he meant to them.

***

I know there will be moms reading this who have lost a child and are suffering like I do. I want them to see me as proof that life does go on. It's so hard – I still have weeks when it feels like one step forward and two back. I'm known for always having a smile on my face and it must be easy to assume that because I'm married with three children I must be OK now. I am very fortunate to have what I have now, trust me – I know that more than the next person. I appreciate every breath in my babies' bodies, every kiss and cuddle and every happy moment because I know how precious life is. But I still have nights where I lock myself away and scream and cry. There are still moments where the guilt I feel is intolerable. I can never be 100 per cent happy. A piece of my heart died with Kamran and I will never be whole because he is not here.

It takes time, but you get better at living with the grief. I used to wish I could flick a switch and get my life back to normal, but I've slowly learned to accept that *this* is normal now. You find strength in your loved ones and your happy memories of the person you lost become more and more sacred. You naturally find your own ways of coping. For me, it's making sure Kam is still a big part of our lives. His picture is still all over our house and we talk about him constantly, almost as if he is still here. I can't bear the thought of him being forgotten.

Even now, several years on from Kam's murder, I get people contacting me online, asking questions about what happened. The nicer ones say things like, 'I don't know how you've done it. I couldn't go on if I lost my child.' I understand what they're saying, but even a well-meaning comment like that makes me feel that somehow I've done the wrong thing. What would *you* do? Would you spend the rest of your life crying into a pillow? The truth is, you don't know how you'd cope, and the sun keeps on coming up every morning whether you want it to or not.

I wrote this book as a way of getting some closure, to finally put down in black and white everything I went through so all the people who were touched by Kam's death, all the people in Birmingham who heard about the case, all the parents who possibly jumped to conclusions and passed judgement on me, can read the truth, in full, for themselves.

It's not been easy reliving everything – there are things in this book I hadn't let myself revisit since they happened. But I did it for all the grieving moms out there who are desperately looking for hope. And I did it for Kam. I want everyone to see his beautiful face on the front cover. I'm still so proud of him – I want the whole world to know his name and how loved he was. I'll never get over losing my gorgeous boy, but now, even on the days I feel like I'm right back at rock bottom, I can see a chink of light and know that tomorrow, or maybe even the next day, life won't feel so desolate.

I guess my message is, never ever give up. Even when you don't feel like you're surviving, as long as there is breath in your body, you are.

***

I miss you Kam Kam and I'm sorry. I am trying to give your brother and sisters a happy childhood, and I'm trying to help other children too. I will always love you.

ACKNOWLEDGEMENTS

To all my friends and family who have been there for every step of my journey – thank you. And to Mom, Dad, Stacey, Noel and Thierry, you are my shining stars, my guiding lights. I owe you everything x

We are a small and growing charity based in the West Midlands. Our mission is to help children who have been on the receiving end of child abuse.

To get involved or donate go to:

www.sharingkamscuddles.com